MW01294345

Day by Day to Alaska

First floating dry-dock on Puget Sound, at Dockton, Washington, in Quartermaster Harbor on Vashon Island. Grandpa Petersen worked here after coming from Denmark via Wisconsin. My childhood days at Dockton helped shape my dreams that one day led me in our boat, *Day by Day,* from Sandy Point, Washington to Sitka, Alaska, and return outside Vancouver Island. In this book I share numerous experiences.

Day by Day to Alaska

Queen Charlotte Islands and
Around Vancouver Island

Gary,

Enjoy! Follow your dreams.

An Adventure-Guide
by
Dale R. Petersen

Dale R. Petersen

Trafford
Victoria, British Columbia, Canada

©2000 by Dale R. Petersen. All rights reserved. No part of this book may be reproduced or transmitted in any form or by any means, electronic, mechanical, photocopying, recording or otherwise or stored or retrieved without written permission of the author.

Published in Victoria, British Columbia

Co-published with Post Point Press (Bellingham, Washington)

Brand names and product names used are trademarks, registered trademarks or trade names of their respective holders.

Canadian Cataloguing in Publication Data

Petersen, Dale R. (Dale Roger),
 Day by Day to Alaska, Queen Charlotte Islands and around Vancouver Island

 Includes bibliographical references and index.
 ISBN 1-55212-348-0

 1. Petersen, Dale R. (Dale Roger) --Journeys--Alaska. 2. Pacific Coast (B.C.)--Description and travel. 3. Pacific Coast (Alaska)--Description and travel. 4. Boats and boating--British Columbia--Pacific Coast. 5. Boats and boating--Alaska--Pacific Coast. I. Title.
FC3845.P2P47 2000   917.11'1044
C00-910247-7
F1089.P2P47 2000

TRAFFORD

This book was published *on-demand* in cooperation with Trafford Publishing.
On-demand publishing is a unique process and service of making a book available for retail sale to the public taking advantage of on-demand manufacturing and Internet marketing.
On-demand publishing includes promotions, retail sales, manufacturing, order fulfilment, accounting and collecting royalties on behalf of the author.

Suite 6E, 2333 Government St., Victoria, B.C. V8T 4P4, CANADA
Phone   250-383-6864   Toll-free   1-888-232-4444 (Canada & US)
Fax   250-383-6804   E-mail   sales@trafford.com
Web site   www.trafford.com   TRAFFORD PUBLISHING IS A DIVISION OF TRAFFORD HOLDINGS LTD.
Trafford Catalogue #00-0012   www.trafford.com/robots/00-0012.html

10   9   8   7   6   5   4   3

To my wife, Cynthia, who has been my lifetime partner of forty-three years and my cheerleader. You are the only one who really understands me. Although you did not join me on all boating passages, you support me in my adventures with the sea. You know that I "march to a different drummer!" Thank you for being patient as I cruise and write.

Disclaimer

The author tried to make this book accurate. It is possible that there will be errors, omissions and differences of opinion from other widely regarded sources. Before a cruise of any duration is taken, the skipper should be adequately skilled and obtain all necessary equipment and navigation aids to make safe passage. It should not be assumed under any circumstances that the author's passages may be made safely by another skipper in the same or different vessel. *Many passages are considered extremely dangerous at various times. Any skipper, attempting any passage is fully responsible for all judgements and safe passage of vessel and crew.* While this book offers insights, suggestions and advice, only US and Canadian government charts and cruising guides should be considered reliable. Even then, the skipper must make intelligent decisions based on the weather, rules of the road, condition of his/her vessel and other factors.

Unlike some ventures, no one bankrolled this journey or book. The products and services used for this cruise and endorsed by the author are done without remuneration. Likewise, criticism of products is not done to devalue those items, but to warn consumers of one person's experience. The author hopes that such feedback will result in better products in the future for the boater.

Comments by the author are his own and do not necessarily represent the views of the editor or publisher. The author has tried to be diligent in giving credit where previous ideas and information influenced this book. The publisher, editor and author assume no liability for errors, omissions, or for any loss or damages as the result of using this book.

Contents

Illustrations

Preface

Day by Day, Day by Day,
Oh dear Lord, three things I pray:
To see Thee more Clearly,
Love Thee more Dearly,
Follow Thee more Nearly, Day by Day
(Public domain, "Day by Day")

The name of our boat in which I made my Alaskan and side trips, is *Day by Day*. It is also the name of a prayer and a hymn as well as my theme song and message aboard!

Oh the mountains and the sea!
How they bring out the adventure in me!
Which to choose is a great choice.
Each is an expression of God's voice.
Go by 4x4 or go by boat,
Go by road or go afloat.
The true adventure is to go alone,
And view all of God's creation as if it were my own.
From the mountains I love to view the sea,
From the sea I like to see the mountains looking back at me.
To say which is best is hard to do,
It all depends upon your point of view!
(Dale R. Petersen, "Oh the Mountains and the Sea")

In 1972, I was inspired to start the poem above, while on a beach during a family cruise in our boat, *Seaspell,* in the British Columbia Gulf Islands. I was born in Montana, which means mountain in Spanish, and I married Cynthia, a name which comes from a mountain in Greece. Next to the sea, I like mountains best. Going to Alaska by boat, you can enjoy both. Little did I realize in 1972, I would make my Alaskan boat trip alone as the poem suggests. It took me 22 years to figure it out and make it happen!

Credits: God has been my ultimate guide in life and on my many cruises. Countless persons and publications contributed to my successful Alaskan cruise and side trips. I thank all of those whose prayers, advice and services were with me "day by day." For all those who helped me get this book published, I am forever grateful. Pivotal ideas came from Terry Peterson, Robert Hale, Matt Morehouse, Francis Caldwell and Jack Bazhaw.

Cover photographs by Cynthia Petersen.

Dockton sketch by Richard K. Shideler.

Map base courtesy of Craig Herd.

Introduction

Day by Day to Alaska shares what it was like to take a twenty-five hundred mile solo-cruise in twenty-three days from Puget Sound to Alaska and back outside of Vancouver Island in a twenty-one foot Bayliner Trophy powerboat. That 1994 trip was my thirty year dream cruise and central theme for this book. God led me in an extraordinary way on that cruise. While I did have challenges, they were met. I share many lessons learned on that trip, and during my over fifty years of boating. Hopefully, *Day by Day to Alaska* will inspire youth to seek adventure and learn how to overcome adversity whether in boating or in life.

Some might say on my 1994 trip I was just lucky. My book reflects eight major trips north, including two to Alaska. I have been around Vancouver Island twice. Each of my four trips to the Queen Charlotte Islands was a different adventure. I crossed Queen Charlotte Sound ten times, eight in *Day by Day*. Side trips to Olympia in 1995 and Skagway in 1999 reflect adventures not part of my 1994 cruise.

Safety afloat is so important. I give you what I believe are important safety rules if you boat in small or large vessels. My hints, tricks and planning ideas should help you make your time on the water more enjoyable. I also share some of my philosophy on a number of issues, marine and otherwise.

Religion has played a big part in the formation of America and in my life. I give you my testimony as it relates to boating and life. Finally, I share how my faith helped me overcome cancer, so I can still fish and cruise. This is my story shared in the same way I cruise—mostly alone and to my style. If you go where I went, your experiences will be different—guaranteed—things change rapidly, especially on the sea. This is an adventure-guide that can help you plan and make short or long cruises in a small boat. My sharing could be better, but if you find a better book, buy it!

Happy reading and God Bless you in life's journey!

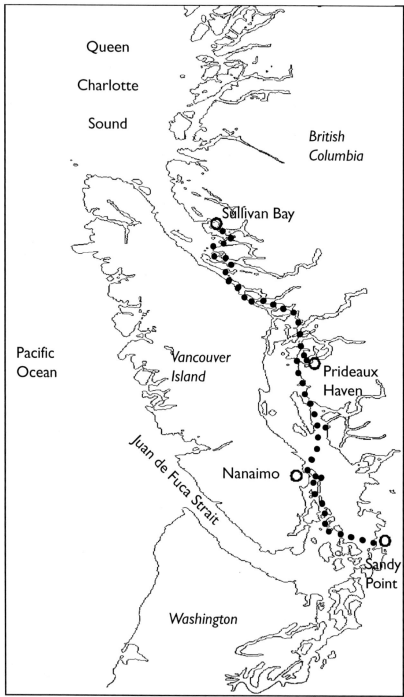

Day 1 through Day 3 route.

Sandy Point to Sitka and Back

Sandy Point to Sullivan Bay

Day 1—June 7—85 naut mi, Sandy Point to Nanaimo.

Today I head to Alaska in *Day by Day*, the most special June 7 for me
ever. For too many years I wanted to do it. Well, now I am! By 1230,
all loaded, the last item is checked off my to-do list. About an hour
and a half after a minus 1.1 tide I struggle to launch on a steep,
slippery ramp. Admittedly, a rough start. It is tricky, but I make it.
Persistence pays off.

At 1345, after picture taking, Cynthia sees me off. There is no
cheering crowd to say farewell, just my loving wife of then thirty-
seven years saying good-bye. Heading out, I am sad. Why not happy?
Sad because I don't want to leave her. This trip is selfish of me! But I
go with her blessing. In fact her last words to me are from the Bible
in Numbers 6:24, "The Lord bless thee, and keep thee." Be joyous!
Several people offer to pray for me while up north and others say
they did while I was on my trip. What could be greater than that?

Leaving, Cynthia and I wave endlessly. What a wonderful send-off!
While I wish she could go with me, we both know my going alone is
best. Heading north, we keep waving as long as we can see each
other. Even when *Day by Day* is a mere speck in the distance, Cynthia can still hear the faint roar of the MerCruiser propelling me at
last on that lifelong dream.

Through the San Juans, playing my favorite tape with my theme
song, "Day by Day", by the Hillside Singers, I sing along. This is
living! Unreal! I am actually doing what I had so long only hoped to
do. Savor every moment. Before long it will be over. But I will always
have the memories. From the start I try to live each day to the fullest
from daybreak to dusk. I learn this is impossible day in and day out,
but it is fun trying! I soak up everything I can, because it is all so

special to me. What if I miss something? Then that is my excuse to go back again someday.

Going through the San Juans, Uncle Mitch's words of many years ago still echo in my ears, "We were seine fishing and our net was full. We got twenty-five cents for each sockeye and we would throw the humpies back." Nowadays, if a seiner gets a bushel of fish they are lucky. Where have all the fish gone? Pacific Northwest population growth and development has taken its toll. The answer is for all parties who have knowledge and an interest in salmon to identify all the problems and all possible solutions. Once solutions are agreed to—act. Salmon and herring are both on a decline. Actions were not fast enough, for in 1999 the National Marine Fisheries Service listed wild Puget Sound Chinook threatened under the Endangered Species Act. This is but another example that if we do not take responsibility for our affairs, the government will take over. This is not a good sign. Let us hope the salmon fare better as a result of this action. In the interim, raising hatchery marked fish and allowing only those to be caught, where the wild species is in danger, seems like a good approach that is being started. Wild natural fish, with their genetic superiority, must be allowed to increase and flourish.

My first day out, the water is calm and pleasant with a small lump created by the tides. The ride is soft, but we (*Day by Day* and I) feel heavy. We are! On our first bareboat trial run, I recall how quick to plane and fast is our V-6. Our neighbor, Jack, reminds me, "She will never run faster." Now with our load, including 103.5 gallons of gas at the start, we are slower but better prepared. As I look around the cabin, I am amazed how organized and neatly in place is everything. A well-found ship!

The quarter berth and two below-berth lockers are full of food, clothing and safety gear. Twenty-one charts are rolled and neatly labeled and stowed in a box tightly fit into an overhead opening above the quarter berth. The forward seat at the port dinette holds two boxes of food secured with bungee cord. Behind the table-leg I put two stacking bins. The top bin holds my library of all the books and pamphlets I think I will need. The lower bin is handy for safety and other essentials. Nonslip place mats on the table hold the charts, chart book and boat log amazingly well in most seas. Topside, the inflated dinghy holds the crab ring and salmon net. The two extra fuel jugs stow nicely on the aft deck. The primary anchor rides on the bow pulpit. Both outboard tanks stack neatly, with the help of bins secured with snubbers, along with the outboard and one cooler chest on the transom swim step. All extra space is filled. Yet I can move around freely. For me it is excellent. Add another person and critical mass is exceeded!

Typical partly cloudy Pacific Northwest skies do not bother me as we head for Bedwell Harbour to clear Customs. They are actually at South Pender on South Pender Island. The floats and Bedwell Harbour Resort sit in a rock-carved bay with clam-shell beaches which are tidy and inviting. With a swimming pool and excellent accommodations, Bedwell Harbour Resort makes a nice alternative for American boaters looking for a change from the San Juans. On this day it is very quiet with the floats less than 10 percent filled. This is the kind of place you would like to spend awhile, like our family did years ago in *Seaspell*. The staff is very polite here and they make you feel welcome. I buy a Canadian fishing license for $46 Canadian so I can always be ready to catch my dinner! (In 1996 the license has increased to $108 Canadian.) Fresh water is scarce here and it cost $3 to dump garbage then.

At 1600, I realize I have been so preoccupied that I have not eaten since early breakfast. I eat, drifting in the harbor recalling pleasant past memories here in two previous boats. Cynthia packed me one of her super brown-bag lunches, so now my lunch is dinner and I am ahead of the meal schedule! I always enjoy the passage between North and South Pender islands. It is picturesque and narrow, but small boats can enjoy passage except at low tides. Take it slow and easy.

In alternates of sun and June sprinkles, we proceed north through the pleasant Gulf Islands in calm seas. Near Active Pass, I watch for ferry traffic. At our 1700 passage in Trincomali Channel I see three BC ferries. Going north in 1996, I count nine ferries during the time I mosey along in the vicinity of Active Pass. The Gulf Islands are a popular American destination. While I often intend to spend more time gunkholing in these islands, it seems I am always just passing through with just a few stops here and there. Since my 1994 trip, Cynthia and I check out some new areas. I encourage any boater to spend a week poking around every cove in the Gulf Islands. They are less crowded than the San Juans. In 1998 I discover Portland Island, Princess Margaret Marine Park, in the fall. It is nearly unoccupied and a great place to anchor and hike. It reminds me a little of Sucia in the San Juans.

In Active Pass, Cynthia and I once stay at our best bed and breakfast ever, Maynecliffe. Run by Doreen and Ralph you can marvel at the quietude, the view, the BC ferries passing below you, the fine facilities, the great food and gracious hosts. Curl up by the fire and read about Gulf Islands history.

A highlight for me is the area around Telegraph Harbour between Kuper and Thetis islands. After looking into Telegraph near the marinas and watching the boats that are watching me slide in and out, I stop at Capernwray Harbour next to the ferry dock on Thetis. On a most perfect evening with sun and calm, I walk ashore hoping to find Charlie, manager of this Torchbearer Bible School. This is one of twenty-two Centres worldwide, where Christ is proclaimed through short-term and practical Bible training, conferences and evangelistic outreach. I learn about Charlie, but never meet him, as a result of our visits to four Torchbearer Centres in Europe. The original Torchbearer Centre is at Capernwray, England. I correspond with Charlie, but I miss him this evening since I am behind schedule. Rather than wait his return, I decide I to be on my way.

It is fun going around Dayman Island where we anchor in *Seaspell* in July 1972. At that time the island is uninhabited and the only cabin on the island is for sale. Correction. The island is inhabited. Raccoons! Lots of them feeding on the plentiful shellfish. Cute. This time, no raccoons. Just more cabins and no trespassing signs.

After a quick run to Silva Bay and the Flat Top Islands, I renew acquaintance with an area Cynthia and I visit in June 1978 in *Nadja* on our return from up north. This evening is still and beautiful making it fun to ply the waters in these narrow passages running both against and with the tide. So quite and peaceful—a perfect evening. A 21-ft boat is ideal for this kind of cruising—quick, nimble and comfortable.

About 2100 near dusk, we enter with ease, one of my favorites, Dodd Narrows, against a five knot current. According to *Sailing Directions* the maximum tidal stream is ten knots. In 1972 on our first passage through Dodd Narrows in *Seaspell*, we scoot smoothly with the current near maximum velocity. I recall then a one-lung, double ender is pitching and rolling along the shore in the slower current, bucking it, and going nowhere.

When my brother-in-law, Rich, and I make our February 1995 cruise to Princess Louisa, we buck the current at about six knots. *Day by Day* has no problem then, but we follow an ocean salmon troller going our way that provides quite a thrill for us, and I am sure the skipper. As we approach the Narrows from the south, the troller is rolling extremely from side to side. As she gets closer to the swiftest part, in addition to the dangerous roll she appears to be zigzagging nearly out of control. Suddenly the troller rolls hard to port with one of her upright trolling poles close to the water, then she twists 90 degrees toward the rocky Mudge Island shore. As we follow slowly close behind, I think for sure the troller is going to crash into the rocks and I am preparing myself for some type of rescue. The skipper must have backed down fast. As we pass, she is in neutral as the skipper wisely waits for the current to pull her away into deeper water before trying again. Her second attempt is made safely but not without rocking and rolling.

It could be a great video, but Rich and I watch in disbelief until it is over as his camcorder rests in the bunk! Now I know why friends in bigger, slower boats make sure they pass near slack water as the tide rips can turn them out of control in an instant. Most boating articles on Dodd Narrows offer similar warnings. Smaller, fast-planing boats skim the surface with little adverse reaction. Fast or slow I never experience danger in Dodd Narrows in any of our three boats in any tide. You must watch for logs and drift that can come up out of the water at you like a torpedo. Now with more development, observe those speed limits. It is amazing how large boat wakes react in the current making it unpleasant for those in boats and on shore.

Rich and I talk about cruising to Alaska together for years. We make many fishing trips together. But the way I am loaded, there isn't really enough room. Besides, I am not sure he would agree on everything I want to do! It is Cynthia who wisely suggests I go alone. That proves to be a good choice.

By 2200 I am at anchor in a the little cove just south of Shaft Point, Midden Bay, on the west side of Newcastle Island. The island is a pleasant marine park, with deer and geese, just to the north, and across the channel from Nanaimo. From my anchorage I can see the lights of town, posh condos and the nearby BC ferry dock. At night, the ferries themselves look like a lighted four-story condo on the move! Nanaimo is a nice city with good shore facilities nearby for the boater. So ends day one, as I recall pleasant family boat visits to Nanaimo in the past. One time I hike all over Newcastle Island— great for exercise. I have also anchored in Mark Bay on the south end of the island where you usually have lots of company.

Cynthia in Day by Day *at Nanaimo during our 1997 visit.*

Day 2—June 8—109 naut mi to Prideaux Haven.

I sleep well, awake at first light and am up by 0500. A deer nibbles the new growth along a pastoral shore among the trees and rocks. Overnight, I left the outdrive up. I figure if I drag anchor at night into the shallows I don't want the outdrive to hit. This morning I forget to lower it before starting. I put the outdrive in gear and the engine stalls. After this happens several times, I discover the problem. The u-joints can lockup in the outdrive. This is bad practice and potentially damaging. MerCruiser should certainly have a kill switch for that situation to protect *incompetent skippers* from the repair shops! I check out the adjacent Esso marine station that is supposed to open at daylight according to my 1978 outdated cruising guide. Well, it isn't, so rather than wait, by 0611 we are past Hudson Rocks running 336 degrees magnetic across a calm Strait of Georgia heading for Welcome Pass.

My new battery operated Remington travel razor gives me a quick, clean shave while underway. The six ounce can of orange juice is handy to sip as I cruise twenty knots at 3,500 rpm. The crossing is pleasant and a far cry from our two previous *Seaspell* crossings which, in a word, were uncomfortable in both a northerly and a southerly. In addition to a light lump this time there is an occasional light chop. The crossing seems fast. When it is rough, it can seem forever. This time we cross with no other boats. In our first crossing in *Seaspell*, we follow two bigger boats that helped knock down the bigger waves. On this morning the east side of Vancouver Island is bathed with sunshine while the mainland side is hidden by dark clouds low into the steep fjords. Welcome Pass is a friendly looking place with colorful red and white buildings on Merry Island. A tug and log-boom tow block the passage north of the island, so we slip past the south side. We stop and drift on the inside of the light as I eat a bowl of Wheaties and a banana. No restaurant has a better view or a heathier fare!

Once you leave Nanaimo, there are essentially three ways to go north or west, however you view your travel. One way is to cruise the south shore along the east side of Vancouver Island. Cynthia and I did this going north in *Nadja* in June 1978. It is a rather long, dull drag, but it is a quicker and shorter way if getting further north is your primary objective. On that day the wind was 15–20 knots SE with a heavy following sea. *Nadja*, which used the same hull as Vietnam river patrol boats, was such a great sea boat so it was a comfortable and easy ride. We anchor at Henry Bay. There is a nice sandy beach on the north inside of Denman Island. A 1995 visitor's guide promotes Denman and Hornby islands as the "undiscovered Gulf Islands."

Another way north is to pass to the south of Texada and poke around Lasqueti Island en route. We do that in July 1973 when our family returns from Princess Louisa Inlet in *Seaspell*. We find Strait of Georgia too rough to cross in a southeaster so we duck in around Lasqueti. When I help bring the seiner, *Pursuit*, south in May 1979, we pass this way without stopping. After a calm trip all the way from Petersburg, we found a nasty northwest behind us making the seiner yaw and hard to steer. I have made several passages this way in *Day by Day* since my 1994 cruise. In my encounters with Strait of Georgia over 70 percent of the time crossings are rough. Salmon Point Resort-RV Park Marina is an excellent port along the south shore south of Campbell River if coming by land or sea. Cynthia and I have a good stay in 1995.

This time we take my favorite way north with a fair Malaspina Strait. Many Canadian lights and lighthouses are still manned and buildings well maintained. In the US lights are automated and buildings falling in disrepair. Canadian taxes are higher than in the US and the debate is on whether to automate and no longer staff Canadian lights. In the meantime, they are always a joy to view because they are picturesque. Being alone on this trip, I am with God only, uncomplicated, without human distractions and a chance to soak it all up—refreshing for the soul. When you go by yourself you also find out what you are made of, particularly in adversity. You also have the option to go someplace when you want in a moments notice. For example, in 1998 returning south, I discover beautiful Anderson Bay on the SE tip of Texada Island along a treed and rocky shore. A lone sailboat is anchored in a spot that gives you a view of mountains and ship traffic.

Today I take my first look into Smuggler Cove Marine Park. What a neat place! Nearly rock-locked and surrounded by trees, it is the perfect setting and so protected. Two sailboats are at anchor. Three private docks and cabins are on shore, two with flowering baskets and shutters. Reminds me of a mini Prideaux Haven with some development. Near the entrance, a larger fallen rock from the wall is supported by a smaller one as though a worker was trying to replace it. Better you come discover and explore this place and stay overnight! I did myself in 1997—it's great for hiking and rowing.

If you want a bigger place to stay, Secret Cove around the corner is a good choice with fuel and other items. Rich and I moor there overnight in *Day by Day* in February 1995.

My next point-of-interest north to Alaska is Pender Harbour. Lots of new houses and condos since my last visit in the seventies. Pender is a nice retreat from Vancouver, with some good facilities. Once in *Seaspell* our family overnighted here at Irvines Landing and we had our first hamburger helper! Funny what you remember! On another trip in October, Rich, Arlen and I launch at Irvines Landing for our first ever visit to Desolation Sound. It's hard to believe Arlen was only about twelve then. Now as a grown son, I miss those days. Arlen was always a good mate. Boating since diaper days, he took a boating class with me once and got a better test score than I did! Besides keeping a tidy ship, he kept me out of trouble on the sea more than once. Pender reminds me a little of the Maine coast, except for the redder rock there, and more trees here. This place is nicer than Sandy Point, but so are the prices! Ice at Irvines Landing is $2.50. Rock walls hold houses very high up and some are on piling, clinging to the rocky shore. A charter boat skipper volunteers, "For Spring's (King or Chinook) use live herring by the piling at the cable crossing (north)." Somehow I do not feel like fishing. Like the ducks and geese, I am urged northward. Besides I still have too much perishable good food from home aboard.

So far, this trip is as I envision it would be—a dream come true! Pleasure boat traffic is very light. This morning the wind is with us past Grief Point in sunny and cloudy periods. At Westview a most cooperative gas dock lady at the Chevron dock helps me take on fuel and water. Such an orderly dock at Westview; full of fishing boats and expensive yachts from the US to over 40-ft, some heading to Alaska. But we are the smallest. Most interesting is a two-story fish boat converted to look, to me, like a Mississippi River Queen painted pink and yellow and adorned with flower pots. I see the 48-ft *Tolly* and wonder if she belongs to the owner of Tollycraft. Later I discover she is owned by R. M. Tollefson, who on his business card with a picture of *Tolly* boasts: "Ex-designer & Builder of Tollycraft Yachts—Confirmed Bachelor, Old Man of the Sea—Too Old and Tough to Kill and Too Young in Spirit to Die." I like that. Now I wish I could have met Tollefson. Sounds like a neat guy with a sense of humor!

Along the way, natural and man-made surprises and pleasantries always keep my interest.

The ferry *Queen of Sidney* slides in as we slide out. Lots of tug and tow traffic today. Since I heard glowingly about Savary Island, I think I will check it out. Well, I spend way too much time tiptoeing through the shallows and making sure the GPS will keep me off the rocks. It does, but frankly, I am disappointed. It probably is better later in the summer to swim in the warm waters where the tides meet. Not today!

I skip over to Lund which is always a fun place to stop. It is a small tidy, quiet port at the end of the road. A sign suggests it is the start of a road that ends in Chili! Lund is a good place to launch a trailerable boat to shove off to Desolation Sound, although you have to take two ferries to get here. The historic Lund Hotel is a memorable place for Cynthia and I once. You won't starve in Lund. Nancy's Bakery near the hotel will make your day if you have a sweet tooth. The Hotel and restaurant are closed in 1999.

By 1550 I am off to Prideaux Haven, past the Copeland Islands Marine Park and through scenic Thulin Passage. Several boats are anchored in the Copelands. In 1997 I spend more time poking through them. Soon we are in Eveleigh Anchorage, and with the outboard only, I very carefully idle between the rocks into the Haven. Wow, more boats here than I ever saw before! I count eighteen. On our first trip here in October 1974 we are the only boat. In June 1978 we are one of five other boats. In July 1995 I count fifty-five. In 1997 there are fifty during my August visit. In 1998 there are fifty-three boats including ten in my favorite Scobell Island anchorage. In 1999 I count ninety-four boats. But today, I hold my breath as I came around the corner to my only and favorite spot—no one there! So for the third time in three different boats, here I am in paradise. From the *Seaspell* log I wrote on October 12, 1974: "Call it anything, but call it beautiful—that's Prideaux Haven." From my *Nadja* log, June 14, 1978, I penned: "Prettiest spot I've ever seen—It's beauty is—indescribable. Beautiful is inadequate: God lives here; vegetation…unique; water…crystal, calm; air…fresh, aromatic; silence…except…crows! Taste and feel the presence of warmth, peace, freshness, infinity combined." On June 8, 1994, I wrote in the *Day by Day* log: "Same heaven as ever!" In 1997 I wrote "If heaven is as nice as Prideaux Haven, it will be a wonderful afterlife." In 1998 my words were, "On a Sunday, I feel close to God here." In 1999 I wrote in the log, "God's beauty here heals."

I have fun rowing in the dinghy around Paige Islets and follow my old footsteps on Scobell Island. Nearby, Harlan and Ann are anchored in their motor schooner *Askov*, which is the name of a Danish school in the town where Harlan was born. They are a delightful couple from Orcas Island, who with their cat, are on a six week trip around Vancouver Island. Their vessel is the perfect ship to make a cruise in style and comfort. They have been to Alaska in her and outside Baranof Island as I plan to do.

Two disturbing changes in Prideaux Haven since my previous visits are: A sign said not to take oysters as the water is polluted; an inflatable with young people storms through at high speed. For the most part, only the crows are the noisy ones.

In 1997, for the first time, my favorite spot is taken so I anchor near Roffey Island with three other boats including the Park Ranger. It isn't so bad. After seeing the Ranger take a dip in the saltchuck and reading 70 degrees water temperature on the sounder, why not? I row to a nearby slanted rock and gradually slip into the sea. Delightful! Next time I did bring saltwater soap. If you try regular soap you are in for a rude awakening. You'll think you put butch wax on! Boulders in the water look like a Roman pool when looking down from a nearby perch on Roffey Island.

Before bedtime I discover oil on each side of the engine forward. It turns out to be from the power steering which was replaced under warranty back home after the trip. The warranty ran out on this trip but I send a post card to my home dealer documenting the need. Fixing at no cost back home was no problem. Also on this trip, at times the oil pressure gauge will vary between 20–65 psi. With a slight touch of the throttle up or down, pressure will return it to normal. "Cheap gauges," said one mechanic on the trip. In 1998 I replace the sender—that was it, not the gauge. It is nice to be a great mechanic, but part of the fun of an adventure is figuring out how to get your self out of a jam. Develop alternatives and choose a solution after considering comparative advantages.

Day 3—June 9—133 naut mi to Sullivan Bay.

Areas around Prideaux Haven offer considerable territory for you to be the *Captain Vancouver* of your day if you overlook a few other boats. Numerous islands, intimate coves, varied width passages plus mountains make it a splendid boaters paradise. Plus, I have always found these waters calm. I have not found it so crowded you could not find a gunkhole to yourself. In June 1978 Cynthia and I find sunshine and water warm enough for swimming even though the week is punctuated with showers.

On this day, I leave a quiet anchorage at 0445 on a glass-smooth surface. *Day by Day* slips by Martin Islands on the inside and one lone fisherman. No other pleasure boats are out this early. We quickly pass Refuge Cove where we stopped in October 1974 and which has boater facilities. In fact since, it has been one of my favorite stops as it is for everyone it seems. It is a combination of the past with just enough tourist touch to make it a cozy cove that feels like home. I am so intent to head north that I completely forget about the bakery in Squirrel Cove, normally a must stop for boaters. Well, I am too early and I didn't call my order in the day before. By 1998 it was gone and a new restaurant replaced it. On this morning I reason that my waist line doesn't need the best cinnamon rolls around! Instead, I eat my Wheaties and banana at 19.2 knots up Lewis Channel with no-hands steering. Power assist steering is a great adjunct on a boat of this size. It is the next best thing to an autopilot, which we did have on *Nadja*, but we do not have on *Day by Day*. That is a desirable option for cruising alone.

We pass a colorful black, orange and white tug towing a huge logboom at Raza Island. We check by Church House on the starboard hand at 0608. It seems like fewer houses here now than in 1974. At that time we tied *Seaspell* to the dock, only to be greeted by barking dogs and unfriendly stares out windows. We quickly get the message we are not welcome. Now it looks like no one lives here. This morning we hop a Bute Inlet-bound fishing vessel wake. For the fourth time in twenty years, this morning I pass Stuart Island, Big Bay and a series of rapids and passages much quicker than I like. Big Bay is such an inviting, well-groomed, beautiful area that beckons you. I reason it is close enough to home that someday I can return to take it all in. And I since have done just that. Our former dentist, Ray, skipper of the *Argee*, told about the unique yacht club here with, as I recall, only four chairs! Ray said the outboard museum in the Liar's Lounge, where fishermen gather, alone is worth a visit. Lots of bait is jumping along the way this morning. Now we are doing up to twenty-four knots as we get an added push from the current through Yuculta Rapids, Gillard Passage and Dent Rapids. The water is as smooth as glass except for occasional turbulence that only gives us a slight nudge and temporary engine rpm rise. We dodge the few whirlpools that add interest to an otherwise tempting surface. I want to fall in love with every place along the way—it's that great!

At Stuart Island I find watching the timid approach the Yuculta's rather entertaining. I often am overwhelmed when the superrich come and go in some of the largest most elegant yachts I have seen ply these northern waters. Then I appreciate the plain and simple craft that show up too. At times my humble vessel seems luxurious. I am just grateful I can enjoy boating in these parts which to me is the best between Puget Sound and Alaska.

The boater should really schedule passage through the above rapids and passes at slack water or at a low current with you. I only casually look at the current tables, and decide I will go, look and wait, if necessary. As has been the case so much on this trip so far, God is guiding me all the way in harmony. It really seems like a good day to travel, and to fish and explore later. Sun and showers touch us today, so typical of this area in June, and just perfect if you are a true Northwesterner, as I am. On Cordero Channel we pass the first active logging camp I see on this trip. If you have time and can get a reservation and like German meals, eat at Cordero Lodge. I did once, and found it to be better than any in Germany I experienced.

On one trip I anchor at night in Cordero Channel near Greene Point Rapids. In full moon early the next morning before daylight, I gently head seaward at six knots guided by radar—delightful. That same trip I deliberately went through as many rapids as I could both with and against the current, some near maximum flow. If you are a skilled navigator and are watchful of drift wood, you can have a good time. I always do, but with some apprehension the first time. Fast tourist boats from Campbell River run up and down and turn sharply in Upper Rapids, something I would not do. I find Beazley Pass near Surge Narrows the most challenging.

Twice I enjoy stops at Thurlow Bay and walk the long dock envisioning what it was like in it's heyday. Both times the place, including the lodge and acreage, is for sale. Each time I imagine what it could be, and temporarily I see myself in that plan until reality hits me. It is the only place where I have been hit up for a dockage fee shortly after landing.

On through Greene Point Rapids. Going down Chancellor Channel this morning is like going down a smooth river with the tide and light wind. I stop at Kelsey Bay, which used to be the ferry terminal to Prince Rupert and a good place to take on fuel. Much to my surprise, most facilities are shut down or decaying. No gas dock is here. For those who wish to trailer this far north to access some very special country, there are two boat ramps. One is free behind the mill. The other is next to the abandoned ferry dock adjacent to the boat basin. For the later, launching was $5 and parking $2 per day in the lot next to the charter office. I leave a rainy Kelsey Bay, after flipping the inflatable on the hardtop up-side-down so it would not be a bathtub. If you go by way of Seymour Narrows, Otter Cove proves to be a good stop for me one night, all alone. If you go through Seymour it is good to go with the current which I have done to about eight knots. I would not want to do that in an opposing wind, however, so beware!

We enter a calm Johnstone Strait where a tug and tow is going no where until the tide turns. The morning ebb helps us as we pass a pleasure trawler and two motoring sailboats going our way. Don't they usually motor? Johnstone can be nasty, so I view today's calm as a blessing. Pretty varying shades of gray outline the distant mountains and hills beyond the far shore as the misty showers water the forest. A helicopter goes by in our direction at three hundred feet, below the damp ceiling of gray. After numerous passages this way, in 1998 I have a delightful stop at Port Neville to find a Government wharf and of all things a Post Office, but no store! The onetime store was in the now abandoned two story log home of Lorna's family. Lorna still lives on the family acreage with her daughter and mother nearby. Lorna will give you the history of the area. I even bought a stamp so I could mail Mother a letter post marked Port Neville.

I was anxious as we head up Havannah Channel into Boughey Bay. On June 12, 1978, Cynthia and I anchor here in *Nadja*. We are thrilled at dusk when a mother bear forages while her two cubs play close by on the west shore nearby. I am foolish enough to think I might see the same thing midday today. While I do not, I ease my mind with what might have been. We then motor slowly up Chatham Channel where I hope to see a repeat of our two passages in June 1978. On one, we count twenty-three eagles in a half mile scooping salmon ahead of us and a black bear on the north shore. On an other trip, I saw a bear combing the beach at low tide in this area. This time I see only two eagles watching the beach and an outboard fisherman zip by with lures fluttering in the breeze. In the channel, a tug not much bigger than a log truck is towing a boom of, by my estimate, 240 log truck loads. That's water power!

The disappointment of the day is pulling into Minstrel Island Resort to see the declining state. In 1978, we relish the place when we stop here twice and moor one night. At that time, a small coastal freighter with charm of long ago calls and unloads supplies. We play tag with her as we crisscrossed our pleasure and her work paths one day. There were more boats here at the resort then, both pleasure and trollers, some of which we knew, or had common contacts. Even Tom, on the Canadian fishing vessel *Barbara* who has property at Sandy Point, gave us a salmon then. Today Minstrel does not look like former times. The hotel was torn down in 1987. Today a mobile with a large "Pub" sign on it does not match the early delightful character of Minstrel, which is captured in my memory, and much earlier, on post cards for sale here. The freighter doesn't call any more and the mail must be slow, too. The first postcard I pick up to buy is stamped and addressed to someone written a month earlier! The next two I pick up are the same! At least I help the mail get going today, even if the clerk doesn't seem surprised. After topping off the gas, I am glad to be on my way. On other trips I find Lagoon Cove just around the corner, a nice clean place, but without the character of Minstrel. My idealism would have Minstrel restored some day. Looks can deceive. In 1999 I went into the Pub and have the best seafood chowder ever.

It goes without saying, from the San Juans to Alaska, there are three features you see constantly: water, trees and mountains. While I do not comment on them much, they are there! Perhaps it is the common reoccurring of these earthly gems some people find boring. To me they represent the ultimate amenities of God's creation along with other living organisms. Our travel north makes them appear as if they are constantly being arranged for our joy.

Looking at the charts and trying to find an alternative route to Echo Bay from our 1978 trip, I decide to try Clio Channel and Beware Passage after reading in *Secrets to Cruising North to Alaska* that Hugo Anderson has passed that way several times, suggesting north to south is best. No problem going through The Blow Hole, but we go slowly. Clio is easy. Beware is well named. At the south end I find it confusing and rock-strewn so I am extremely cautious, running with outdrive in the upper range and periodically stopping and walking forward on the deck to better see the bottom as we drift. My opinion is that this route is not worth the hazards involved. It is not fun or necessary, although it is for those who commercial pot fish in the channels. In 1999 I do go through Canoe Passage but it is strewn with kelp. The only place worth further exploring in this passage as I did in 1999, is the deserted Indian village of Mamalilaculla. It is in a nice setting which had modern buildings at one time. During my visit the grandson of the last village chief is here giving tours. I make a small donation as part of the effort to maintain the site. On three trips in this general area, I do see a few isolated pleasure boats at anchor.

My next stop is Echo Bay. There have been a lot of improvements since our previous most northward call in *Nadja* on June 12, 1978. I recall it as being a small, quaint place, and I am having a difficult time relating to all the changes, including the use of a section of the original Lake Washington floating bridge near the entrance, which is the foundation for the store and gas dock. Nancy and Bob have run Echo Bay Resort since 1981. They still sell gas by the imperial gallon and they take Discover card. My kind of place!

Speaking of gas, the most embarrassing item on our Bayliner is the gas fill location. The fill cap is vertical on the transom. From here the hose to the tank runs nearly horizontal which means almost uphill when loaded and sitting still. Once the hose is to tank elevation it runs level again from starboard to amidships. As you fill, air tries to escape up the same fill hose, meaning gas spills back into the bay. The air vent is real clever too. It runs the length of the tank inside from the forward end to a hose at the after end of the tank, then vents overboard on the transom. Prior to my putting on a $52 in-line Racor fuel/air separator, periodically during filling, gas would spew out the vent into the water or onto the service station driveway when filling on the trailer. This check valve stops that, but makes fill-spout back spills worse. When I confronted Bayliner, they said you must fill very slowly and that they would not correct the problem. During my awkward filling at Echo Bay, Nancy asks, "What is wrong?" as do most gas dock attendants. I explain the above, after which she asks, "Did they ever hear of gravity?" Now I always use absorbent pads to catch any fuel spill. When Nancy asks if I am traveling alone, I explain I would like to have my wife along but that no way would she be cooped up that long in a small boat, to which Nancy comments, "She is the sane one!"

After looking around and trying to recall how it used to be, I tie up at the Echo Bay Marine Park dock at the head of the bay and eat dinner aboard *Day by Day*. I always tie up here and usually have the dock to myself. It's a pleasure to walk to the one room school and the shell laden beach. Often I row around in the dinghy. It is a fun place. Moorage with electricity is available at one dock. Salmon fishing is reported to be slow here as evidenced by few boats. No wonder, with past fishing pressures and the destruction of salmon habitat. I recall reading recently about an area near Echo Bay where Ronald W. Miller (Calhoun, *Vol. II*) observed the catching of over five hundred big salmon in years past. Not any more. The one that makes me want to cry is the Nahmint Bay story in Alberni Inlet. The January 20, 1977, *Everett Herald* wrote glowingly of catching fifty pounders right beyond the resort float. The article warned of future fishing declines. In 1993, imagine my shock when I went there to sample my long held ultimate fishing venture to find the bay closed. The resort is a ruins. The bay is dead! This story is repeated over and over. All parties had better get serious and save the Pacific salmon now.

Today one person does bring in an impressive thirty-eight pound ling cod. An eagle in a nearby tree is being given the *what for* by two crows. It is noisy and intriguing to watch. Opposite the main resort on the north side of Echo Bay, house boats add to the color where James and Muffin run the Windsong Sea Village Resort. Besides their gift gallery, they can offer you float cabin rentals or adventure tours. The setting and comfortable resort facilities at Echo Bay make you want to linger awhile. I always try to stop here as long as I can. Showers are reasonable. Its the kind of place I would like to stay all summer. But then I would have a hard time seeing me in one place very long!

Now it is time to roar off. I want to visit Simoom Sound but become confused of it's whereabouts from my chart book after I see Simoom Sound PO next door to Echo Bay and not being able to find the post office, which turns out to be at Echo Bay now. By the time I figure it out, I am half way to Sullivan Bay reached by Penphrase and Pasley passages and Sutlej Channel. This country is great and deserves a return one day to check it all out which I do on later cruises. It is like wilderness; I am alone and I love it! In my view, the inlet areas north and east of southern Queen Charlotte Strait is as alluring as it comes. Sullivan Bay is worth a visit where I find moorage for $10 and a shower $4. It is a city on floats. Other than fuel tanks on the hillside, the rock-ribbed shore provides no place to build except on the water. It reminds me of Knott's Berry Farm in the forties. Clever little signs decorate the many small buildings along the floats like: "Sullivan Bay International Airport" where seaplanes land; "Aquarium" for rest room; "Pot Hole Department" for tool shed; "Sullivan Bay Power Co." for the generator shack, brought smiles to my, at times, childish nature. An open-air sawmill on one float cuts logs into lumber for the "city." Pat and Lynn, owners of Sullivan Bay since 1979, express their humor and friendliness at Sullivan Bay in a number of ways. I love it!

During my fueling, Pat and I get into politics. Pat is a very helpful person. In 1999 my engine is running rough. I and all of the so-called experts along the way could not seem to figure out the problem. After hearing about it, Pat said quickly, "Spark plug wires," after which he promptly gave me a used set. Changing one wire made the engine run like new again. So Pat is my hero in politics and engines!

Sullivan Bay has floats under individual homes. Some simple. Some elaborate. One has a picket fence around their float yard. There are some homes here on concrete floats as nice as any home at Sandy Point. Then there are some creative architectures. Sullivan Bay is also a haven for big US pleasure boats. One such is Haggen's *Check Out* of Bellingham, owner of the grocery chain bearing his name. His refurbished, large Uniflite is better than any model the company produced with her posh enclosed command bridge and green colors. She dwarfs *Day by Day* moored behind her tonight. Not to be outdone, nearby is a 100-ft east-coast yacht. As with every stop on my journey, *Day by Day* is always the smallest "yacht," although kayaks here are the smallest traveling craft. I am always grateful for my v-berth stateroom with head where I sleep well. Regardless what the literature says, this boat sits three, eats or fishes two and sleeps one. Surprisingly our 16 and 17-ft boats actually carried four people under cover better than this boat. As with most things in life each boat is a trade-off. This Trophy is a better boat for my style cruising than our 31-ft one was. As I age I should be more tolerant, but I also want more space!

Several boats are here tonight waiting to head north. All are bigger than us. The smaller of this fleet is *Saddie*, a 27-ft diesel Sea Sport owned by Pat and Loren from Bellingham. Even she is a "ship" to be admired and the only one in the waiting fleet that can cruise at *Day by Day* speed. I am amused at a seemingly unprepared couple cruising in large wooden boat. They made it from San Francisco but are without adequate charts so are tagging along with a Seattle boat. I later see them in Ketchikan, so more than luck is with them.

The evening float talk is about the gale warning posted for some time now. I state I don't think it is going to happen as the barometer is steady. Further, I announce I will be leaving early if the barometer stays constant in the morning and the automated sea and wind states are favorable. The consensus by the others is that they will meet at 0800 tomorrow to decide what to do. I plan to be long gone by then. Pat and Loren say they spent several hours that day programing their GPS with waypoints. *Gulp*, I have not done that and I do not know how! I do get good tips on places to duck into if necessary south of Cape Caution. In a neighboring pilot house I see a skipper doing his cruise planning. I decide I had better do my homework! So I do the best I know how. I make a list of bearings, distances and longitudes and latitudes as my waypoints. Rather than be in my GPS, they will be on paper and be my guide. After determining nine waypoints to Cape Caution, I am at least part ready before I bunk down.

Sullivan Bay to Ketchikan

Day 4—June 10—146 naut mi to Oliver Cove.

I awake after daylight, later than I expect. The barometer is 30.23, the same as when I went to bed and the local water is calm with no breeze. The automated reports are all favorable but the gale is still forecast. Normally you don't mess around with this kind of report because they tend to be more right than wrong. Besides, I have lain awake nights at home trying to imagine what my crossing and this part of the Queen Charlotte Strait might be like. This time I sleep through that nonsense and feel confident and refreshed. Before leaving, I decide to rap on *Sadie's* cabin and see if I can arouse Loren and interest them in an early morning crossing. Loren steps out and says that they will stay. They are prepared to hole up several days if necessary until the threat of the gale passes. Now I know why I travel alone! Most laugh at my independence.

In 1979 I steer the *Pursuit* across the middle of southern Charlotte Strait in the dusk and dark of night. She is 44-ft and two of us keep watchful eyes on the chart, radar and into the darkness. This time I am it! Plus, I have never been along this western shore, and my charts are inadequate.

At 0515, I fire up the Chev V-6, only to have black smoke roll out the exhaust. After two carburetor rebuilds on warranty, now this! Does anybody still believe carburetors are better than electronic fuel injection? Not me! This is exactly why I have argued with Mer-Cruiser why they should be using fuel injection as GM does with this engine in Chevrolet S10 pickups and Blazers. By 1999 they did on this model, giving fifty-five horsepower more than on our engine. This is but another of my arguments how MerCruiser is slow to adopt new technology on their outdrive power. This has been true for all three MerCruiser's we have owned. They were slow to adopt electronic ignition. The V-6 MerCruiser did not have multi-port fuel injection, even by early 2000.

Now that I have that out of my system, we glide into calm channels by ourselves at 0525. With great anticipation we slide into Patrick Passage and down Wells Passage at twenty-five knots. At long last we enter Labouchere Passage into Queen Charlotte Strait. My

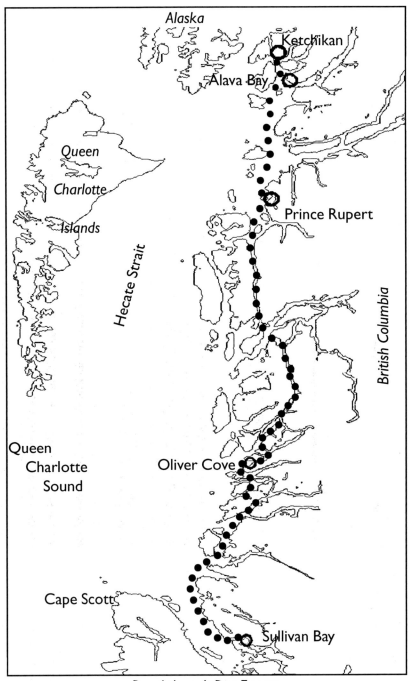

Day 4 through Day 7 route.

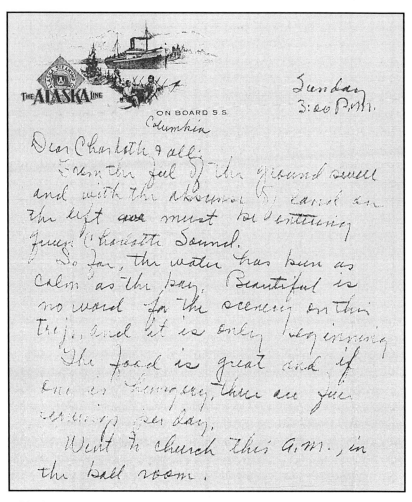

My first awareness of Queen Charlotte Sound is from this August 1941 letter from Dad to Mother, written while crossing on the way to Seward.

strategy is to just nose out and turn back if conditions are unfavorable. My heart leaps as I find a perfect morning. The early sun paints a peak orange. Three peaks with snow remind me this is north country in June. Is this right for me being out here this morning? I can only say it looks and feels right, but only if God directs my path. This morning it all seems we are given a *go*. For me, this has always worked on important things. For little things that go wrong, it only keeps me humble.

Beside me on the table are my rough notes of the night before with waypoint data if needed. My fellow dock cruisers last night were helpful to point out that Blunden and Allison harbors are good refuges going north before Cape Caution. Since this trip, I have been in both.

Passing between Lewis Rocks and Numas Islands I decide to cut the corner of the two chart book headings of 195 and 275 magnetic. No point of using extra fuel, and besides it looks like a piece of cake. If I were a group member, I would still be back at Sullivan Bay. There are no other pleasure boats out with me, but in the main channel it looks like considerable commercial traffic. The Canadian gillnet fleet is going north. At least I have company. That is very comforting, even though they sound foreign on the radio and I can't understand a word. I guess they are from Vancouver. What ever happened to all the Scandinavian and Yugoslavian fishermen (called fishers today to be politically correct) who were around when I was a kid? Times do change!

Anyway, it is nice out here. This is the farthest north I have ever been in any of our boats. This coast is not as intimidating as I pictured in my mind. In rough water your notion undoubtedly changes. I zip north toward Richards Channel munching my low fat granola bar. Together with orange juice it makes a good ocean breakfast when you are underway. Near Jeannette Islands we pass the first of a number of gillnetters. The headings on my ancient *Evergreen Cruising Atlas* are working fine.

Then I see a BC ferry going north further out and a tug and tow ahead going our way. The Canadian gillnetters seem to travel in pairs. Smart! To date I have yet to see a smaller vessel than ours going north. As the fishing vessels grind away, I wonder what they think of my smaller, faster boat. Do they think I am foolish or do they make other curious comments? It does not matter. Displaying our Furuno radar and radar reflector, we look nautical and serious.

We pass close to Harris Island and Dickenson Rock to the outside. While the chart shows a light on Harris, many of the new lights, while powerful as a lighthouse, have no character. Strictly functional. I want to explore Nakwakto Rapids on this trip, but I wait until 1996. Today it is northward.

At 0735 I notice a sandy beach on shore. This coast is scenic. In 1998 in ideal weather I anchor just south of Cape Caution at coordinates 51° 08.49'N, 127° 43.43'W, and explore a postcard-picture cove with a sandy beach partially sheltered by a small island. I was positive no one else had ever been here. When I enter the woods off the beach near where I land, to my surprise, I find a well-hidden shelter from the wind, complete with driftwood benches and dry firewood. It is so neat and tidy that it could be someone's sanctuary in the wild. Obviously, I treat it with great respect. This cove could also serve as an emergency anchorage in a storm.

A sandy beach just south of Cape Caution.

Although there is no need today for my GPS waypoints, I do eye the readings as I near each one just to verify both the GPS and I are correct. So far so good! I am feeling like an old salt and in love with this boat as she carries me safely toward the land of the midnight sun. Somehow the Trophy seems big, high and proud above the sea. Her 12-volt outlet (in 1999 I added a second one) powers the GPS and when needed, my laptop computer, a 12-volt vacuum, spotlight or emergency CB radio. I consider CB's junk with cluttered meaningless chatter, but in an emergency they may be the best contact with someone on water or land. My goal is to avoid CB use. I prefer the more professional VHF radio and it should be used as such. On this trip, I do not have a cellular phone on board but I did in 1999. Like VHF, cellular does not have 100 percent coverage.

At last at 0751, we pass within twelve hundred feet of Cape Caution in five fathoms as my atlas shows you can. Only on a smooth day! Otherwise move off shore. The Cape is so named for good reason and should be given a wide berth in rougher seas. My new *Marine Atlas, Vol. 2*, shows passage three-quarter mile off shore; still too close for some days. By 0800, when the Sullivan Bay skippers meet to decide what to do, I am nearly across Queen Charlotte Sound! We run on the outside of Egg Island and head for Dugout Rocks. On later trips I learn to favor passing inside both Iron rocks, Egg and Table islands and close to shore near Kelp Head, dodging the rocks, using just three headings and Chart 3934, when going to Rivers

There really is an egg on Egg Island!

Inlet. The sea-foamed broken surface alerts you when rocks are near. In 1998 in perfect conditions, I anchor on the east side of Egg Island and scramble up the steep bank to the lighthouse where I meet the light keeper and his son. They give me a tour, tell me of their duties and describe what life is like in isolation. It sounds appealing! The lighthouse on Egg Island is high above the sea, yet stories tell the horrors of days when it was not high enough, destroying the original light. It is hard to imagine such a mean sea. I felt privileged to get a pass on this day and on each of my trips north. At 0817, I eat my first KitKat candy bar. I only brought four of these onetime favorites, but after a smooth crossing of Queen Charlotte, I deserve one! When it is so calm I wish we had a 350 engine and could cruise thirty knots. But today, I am grateful just to make it across.

Before leaving home I got a haircut from Marlo, our former neighbor and a barber. He has never owned a boat, but he has caught more big salmon than I will ever dream of catching. Pictures of his catch hang in his shop to prove it. When I told Marlo of my boating plans, he told me how to fish Rivers Inlet. So at 0830, I turn on the sounder to find the area teeming with fish on the screen. Excitedly, I put the gear in the water the way Marlo told me to do. After awhile, I wonder why no strikes. Checking the sounder I note it is on simulation mode! No fish! In fact, on the proper setting the water is sterile. Another clue should have been that no one is fishing today. Only two divers are nearby, perhaps after some seafood.

Lots of boat traffic consisting of large yachts, cruise ships and commercial vessels pass by Rivers Inlet while I am here. After nearly three hours and no bites, I explore Klaquaek Channel with caution since I do not have adequate charts. It is a perfect protected place for lunch or for anchorage with many islands including Penrose Island Marine Park.

While I am searching these unfamiliar waters, a fast small boat approaches. It turns out to be Jim, the owner and operator of the old cannery, Goose Bay Fishing Resort, who asks, "What are you up to?" To my reply, "Fishing," he says, "You're a month too early!" This, in spite of Anderson's claim that he caught twenty-five and thirty-five pound Chinooks in May 1984. Jim is very accommodating and offers his services if he could be of help. I see him later after I use the outboard to motor through a shallow channel into Darby Channel when Jim says, "We don't go that way." Well, I made it, but I must admit I did not have an adequate chart. I reason that since we brought the fishing boat south with just a chart book, that my twenty-one charts and two chart books will be adequate. They are, if you follow the main channels but if you explore off the beaten path as I have since, it is good to have more charts. Some of my old charts in the seventies only cost $1. Now they are about $15 and no limit on how many you could buy. My budget and space restrained me. It did not dawn on me at home that I might need more detail. So I proceed in out-of-the-way places with extreme caution.

I decide to forgo further exploration of Rivers Inlet and Dawsons Landing. I reason someday I will return to fish, and I have. As we depart, an eagle watches us as though we don't belong here. We head up Fitz Hugh Sound with a light breeze behind us and light rain. About twenty dolphins are feeding on the eastern shore. At first I think we are near rocks so I stop to check. Soon one of the rocks came within twenty feet of the boat!

Colorful scows never stopping hauling equipment to Alaska. I stop to chat with a couple in a 24-ft sloop going our way. They are from California and plan to go as far as they can all summer. They like the rain and not having to buy gas as they sail north at nine knots. Without thinking, I tear off too quickly leaving an arrogant power-boat wake. I feel badly about that afterwards.

At 1518, I get a big skipper's wave from a troller-long-liner heading south. He probably has a load of halibut to sell in Puget Sound. Lots of other fishing vessels heading south too. I wave at a gillnetter as I pass the same way. He does not wave. He probably doesn't like tourists!

Going by yourself is really good for the soul. You set your own schedule. You test your self and it tells you if you are really a mariner. The rainy-calm now reminded me of my commercial trolling days at its best. I take a swig of ice cold cider from the jug in the ice chest. Just like the days when I would drench my parched throat after pulling fish on a warm day on the ocean.

As I pass Fog Rocks to starboard on Fisher Channel, I think, unlike our previous Bayliner, no leaks. Oops, I spoke too soon! Three of them. One runs back into the sink. That's handy! The other drains into the storage under the aft dinette seat. Not so handy! The good news is that this Trophy has a fiberglass cabin sole (floor) so leak water runs to a drain and keeps the berthing area dry. I like the gentle rains. They wash the salt off the boat.

At 1700, we arrive at New Bella Bella, a native fishing village. After topping off the tank, I relax in *Day by Day* at the float, as I have dinner aboard after a call home. The BC ferry *Queen of the North* calls at the dock while we are here with passengers and freight only. Now there is vehicle service to a new terminal south of town. The Heiltsuk Hotel near the dock accommodates overnight stays during my 1994 trip, but is now closed. On the dock, a van bumper sticker has a good reminder, "God Loves You." Amen!

By 1900 we head out in the wet, but not wild. A chemically treated anti-fog cloth works well since Bayliner does not give you defrosters like Sea Sport does. But our 21-ft costs about half of their 22-ft, so the rag is a bargain! The closer we get to Ivory Island, the rain and fog thicken. The radar is useful to help me spot the channel to Reid Passage. At 2000 near Ivory Island I am punchy with fifteen hours at the helm. For a long time I can't figure out why the VHF has so much static. Finally, I discover the bilge blower is on! I have a lot of respect for the continuous government VHF marine broadcasts in US and BC waters. They may not always be accurate, but it is comforting to have them, even though they don't give up on the gale that just will not come! We anchor alone and peacefully in Oliver Cove after using the cruising guide harbor chart. I go to sleep in a very bright drizzle, at 2145, that softly patters the deck above.

Day 5—June 11—168 naut mi to Prince Rupert.

Dampness is the villain in a small boat. No, today is not like that boat show in the warm, dry Kingdome (now demolished) when you drooled over those sleeping quarters! Between the window leaks and water vapor on them, I am glad to get dry heat. The engine heater is super but I need a window or two open a bit to let damp air out. When running in the rain I roast myself trying to dry things out. After a day's run, the engine is a great place on which to dry non-salty wet things overnight. Just don't forget to remove them before the next day's run.

On the water, there is wider freedom to explore and to travel as you please. You can travel in a kayak or on the biggest ship and go literally anywhere in the world. I am fascinated by the wide variety of watercraft you see when you boat. It also amazes me how well disciplined skippers self-enforce the rules of the road. With that observation in mind we leave Oliver Cove at 0555.

I use the radar as another pair of eyes. Admittedly, it is difficult to locate the pass south of Lake Island to go up Mathieson Channel with just the chart book. The current is ebbing about three knots against ocean swells creating a breaking bar condition and visibility is not that good. I ease *Day by Day* slowly forward at about three knots and 1,500 rpm with a close watch on the bottom with the electronic charting sounder. Ideally, we would wait for a tide change, but slowly and surely we pass the shallows and mildly breaking waves. This is the roughest water so far and I am impressed the way my vessel handles.

The rest of the trip to Jackson Passage is easy, but it is a Furuno day. Radar is awesome. It serves better than a second wiper on the port side, which I do not have. My motto today in the rain is: Better a leaky boat in BC than a dry one at home in the garage. Drips show up in the v-berth on the starboard side. I ingeniously rig foil, pans and a cottage cheese container to keep the cushion from getting soaked. I wear shorts inside since it is so hot with the heat on high and wear Helly Hanson's outside in the rain when I must. My living space is limited and even more so when drying things out. One thing about Bayliner, no charge for the leaks, they come standard. At least that has been my experience on two new boats. Our Uniflite leaked too in heavy spray and at the time they were considered a high quality boat.

By 0745 we enter Jackson Passage by following the red line on the atlas. We get a three knot push on the ebb thirty minutes before a 1.8 ft low as we ease our way down this picturesque passage at six knots. This is one way to increase fuel mileage. It is hard to steer as the boat yaws and over steers past mini waterfalls and dense vegetation along the rock-hemmed shore. Anderson, my atlas and *Sailing Directions* all advise passage only at high slack, at least for large craft, but we have no problem. On this route you avoid the ocean exposure of Milbanke Sound.

We quickly cross Finlayson Channel and follow a smaller cruise boat *Spirit of Alaska* into Klemtu. She is a good snow plow as there is a lot of debris in the channel. People are crowded on board like cattle. Not my way to travel! We arrive at the gas dock at 0855 but it does not open until 1000. Watch your fenders here. Passing boats don't slow down that much and their big wakes will toss your fenders on the float. It would be nice to have a diesel and pass by these expensive gas places and not have to wait. We could have made it to Prince Rupert without refueling but it is good practice to have plenty of fuel for possible side trips or extra distance travel in case of bad weather.

Day by Day has an excellent Visa portable marine head in the v-berth. It is nearly as good as the Thetford we had in our motor home. I must say though, it is a lot better for just one person than for a full crew for a lot of reasons!

As we leave Klemtu, an eagle flies across our bow unconcerned about all of the boat traffic. Next is one of my favorite spots: Sarah Island (Boat Bluff) Light facing across the narrow channel to Jane Island. Five red-roofed buildings perch on a rocky slope toward two deep, narrow passes that look like an ideal place to live, work and fish. You sure would get a close look at all boat traffic. The narrow reaches from Klemtu to Prince Rupert appeal to me on all three of my passages to date. No spot intrigues me more on this leg than Butedale, a well-lit cannery in former days, next to a generous waterfall. In the past my skippers would pass quickly. This time I am at the helm and I will take a closer look. Unfortunately, there are no more lights here and the facilities are failing. It looks like some materials are being salvaged. Butedale will never be the same. Some-how the "Welcome to Butedale" sign does not match the atmosphere today. Workers at the site show no interest in our presence. Fortunately, the waterfall will remain and be special. On a later trip I give you an update.

These channels stretch your neck as you try to see the craggy peaks and waterfalls that ribbon their way from snow line to sea level. Except for some nasty chop on Wright Sound, we pass over calm or slightly rippled water. You have to watch for the ever-present drift-wood. Lots of it today. And lots of passing boats both ways to keep your interest. Almost like I-5! Well, not that bad. Today is punctu-ated with heavy rain showers that pass like translucent curtains, then sun patches. Very pleasant really. Radar is helpful, but not mandatory today.

Be sure to look into Lowe Inlet, a marine park, as you pass. From the south the rock in the inlet looks like a polar bear. Too many times I went by and fail to see the falls or use the anchorage. I will always remember Grenville Channel. It was here in May 1978 I first used radar when it was my turn at the helm of the *Pursuit*. It was night but you couldn't go wrong. Those rock shorelines look like fencerows. Just stay between them! Today, the sea is generally glassy except for a jolting wake now and then. We do meet a Washington trawler, *Victory*, heading south leaving a seemingly innocent wake but the short and sharp wave knock a nut loose from overhead. Where to, I know not to this day. It is a real kidney buster and for sure tests our Bayliner 5-year hull warranty! When cruising Grenville, just follow the distant V's formed by the mountains to the sea. It's that easy.

The water is clear and blue most of the day, but as we near Calvert Point, it is very green. You see the tide-change line distinctly in the channel. Then we cross the biggest wake of the day from the tug *Ivar Foss*, going our way. Thanks, Cheryl! Our daughter is a CPA for Foss Maritime, who started boating with us since she was nine months old. Don't we still sometimes blame our kids for everything? After that uncalled for comment, I was positive the chart book was in error too! As I round Gibson Island, heading for Kennedy Island I notice the land and sea do not match the chart book. At Lewis Island, I stop to figure it out. Oops, I am looking at the chart up Petrel Channel on the same page below, which looks quite similar. Finally, I admit I am wrong and continue into Prince Rupert. The Skeena Delta is not fun at all. The water is dirty and the low-lying islands, numerous markers and boats everywhere confuse my weary mind. I have read where long periods on the water running in a boat can give you alcohol-like tendencies. I think I have them this evening!

After fueling, I raft next to a small, old troller in the Rushbrooke boat basin on the east end of town for $8.49 for the night. The lady in the port office asks everyone to write down in a book the origin of their boat name. It is fascinating to scan the list to see the reasons. Source of a book someday? A Bayliner owner planned to do just that, as we owners got letters inviting us to submit similar data. When you read the "Day by Day" poem at the beginning of this book you probably guessed the origin of our boat name. One time running to Neah Bay in *Seaspell* near Race Rocks, I was listening to the then popular song, "Day by Day", when I said to myself, what a neat name for a boat. Three boats later it is on our best boat of all. Today, there are lots of boats in port, many double rafted. Before bedtime, I take a needed energetic hike to town for groceries.

Day 6—June 12—110 naut mi to Alava Bay.

By 0430 we make an early run out Venn Passage to Metlakatla Bay in the early light which reminds me of a wide St. Joe River in Idaho. A red sky predominates as we head 310 magnetic toward Ketchikan only sixty-three miles away. The closer we get to Green Island, the stronger a NE breeze is blowing out of Portland Inlet. Sun shown under a sudden cloud, that looks like a dome cover on a stadium. For the first time, we are planing along in a beam sea taking on spray. I am glad to pass behind Green Island but the reprieve is short. Soon I will have to decide to go on or wait some place. The forecast still calls for a gale, but it appears the water is calmer ahead as we leave Whitly Point. It is only twelve miles across and by closing a mile every three minutes, I reason we will be in greater shelter. It works. With each mile the water smooths. I am grateful for my nautical sense and for God answering my prayer thoughts and guiding me safely. I realize I have to be humble, and not smug, about my accomplishments.

Before starting across Dixon Entrance I think about getting the dinghy down, but do not. I want the cockpit as clear as possible in case I needed to use the outboard, should we lose power. I am amazed at the hull design and how we cruise in almost every condition, especially in a beam sea. By 0710 we reach Tree Point in a glassy calm. I stop the boat and kneel in gratitude. We made it to Alaska! It is Sunday morning so I have my devotional adrift on the sea. The rocky shoreline reminds me of the area around Race Rocks. I enjoy a breakfast and take some pictures. Now when I sit in the boat at home, it won't be all dreams. There will be memories too. On this morning I reflect upon the many years of dreaming and talking to others about such a trip—now here I am!

On this trip I find moist towelettes (we call them Handi Wipes) to be of great value for washing face, hands and body as a mini-bath. I thought if they're good enough for babies, they're good enough for me! By now I realize I am fully living on the edge for most of the long daylight days and it is so great! I love it! When I am up north I admit that I leave all my cares of the world behind. And probably my responsibilities. Is it selfish? Yes. Maybe one day my book will repay the world with joy and information. I hope so.

By 0811 we are off and running again toward Ketchikan and arrive at 1021 with the tide. I finally clear Customs by phone on the sixth attempted call two hours after arriving. Ketchikan is a very busy place with boats, planes and cruise ships coming and going. In a short while we have sun and showers. I tie up at City Floats to run errands including getting an Alaskan fishing license at one of the neatest stores I have ever been in—the Tongass Trading Company, where they have things for the whole family. Their commercial fishing department is the best I ever saw. I reluctantly buy more

You see a lot of cruise ships at Ketchikan.

charts after realizing I am a bit weak on information between Sitka and Craig.

Since we make it to Ketchikan two days quicker than I plan, we have extra time to go around Behm Canal or go to Elfin Cove. These are two unplanned, but very desirable destinations. When I call Cynthia, I suggest she come up and we get an apartment and stay all summer. "No?" I came close to getting a job here once, so maybe a mini-stay would satisfy that unfilled longing. It is fun to watch people commute in small skiffs to and from town and the adjacent islands. One woman, as she lands her skiff, carries a baby in one arm and garbage and a canvas bag in another. Bob, the skipper of the Bellingham fishing vessel *Desire*, is selling whole halibut off the boat for $2 per pound. I should have bought some rather than three State and Province licenses for over $100! Watch out for the creosote on City Floats! Lots of it.

The intensity to try to do everything I want in a twenty-hour day is staggering. It is like cramming everything you ever wanted to do by living in Alaska for one week! You can't, but it is fun to try! There is so much I could share about my short stay in Ketchikan, but better yet, why don't you come and enjoy it yourself? It's a great place! I do feel insignificant though in our small boat next to the cruise ships; walking around town I am lost in the crowd of passengers. While next to one cruise ship I was thinking for about the same money as my trip, I could be on a ship and have great meals. I quickly dismiss that idea. I like my way!

I decide I will try fishing, then go around Behm Canal since I am ahead of schedule. Before leaving, there are the usual fueling and associated tasks to do. Gas prices are very reasonable in Ketchikan. They are very high in BC. The problem I have here is that for some reason I cannot get the boat to take fuel at the Union 76 dock without constantly spilling over. I finally quit and go to dump the head in the cleanliest restroom in town. Unfortunately, I plug up the toilet in the process and flood the floor with you-know-what! What a mess! I do clean it all up. Do you suppose this is how Ketch-i-kan got its name? It certainly caught mine! After a shower I am finally done after spending next to no money here. I give the attendants $5 for putting up with me so they can get a snack. I have little trouble filling at Chevron.

Fishing near the edge of town at Mountain Point like all the rest means no fish! Next we have a peaceful calm cruise to Alava Bay at the south end of Behm Canal. I hope to have the place to myself, but there are four other boats here. Two well-found Seattle trollers, the *Nina* and the *Josephine*, have the only Forest Service buoy intended for the Service's cabin users. After dropping the hook, I cannot start the V-6 to set it, as I fail to leave the engine running. I am tired and after a meager setting of the hook with the outboard, I think maybe in the morning the engine will start.

Day 7—June 13—42 naut mi to Ketchikan.

I awake early and think, all this big country, and we five boats are all squeezed into this small bay! Anyway, it is beautiful wilderness country. In the bays you get the feeling along Behm Canal you are at some large, scenic, high-mountain lake. I row the dinghy ashore to check out the Forest Service cabin, which is clean, comfortable and well stocked. They are left unlocked but you must get a permit for $25 per night to use them or risk a $500 fine and six months in prison! For more information on cabins or to get a permit contact Misty Fiords Ranger District in Ketchikan.

The engine starts fine. By 0630 we are underway to Harris Island to catch a halibut. After fishing one spot, I decide to move to another, but, again the V-6 will not start. After a few tests, I conclude it is the electronic brain. So, I fire up the 8 hp Mercury outboard and start for Ketchikan, twenty-six miles away. I try trolling part way but I soon lose interest in that and think I'd better concentrate on getting there as fast as possible. The weather is ideal and the water calm. On the way, I study the GPS manual and learn to program it, so it is a good day and we were still a day ahead of schedule.

We average three knots, and reach Ketchikan by 1630. The Chevron dock attendant helps me locate a combination Bayliner and Mer-Cruiser dealer, a fortunate find in SE Alaska. I soon learn a free *Southeastern Alaska Phone Directory* is a valuable resource to have. When I call Gordon, the owner of Gray Marine, I am told that they cannot work on my boat for ten days. Several prayers and phone calls later, I am told his MerCruiser mechanic will see me at the Thomas Basin after work. After rafting next to an older Bayliner Trophy, where I spend the night, the mechanic determines after tests, that our starter is bad. He claims in order to get it out, the engine will have to be pulled! It seems plausible as space is tight. The estimate for all this work is about $850. Another call to Gordon and I have arrangements to haul out the next day and be towed to the shop. Since they are backlogged, I agree to do all the work except to install a new starter, which might be covered by warranty. It expired two days prior! So, for the first time I sleep aboard our new boat with a dead engine.

Ketchikan to Sitka

Day 8—June 14—36 naut mi to Princess Bay.

Last night I have my best sleep of the trip; over seven hours without awakening. Before haul out, I enjoy looking over more of Ketchikan. I am intrigued by a 19-ft Glassply towing, with the current, a full size scow with a fishing lodge and outboard shop on it! She is being towed from winter anchorage to the tug dock so she can be taken to her summer location. You see many different things here. I also visit the Forest Service Visitor Center, where I find a very helpful staff and excellent literature.

After haul out on a perfect morning when I should be exploring, here I am removing the manifold to gain access to the starter. I am not resentful, but grateful that I can speed the work. The good news is that we will not have to pull the engine. When I get down to the last starter bolt, I cannot get it out. I go into the shop to look for help. There I meet Richard, the outboard mechanic from Port Angeles, my adopted home town, who says, "Let's take a look." Minutes later he uttered, "It's not the starter. It's the solenoid," he concludes, after wondering if it was the starter before making a test. So, I put everything back together and Richard changes the solenoid, which could have been fixed in the water last night! As we finish the work, the morning cloudless sky turns to an afternoon shower. But I am relieved and glad. When the MerCruiser mechanic returns and is told what happened, he shrugs, "I have been missing quite a few of my diagnoses lately." When Gordon learns about all this, he is extremely apologetic to me. When I ask about the bill, he says, "You don't owe me anything." Mercury Marine and Gray Marine covered

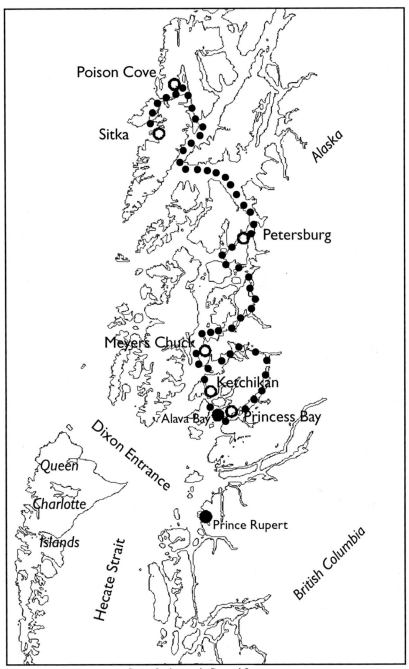

Day 8 through Day 12 route.

the cost. By 1700 we are back into the water. I am still a day early on my trip plans so off we go to Behm Canal again.

The lessons of gratitude I learn as the result of our breakdown are: People are very good to me; the breakdown happens at a very good place and time (it could have been much worse); I learn GPS operation and more about MerCruiser repair; I learn more about Ketchikan; God cares for me. I was saddened to learn in 1999, Gray Marine is no longer in business. Gordon did say it is hard to get good mechanics for a short season in Alaska.

Tonight we are alone tied to the Forest Service cabin buoy in Princess Bay on Behm Canal. This is like wilderness—so peaceful and no other boats.

Day 9—June 15—138 naut mi to Meyers Chuck.

The engine starts easily this morning. We move out early with fog seaward and a golden sun ahead creating a fairyland of a calm canal. The buttermilk ever-changing sky keeps my interest in competition with the boat-less majesty of the canal, its adjacent snow-capped

New Eddystone Rock.

peaks and dashing waterfalls. A sight I shall never forget is New Eddystone Rock standing like a sentinel in the middle of the canal silhouetted in front of a rising sun. Yes, this day is my time and place!

Anderson claims Walker Cove, our next stop, is excellent for ling cod. After a few jigs, something grabs my line and off it went until the leader breaks. I must have jerked too hard to stop the escape and that was it. No wonder fishermen are called liars! Who is going to believe me? Soon we are on our way soaking up the beauty others have described and photographed. No one can truly capture what you see and feel on these God-given days. We make a quick loop into Bell Island Hot Springs. For years I dream of coming here and having a hot mineral bath. I confirm what the atlas says about visitors not welcome. A sign says, "Closed, keep out, no trespassing, no boats." Another reads, "No visitors." So, no bath!

We are the only boat in sight for fifty miles around the Canal—nice. By lunch time we are at Clover Pass Resort. Really a tidy place with cabins, RV space and moorage reachable by road from Ketchikan. Cynthia and I stay here one night in the summer of 1980 when we fly around SE Alaska. There are a lot of good fishing stories from here, but today management says it is slow. Four fishermen bring in three small halibut.

Our third call to Ketchikan completes the 130 mile loop as we take on gas before heading north again. After a calm morning, winds push up good-sized waves to follow us the rest of the day up Clarence Strait. Not a pretty passage by the last day's standards. I am spoiled. During dinner we drift with a 1½ knot set the way we want to go as I read the paper and trail a herring. No fish, but as I am brushing my teeth, I spot a black bear well over a mile north of Ship Island on the beach of Cleveland Peninsula. Through binoculars, I watch the bear chew on twigs along the shore for five minutes until disappearing into the brush.

In 1979 when we brought the seiner south, we came and left Meyers Chuck in the dark. Tonight I am glad to nudge our way into the narrow opening from a roughening sea at nightfall. I drop the hook in the chuck without going ashore. Later I learn that I miss the ladder-access tree-fort breakfast restaurant, Village Arts Co-op Gallery and Meyers Chuck Lodge. Although I saw more of Meyers Chuck than I did in 1979, I wish I could have seen more. In 1999 I do, and tie to the main dock. Several Washington yachts are here. I walk the dock and nearby trail along the cove that connects all buildings. This place is a picture of the past. Some new cabins are sprouting up between former life in the community of a defunct store and a closed modern school for a lack of students. This takes away the person who ran the tree house breakfast spot. The Lodge is

An ideal home site in Meyers Chuck.

closed and for sale. I overhear a woman from the lodge say, "It gets old fast." The old Post Office is closed and the new one is on an island. To me the ideal life is living in the rustic cabin on a small rocky island in the chuck partially supported by piling, with a postage stamp yard. A dock holds a fishing boat and a skiff for rowing to the main float.

Day 10—June 16—110 naut mi to Petersburg.

We leave early with Clarence Strait still rough, but the waves are with us again. We pass between Lemly Rocks and McHenry Ledge into a calmer Ernest Sound. After a miscue into Santa Anna Inlet, I realize it isn't the Anan Bay that I was looking for. I try fishing on Kuakan Point on Deer Island. No dice. We next anchor in Anan Bay. One larger boat at anchor leaves soon after our arrival, so we are alone. I row in shallows to the shore but discover I could have tied to an anchored float closer in, which I do in 1999. I explore the Forest Service A-frame, with oil heat, overlooking a meadow of trilliums and buttercups and the bay. Next I hike the one-mile boardwalk and stepped trail to the famed bear observatory. Today no people, no bear or spawning salmon. Walking back I see a sign that I didn't see coming up, "Warning. Bear use this trail." In 1999 this sign is gone and a lot of fine print explains how to behave in bear country. I do walk noisily so as not to surprise a bear. Get a bear facts brochure from Forest Service, Alaska or British Columbia or use the book in the Bibliography if you are going into bear country. Anyway, this little side trip was fun and scenic even without bear. Ditto for my 1999 trip. Since 1994, additional bear viewing platforms have been added. I understand during bear times lots of tourists come by tour boat from Wrangle, so choose which experience you want. On these trips I do see bear scat, so I blow my whistle periodically. Later while in Montana I learn you should not use shrill whistles as it attracts a bear's curiosity! Okay! Now I carry my boat hook and tap my wedding ring against the metal tube as metallic sounds are to alert a bear of your presence without attracting them. Bells are supposed to be good, too. Advice of bear experts is that you should not hike solo in bear country, as I do, and never run from a bear.

Next we head for Wrangle via Blake Channel and The Narrows. Being under charted, I again make the passage with great caution until I see a planing crab boat come through the tight spot, then I lose all anxiety. The closer you get to Wrangle the dirtier the water gets from the Stikine River. Boy, am I spoiled. I do not like it when the surface is opaque to anything below.

After a restful stop and a brief look at Wrangle, I conclude the main street appearance hasn't changed much from the 1910 postcard picture I saw here. Still I am glad I stopped. Wrangle is my best stop for buying gifts. I also buy two engine belts after thinking I should have them. The parts man confirms that belt failures are one of the top causes of boat engine failure in SE. Of course he is selling belts! The yellow paint on the floats here can make a mess out of your fenders.

We have a choice to take the shorter route to Petersburg up Dry Strait (see *Coast Pilot*; Anderson says don't go that way) or the longer trip through Wrangle Narrows. I opt for the later since I did not absorb it all on my only passage through it on the seiner in 1979. Besides, my trip plans do call for Wrangle Narrows as a must see. I never tire of it.

It is a dull drag to Wrangle Narrows bucking a westerly in silty water down Sumner Strait. Finally, fun begins as we wind our way down a scenic river of tidal water up to twenty-three knots. Numerous homes dot the wilderness-like shores. I had a job offer once to work in Petersburg and I had visions of living along here. So my longing continues, since we did not move here. Seeing all the fast boats heading south after work, I conclude they must be commuters or fisherman. Did I miss something? According to a store lady in Wrangle, her Forest Service husband caught a freezer full of halibut at Anan Bay! She didn't say when. Next time!

By 1730 I am tied to the dock at the Beachcomber Inn in Scow Bay about three miles south of Petersburg. Cynthia and I ate here in 1980 and I remember it as a top seafood restaurant. The Inn is a former cannery overlooking the Narrows. It does not disappoint. My meal of smoked black cod and Snicker's pie is sumptuous. The only thing missing is Cynthia. I call her from the Inn. Mean trick! On the other hand, this is my only restaurant meal out on the trip, and I picked the best to savor for a long time. Besides, I need a break from all

Beachcomber Inn, early cannery, now a restaurant.

those canned foods! In May 1999 I was sorry the Inn was not yet open for the season and remodeling was going on. Gourmet cooking aboard is not an objective on my trips. Quick, simple healthy meals are, as I am very busy and on the move. In fact, on my trips I eat no butter, margarine, mayonnaise (we learned that in Germany) or soft drinks, although I carry all of the above except butter on the 1994 trip. At the end of the trip I feel great and weigh less! After I learned I had cancer, I changed my diet this way most all of the time. My permanent weight dropped twenty pounds and stayed that way mainly by just cutting out most desserts.

We moor in one of the finest managed ports, Petersburg, for $4.45. It is fun to look around town and see all of the improvements since 1980. Not all share my enthusiasm. One port employee complains that there is too much traffic. He says when he moved here, his only access to his house was by boat. What happened? They built a road by it and it has not been the same since. His idea to keep Petersburg the nice little Norwegian village it was intended to be, would be to bar all cars from getting off the ferry and allow only electric golf carts on Mitkof Island. Not a bad idea.

Eagles are thick here, hanging around the boat basin. They swoop down for fish carcasses or bait left around, sometimes getting very close to people. Eagles are so common in SE that I don't usually mention them. When Cynthia and I were here in the summer of 1980, an occasional iceberg would enter and pass by in the narrows. It is a fun place!

Day 11—June 17—124 naut mi to Poison Cove.

After more sight seeing, including the Forest Service Visitor Center, I take on fuel and reluctantly leave Petersburg. I do buy another chart to be safer. As we move out a *murder* is in progress. Eight eagles near the green buoy closest to town circle above a sea gull, like a basket, gradually forcing the sea gull into the water until one eagle captures it. Gruesome!

My trip is very intense. Like a job. I feel I have to keep moving and record everything. But, I love it. Sure beats laying around on a Hawaiian beach or trapped on a cruise ship. I would probably go nuts. I have since been to Hawaii for a first time, but I like Alaska better.

Nothing much of interest after we leave town late morning with a gentle breeze behind us. In fact, it is rather dull to Pinta Point except for me drifting off course toward Cape Fanshaw for awhile. I want to see Kake, but somehow the closer I get, I am more interested in getting to Sitka. As we pass outside West Pinta Rocks, the water is glassy on Frederick Sound toward Point Gardner, a place with a notorious reputation for bad water. So far, so good. About halfway across the twenty mile passage the *glass* turns to ripple with rougher water ahead from a southerly. Now I can see whitecaps. My first concern is the tide rips warning in *Coast Pilot* and in *Pacific Troller*. Since we will pass on the flood, I'm not too concerned. I mentally develop a backup plan if it gets too rough or the big engine quits, God forbid! It finally gets rough enough that I decide to layout the survival suit and EPIRB. I also need to get the inflatable off the hardtop. To do that, we stop and I don my safety harness that Arlen advised I take along. With it over my float coat I felt secure, tied to the boat, as I unleash the dinghy topside. I was careful to stay on the windward side. If I fall overboard, I would not want to be dragged under the boat. Without difficulty I soon have the dinghy in the cockpit and tied down. I am now mentally better prepared for the roughest water yet. At 1537 we pass Carroll Island one mile off shore. We are going slowly, but safely and comfortably. Suddenly, all rough water is forgotten as I watch an acrobatic humpback whale leap, splash and play. Quite a sight! The 20–25 knot wind and confused sea bother me less after the whale show. I am thrilled and never scared, only cautious.

We pass Murder Cove. Nice name in threatening water! And at the time, I did not realize I would be staying in Poison Cove tonight! When I get home, I read some of what went on in the past at Murder Cove in *This Raw Land*. I packed that book all the way to read at slow times. There weren't any. Had I known, it would have been fun to enter the cove and visualize the onetime large salmon cannery and the grizzly bear encounters. Reading about this part of the country gives me pause. It is surprising the number of rugged individuals who succumbed in this area to boat sinkings, plane crashes and grizzly attacks. I do visit the cove in "Side Trip 3" in 1999.

At 1606 I happily round Point Gardner where breaking 4–5 foot waves no longer give us concern. Now the sea and tide are with us for the next twenty-seven miles up Chatham Strait. Sort of boring, but at least we can speedup—surf down and climb the waves. Only twenty-three miles to Sitka if we could fly! Over one hundred miles the way we have to go. The last passage is just another proof of God's care. Lucky, some would say. But it is more than luck. In my lifetime as a Christian in over forty years, there have been too many positive experiences to say it is luck. The more you pray and leave yourself in God's hands, the more you prove what the Bible says is true and that Jesus was right. In this situation, Jesus could calm the sea. We can use that same power to bring us more into harmony with the elements, as this trip is proving.

Before reaching Peril Strait (another positive name!), I look into the v-berth area after diving into a particularly bad wave. On the shelf above each berth is salt water! No time to fuss with it now, but I do slow down. We finally make our turn into Peril against a small, but short, sharp chop that rattles everything. Suddenly, I hear *crack, crack*. I am sure the hull has cracked. I check below. Nothing obvious, except the previous leaks. The bilge seems okay. So we go on. All is quiet. I am puzzled, but relieved.

Going on to Lindenberg Head it seems like it would be a long pull to Deadman Reach! Now I wonder if I will have enough gas to get to Sitka without going sixty miles round trip out of my way to Tenakee Springs. While I would like to go there and to Elfin Cove, I rule it out for this trip. We are right on schedule now. At 1835 I decide to anchor up behind Lindenberg and sort it all out. A deer greets us on the nearby beach. While anchoring I notice the rub rail is gone! Checking aft I discover the rub rail dangling from the stern on each side. As I retrieve it, I see it is cut and abraded. I reason that in the following sea, a large wave forced the rub rail out of its base. These same waves forced water into either screw holes or broke the caulk seal below the rail, thus into the v-berth. As soon as we headed into the chop, the rub rail fell down and banged against the hull. When I stopped to check that noise, the water carried the rail under the boat and was cut by the prop. The rail then was free to trail in the wake, but I did not see that at that time. At anchor I simply wipe the rail parts dry and push them back into place. Then duct tape to the rescue! It works. Dockside at Sitka I re-tape and caulk the rail, a job that lasted the rest of the trip. When I get home, Bayliner sends me a new rail at no charge so I can replace the damaged one. Determining the gas situation is more difficult. Since the gauge is aft in the tank and underway the gas runs aft, the gauge gives a false fuller-than-is reading most of the time. First, I calculate what we should have burned from Petersburg, and what we should burn to Sitka considering tides and wind. If the tank was full at Petersburg we should have just enough. Next, considering how the gauge reads and how the fuel is probably sitting in the tank, using a little geometry, I calculate that we were short 8.5 gallons, but with extra fuel on board we should make it. So, using two methods I am confident our fuel is adequate. After trying to determine the effect of tide on comfort and fuel economy, we finally leave at 1945. The tide works against us giving neither comfort nor economy on this reach. But the water seems a little better now.

I consider staying at Appleton Cove but it is out of the way and it would take more fuel, so we press on. The beauty of GPS is that you can see your speed over ground. That can confirm your probable gas mileage and help you determine if you can make it to the next fuel stop. It looks like we are doing fine. By the time we get to Deadman Reach, the water is calm and we pass two fishing and one pleasure boat. We anchor in Poison Cove, so named according to Anderson for a Russian hunting party who got shellfish poisoning. For that reason, I avoid clams and oysters in remote areas. Tonight at 2200 in daylight I try crabbing since other pots are here. None. The setting here was like a high elevation wilderness lake in northern Idaho.

When we left Petersburg *Day by Day* was very tidy. The sixty miles of rough water and leaks above the bunks have the cabin in disarray. So, we end the day that way but in visible light at 2300. That is why I chose June—lots of light.

Day 12—June 18—56 naut mi to Sitka.

I awake at 0100 and I can still see outside. After four hours sleep I am up. With the tide out I can see why no crabs—steep and rocky. My crab ring would need to get down 100 feet to the flat bottom and eel grass. I don't bother. At this location I can't get AM, FM or VHF reception. Little gnats are bad here but they don't bite. Surprisingly, I do not encounter mosquitoes on this trip. I try some of my military jungle-tested insect repellant while here. It smells good. Gnats seem to like it! Surprisingly bugs are little problem up north. On later trips I carry Citronella insect spray—safer for you. The worst place for mosquitoes is around Prince George, so when I tow the boat that way, I try to stay over night as far away as possible from that area.

As we pull into the Peril at 0500, a tour boat is going our way too. She calls on Channel 16 that she will arrive at Sergius Narrows at 0554. We pass her and buck the current but still make seventeen to nineteen knots. It is fun weaving thru the course. Like so many other passages, writers about Sergius Narrows have painted fearful images of danger. I find it beautiful and fun. At Salisbury Sound we get radio weather again, as a tug and tow came into view. It looks like my VHF will not broadcast. I suspected that at Ketchikan. Somehow I'm not worried.

At Kane Islands I count nine eagles. One in every treetop at one spot. Lots of sport boats are heading for Salisbury Sound. A number are fishing in Olga Strait. Two skippers exchange words as one boat invades another's "territory." Incredible with all of this big country! I saw one fish caught during my thirty minutes try. None for me as I am impatient to reach Sitka. Wow, these new charts have thin paper. More costly and less paper! Perhaps that is part of the transition to CD-ROM. Now you see them, now you don't, except on the CD! In January 2000, a chart dealer said the next step is to eliminate chart inventories and print them on demand at the store. This book is printed that way, too, as orders come in.

By 0815 we are in one of my favorite places, based upon one previous visit—Sitka. We made it! Not only to the half way mark of the trip, but on our main tank fuel as well. It looks like we had ten gallons to spare for 2.4 mpg, or the same as the trip average mileage. By buying a V-6, I thought we were buying economy. Not so! This Trophy is underpowered. The engine hums at 3,500 rpm at cruise of twenty knots. Too many and too slow. But, it does it hour after hour and it requires no added oil between changes. This engine and our last 3.0 Liter, GM 4-cylinder are the only boat engines that did not use oil. The common denominator is that I used MerCruiser 4-cycle oil in those two only. To make the underpowered case for this boat, our 22-ft Bayliner Nisqually had a 302 Ford V-8. She cruised three knots faster and got 2.8 mpg. Two advantages of the V-6 are: More space in the engine compartment (joke) and it uses less gas in rough water off a plane. My V-6 is only 155 hp. Newer ones are fuel injected and produce 210 hp—a good option for repower. In the December 1994 *Popular Science*, I read where a party took a 26-ft outboard powered boat to Alaska. They claimed to cruise at forty mph and still got 2.3 mpg. That must be nice. The boat cost $85,000 and had a smaller cabin than *Day by Day*. I'll take our Trophy any day which cost less than one third as much.

At the dock the consensus is fishing is slow. One guy rattles, "One fish per seven hours here; twenty hours per fish in Ketchikan." That's awful! At least I have an excuse. At the dock I also learn from my queries that it will not be a good time to go outside as I had planned to Cape Ommaney, then to Port Alexander and around Cape Decision. This would have allowed me to see Port Alexander, which I consider a high point, a shorter return route and not have to go the same way twice. Now though, wisdom should dictate. Between a now lumpy ocean, no fishing fleet on that itinerary and questionable fuel availability at this time, the answer seems clear. This means I will not visit Goddard and the hot springs there either. I see no reason to go further south here if I want to do Sitka and leave tomorrow. Besides now I will be able to visit Baranof, which I want to do but was not in my plans.

I spend the day cleaning, drying-out and changing oil. I won't bore you with all the hassles and details. I got engine oil in my mouth trying to get my oil change pump working though! As I wash the oil out of my mouth, a female charter skipper is adamant that I move my boat immediately so she can get her boat out. Both she and the oil in my mouth got out!

After getting $5 moorage with electricity at the north basin, I call Cynthia. I coax her to fly up, so we can spend time together here. She is tempted. If it were not for our eighteen year old Siamese cat, Tia, and some other factors she may have. I enjoy walking the docks and the town and chatting with numerous folks. Soon I feel like I am caught up on things since our 1980 visit here.

The troller *Jaeger*, from Port Angeles, which I have always admired, is here waiting for the July 1 opening as are many others. The Forest Service District Ranger office is new and overlooks the boat harbor.

Posh! Yikes, a McDonalds on the water here. Too bad! Downtown, I find a tempting menu item in a street stand that I have to try. Salmon sausage, made in Kake, on a croissant and Ocean Spray's cran-raspberry drink. Dynamite! I had neither before but I am hooked! It is worth a trip to Sitka alone for that duo.

Back at the dock people bring in a few nice fish from Salisbury. One Alaska native, Barry, chats with me at length. He relates how he caught a 6' 2", 234 pound halibut this spring and had no pistol. A gaff used in several key places subdued the big fish. Not so lucky was Joe Cash on the troller *Flicka*. That story alone is a reason to read *Pacific Troller*. Joe was found dead onboard with the engine still running with the boat run aground. The killer was a 150 pound halibut. Evidence on board showed how it happened and how Joe struggled to live, but lost. Beware of those halibut. Oh, I have! I just don't catch them! (that was true until 1995).

Barry proudly shows me his Glassply that used to be his brother's. At the moment, it needs work so he is dock bound. I got to thinking, Barry doesn't have a boat ready to fish. I have a boat ready to go. Barry has caught a trophy halibut. I have never sport caught a halibut. So, I ask, "Barry, if we were to fish the evening tide change, could we get a halibut?" His eyes light up, "We might!" Soon we had plans to meet at 1900.

At 1900 sharp, Barry, is ready to go with his gear. We head out Western Channel. Endless rocks and small islands dot Sitka's entrance and intimidate all but those with adequate charts or local knowledge. Our plan is to fish at Vitskari Rocks where Barry got his slab. Midway between the last entrance buoy and Zenobia Rock, it is apparent Vitskari is not in the cards tonight. The low dark gray sky pushed lower. The southerly ocean swells lift us higher and more aggressively as we push seaward. Then I notice big fish finning. Kings, perhaps? They look too big for sockeye. Soon we are jigging for the big white fish in a second-choice location. There is a fair drift from the SE. Apparently, we have not reached slack yet. I wonder if we are in the wrong place and if Barry has me on a fish chase. No other boats are out here and it is a foreboding evening. Impatiently, I tell Barry, "Maybe we should forget halibut and troll for salmon back toward the entrance where we saw the finning." He readily agrees.

Barry rigs one of my old herring on my light pole in a manner strange to me. As he lowers it, the herring makes a slow roll in a six foot loop. Within five minutes something jerks Barry's line from the down rigger. After a minor struggle, we net a twenty-seven inch King. Nice fish, but an inch short, so he reluctantly releases it. Soon the fish departed slowly. Barry lowers his gear to ninety feet as he did before. At least our hopes are higher.

A bright twenty-eight year old, Barry, impressively articulates all kinds of Alaska fish facts. He also shares some family hardships. It is sad. In talking further at one point, Barry mentions we are all of God's children and how his dad taught him to give thanks for every thing that comes from the sea. I learn he used to go to church. At that point we discuss some of God's word and I give him a New Testament with a promise that he will read it now and then.

It is starting to get dark, when Barry's pole gets a tug. This time the struggle is greater. Finally, a bigger king surfaces. Each time the fish gets close to the boat, it dives again. Such energy that is painful for me to watch, even though I love salmon fishing. The endless struggle to the end is unusual. It is the first time in my life catching a salmon bothers me. At last we net a keeper, maybe twenty-three pounds. Certainly a record aboard *Day by Day* in its second year of sea duty. We motor slowly to Sitka along the rocky southern shore of Japonski Island. I feel uneasy in the early darkness since I have no detailed chart south of Chart 17324 which cuts off just where we need it. My plan is to buy more charts if we return south. I rely on Barry to get us into the channel connecting Sitka's waterfront.

In the dark we have our photo op, before fish cleaning at the outer float for the purpose. Barry wants to give me half of the fish. As much as I want fresh salmon, I insist he take it home.

It has been a busy day. Aren't they all? Life is fun when lived to the fullest, and I did just that! In good times I like the words in Psalms 46 that can help us in the bad times: "God is our refuge and strength, a very present help in trouble. Therefore will not we fear though the earth be removed, and though the mountains be carried into the midst of the sea." If you have a bad day, Psalms, which means praise in Hebrew, is a good place to start.

Watch for commercial traffic in Peril Strait.

Troller Roamer *for sale at Baranof in 1994 is tempting.*

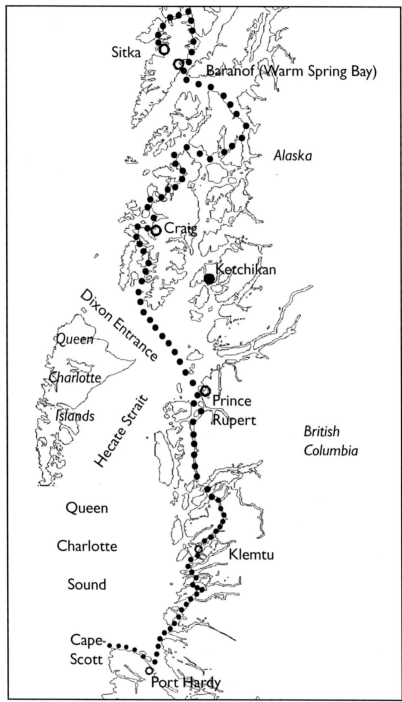

Day 13 through Day 18 route to Cape Scott.

Sitka to Cape Scott

Day 13—June 19—105 naut mi to Baranof.

Father's Day. I miss the kids, but I ran far away for Father's Day! I sleep in and miss the 0400 bite. The forecast is for SW winds. I decide to fish, then work our way to Chatham Strait by Monday when NW winds should appear. By 0845 I lose interest in fishing where we were last night. I stop after a halfhearted short try. Only one bottom fish and a whale sighting. We return the way we went in last night and stop at the boat basin near town. Here I exchange glances with the cruise ship crowd and write some post cards. After all, its Father's Day and I can do as I please! Every day is Father's Day on this cruise! After following the waterfront I would say Sitka must be the eagle capital. They are everywhere. With mixed emotion we head north. I want to come back. There is an element of sadness as the thrill of making it to your destination is reached and you must now return.

The trip back through Peril Strait is uneventful, but pleasant, in fog patches and drizzle, then sun. There are two notables. Just past Rapids Point we meet a tug and short-coupled scow going with the three knot current. They look very domineering in the turn and narrow passage. Giving them a wide berth proves wise. Near Fairway Island we pass another tug and tow. Looking back, a rain shower makes the silhouetted pair look like they are on stage behind a thin veil. Springtime in the north country rewards you with varied gray tones long remembered. On this return, I steer by the feel of it without the chart book. What a difference a day makes! Today I eat a second KitKat bar and play my "Day by Day" music to celebrate the half way progress.

As we enter Chatham Strait at 1515 it looks innocent all the way to Point Gardner. It did not take long to find that we are bucking swells that slow us down. The further we go, the rougher it gets. Then came the wind in our face. It is slow but comfortable at almost nine knots. A sloop and a yawl follow the Baranof shore at a good clip with the wind. Suddenly, near a waterfall they turn and are stationary. Well ahead, other sailboats are entering what could be Warm Spring Bay. It must be the annual Admiralty Island race from Juneau, I reason. Then what about the two nearby boats? Did they miss the day's objective? Or did the rest of the fleet decide to shorten the day and the two fast boats not get the word? Anyway, we keep pounding into the swells while they must tack uphill. Finally, the two sailboats cross our bow. The lagging skipper waves frantically at me as though I am going to run him down. Strange, since we are not on a collision course and we pass safely to his stern. I conclude that he planned poorly, overshot his mark and is now behind in a two boat race to tonight's port. A King salmon jumps out of the water before us in the strait which is now calm.

By 1710 we follow another sailboat into Warm Spring Bay. I am impressed! So glad we didn't pass this place by. It is hard to describe the ultimate visual experience here. The water is clear and calm. The mountains go straight up, topped with snow, of course. Like Prideaux Haven and Princess Louisa, you just can't absorb it fast enough, but they all are matchless places on earth. A waterfall at the head of the bay dominates as it cascades from a basin above. By 1730 we tie to the float that is in the current of a waterfall that seems to be in a contest for the most beautiful of all. Water runs endlessly from the hose on the dock. Homes, the old store closed in 1991 and the decrepit bath house, both on piling, are connected by board walk at bay's edge. A pelton waterwheel provides fossil fuel-free electricity for the residents of which there is only one family today. What to do first? I make the hike to Baranof Lake which could leave a lot of national park lakes to shame. I climb to a knob above to view the lake, Warm Spring Bay, mountains, and Chatham Strait bathed in the sun under patchy clouds. Breathtaking!

Steam and hydrogen sulfide from the hot springs between the lake and the town site hint of the biggest treat of all. Visitors have two choices for a hot bath. One is reportedly in a wooden tub above the falls, which I do not see, or a cattle-watering tank on the porch of the last house, that is for sale, on the boardwalk. A sign says it is okay to use the tank, but leave the place clean. I choose the tank. What could be better than a free hot bath as you view the falls beside you, your boat, the town, bay and snow capped mountains? Thanks, to the unselfish people who made it all possible.

Back at the float, we are just one of two pleasure powerboats, several trollers from down home, a gillnetter, and about a dozen sailboats crowding two-deep, including the two "lost boats" we passed en route here. The skipper of a sloop on the opposite side of the float was not part of the race. He is a pilot and he and his wife live aboard their boat in Juneau. While she went south for a break, he is taking the summer off and sailing alone until she rejoins him. I told him my wife was a good sport to let me go on my thirty year dream. He replies, "If she was bad sport, you'd go anyway and make up later! She couldn't stop you if you waited that long."

Making fish chowder from this morning's catch of the day is fun, cooking aboard on the day that your kid's are to pamper you.

I must say, I would like to buy this town and live here year round. It does show signs, though, of others' failed dreams. If I understood right, the cabin with the hot tank, ten lots, some with cabins (four nearly complete), the store and old bath house, water wheel and water rights were all for sale for $750,000. The store ran through 1990 and reportedly cleared $20,000 that year. *This Raw Land* describes what life was like here in Baranof's hey day. I would have liked that! And the troller *Roamer* is for sale. Hmmm!

People here are interesting—practically all overnight visitors. The former skipper of the gillnetter, *Wampum*, is on a maiden voyage with Jose who is buying the boat. Skipper has a larger boat and a new enterprise—specialty seafood mail order. If you get a flyer in the mail, you know you are rich and can afford the very best at megabucks per pound.

The sailboaters on the race are a crazy lot. They go from boat to boat, noisily, looking for food and drink, then rock each ridiculously. I am glad we do not qualify. It is a great Father's Day as I fall asleep quickly, near the roaring falls.

Day 14—June 20—207 naut mi to Craig.

At 0300 "Knock, knock," on my deck awoke me after three hours sleep. In order to make room for the trollers last night, I moved from against the float to the outside of *Wampum*. We agreed that when she wanted to leave early, we would, too. On a perfect morning, we slide out on the morning glass. So heavenly! I'll have to bring Cynthia here. I don't want to leave.

After a twenty minute crossing, I am ready to fish a placid Point Gardner. Finning fish tease me, but none will bite my choice of lures. An early sun paints the near continuous mountain range on Baranof Island a light orange. The Abe and Al pulsates rhythmically in the seemingly motionless clear depths beckoning the big one. Rips start to appear. An eagle on the point watches guardedly. It will be exciting to explore more, but we must go.

It is good to be planing again. The open window with the cool air blending with the heater's warmth is tantalizing. I stop when herring flip on the north shore of Kupreanof Island. The herring leave as I get my jig out and reappear after I put it away! The break is good, though. By 0850 we are in Petersburg to stop only for necessities. At 1000 we are on our way. We do not beat the tide change, so up Wrangle Narrows we make only sixteen knots. Too bad there are so many ugly channel markers. They spoil the looks of a scenic drive.

The passage down Sumner Strait is a drag again. With a glass surface, bright overcast and three hours sleep, I can barely stay awake. I was going to go into Point Baker, but it seems like too much effort, so we pass. I had planned to go through "The Summit" between Kake and Point Baker. It would have made a nice shortcut. However, my latest reports advise against it, since the markers are no longer maintained. One skipper told me his friend went through there and bent a prop so badly he still talks about it.

Port Protection to Craig is highly rated by some authors. While I find it interesting and little traveled, it isn't as exciting as I expected. Perhaps I am tired. Running into a chop to Shakan Bay wakes me up. Fortunately, the weather is good, but I find several places rather nerve wracking. Most of the route is rock strewn so you need to be on your toes. Several times I have to stop and study details on my inadequate charts. I do have Chart 17387 and 17403, but if I had Chart 17404 and 17405 it would be easier and safer. I feel fortunate to make it through every maze with no damage, until I get into the Craig boat basin. More on that later.

Entering Shakan Strait from the north reminds me of entering a gate to the wilderness with a curved driveway to boot. The dredged Dry Pass section is different and a change, but not that natural looking. We go through at low tide so I see a lot of bottom. High tide would be more scenic. I see my second black bear foraging on the shore about 300 yards away, at 1615, just west of Aneskett Point. We meet a tug and scow loaded with logs heading north at the south end of El Capitan Passage. The current with them makes the tow crab. It would be fun to see them go through the narrowest channel. In about twenty miles through El Capitan, I see one small aluminum boat, one tug and tow and one bear.

We peek into Tokeen from the boat but I do not see the store my atlas indicates. The only life is one person and four big dogs. It seems many of the atlas information items are forty or so years out of date but they keep selling them as current and at today's prices. We should all report new information to help others in the future. The channel north of Tonowek Narrows is well marked. Frankly, I have a hard time reading both the chart book and Chart 17400 going through the islands in San Christoval Channel. I find the channel markings confusing, so we proceed at six knots. It would be nice to have Chart 17404 here. Finally, we arrive at Craig at 1845 after being a little uneasy about the entrance. I follow *Miss Muffet*, a 42-ft Tollycraft from Juneau, into the southern basin. I guess I am distracted with her stop and go maneuvers within the basin, and I do not realize I drift into the unexpected shallows. So for the first time on this trip, I bump our prop. It causes only a minor ding that does not affect top-end rpm. So, if you do enter here, stay to port inside the breakwater and watch for shallows to starboard.

Craig is a modest port compared to most others in South East. I always wanted to see the place, since the Forest Service is here, again with a nice Ranger Station along the boat basin. Another curiosity is where the unsolved murders took place aboard a Whatcom County fishing boat, *Investor*, in 1982. An arson fire killed six adults and two children. The accuser, who had a feud with the skipper, was acquitted after two trials, which to that time was the longest and most expensive criminal case in Alaska's history, according to *Bellingham Herald* reports. After that, I wonder what kind of place this is. I do not ask anyone here about that.

I am more intent on cooking dinner and talking and watching the crew off the *Miss Muffet*. Today with seven aboard they bring back five kings between twenty-five and forty-two pounds, the most big fish I ever saw on a sport boat. The skipper says yesterday they caught seven between twenty-five and fifty-seven pounds. I am awed! The skipper admits they are only after trophy fish. Yet, I am in a Trophy boat and I have none! All are caught at Cape Felix down sixty-five feet on pearl crocodile spoons, herring, or a flasher and big herring. I am torn between going fishing the next day or to take the good weather window opportunity to cross Dixon Entrance. Somewhat puzzling to me is, how would I get all of those big fish home, if I were so lucky? I'll come back again, I reason.

Muffet's friendly skipper flows with information. He says he always fishes either Craig or Langara Island the third week in June. Skipper says he goes out in his 22-ft boat and ties to a buoy behind Langara. I first heard of Langara this past year from Joe, owner of a building supply store in Bellingham, who fishes there every year. When Joe hears about my trip, he said Langara is the place to fish in June. I conclude that another year will bring me back to Craig or Langara to fish. Preferably two of us in two boats.

Skipper says he thinks Waterfall Cannery boats are going to Cape Bartolome to fish. He suggests I do the same or run back through Tlevak Narrows and head south to fish Cape Chacon. I decide on the latter. Skipper is ever so helpful in coaching me on the rest of my route to Dixon Entrance. He thinks I will have no trouble with my limited charts aboard. He is right.

As I eat my simple meal, I watch expert filleting of the big salmon. Then each head and backbone with lots of meat are thrown overboard. That would make a great meal for me! With the high price and scarcity of salmon we must use ever bit of them. Boiling backbones, fins and the like with pickling spices, or gas broiling or microwaving them makes a great snack or lunch. Grandpa use to smile when he had a large salmon head on his plate, wasting little. It was hard for a six-year old to watch, but then I was only 50 percent Danish!

Day 15—June 21—145 naut mi to Prince Rupert.

As I step out this morning, a boat neighbor offers me a cup of coffee. He has lived in places I have been from Wisconsin to Montana, but now lives winters in Olympia and Craig in the summer. He volunteers that Cape Chacon can be rough and that the current in Tlevak

Narrows can be fast. So many people along my cruise route have been friendly and helpful. In these rugged lands, it's good to know, while people are independent, they offer their hand. I try to follow this code of the North. This morning I can't get the forecast on the radio, but the barometer is favorable and a skipper at sea says the water is wonderful. I am fortunate to get Chevron fuel this morning. A fuel barge is at the dock. Once they start pumping it's no vacancy for about four hours and this is the only fuel dock. The attendant is more than helpful to get me in under the wire. I quickly look around town. Not a lot to see. I do locate a pearl spoon to buy. One store is out as someone bought the whole box yesterday. Let's see $5.50 times 24 equals $132! They must be good. If looks and the brochure are any clue, it appears Ruth Ann's Hotel is the place to stay and eat in Craig. Anderson says it is excellent.

Finally, at 0845 we are off. The run to Waterfall Cannery is pleasant. I have known of two parties who stayed there. Ken, from Sandy Point, said it was a trip of a lifetime there to fish and eat well. Where onetime canneries had to ship cans of salmon to get paid, now they get fishermen to pay before they leave home! Ken is another of those who owns no boat, but he catches more fish than I, while it costs him no more than owning a boat. Maybe I will do that, "When I Grow Too Old to Dream." In 1994 they fished out of 19- and 21-ft Olympics. Reservations are required. Most charters around SE are small. Some use a Trophy like ours.

Next we pass though Tlevak Narrows at 0952 near slack. Like many passes, it is narrow, rugged, but easy. It is less intimidating than I imagine. The run down Tlevak Strait is straight with a little wind behind us. Except for a fuel barge, one very large ocean going yacht heading north, and a USCG buoy tender, we are about it on the fifty-seven mile run to Cape Chacon. You get the feeling you are alone in a wilderness. It is nice to enjoy it in good weather. We follow the chart book headings for the most part outside of Round Island and Dewey Rocks.

We have two choices when we reach Cape Chacon: 1) Go back to Ketchikan and take on fuel, which was the original plan; 2) Head directly for Prince Rupert and forty-six miles of open water to Brown Passage, then another twenty-six miles to port but save 115 miles over going to Ketchikan. I won't decide that until we get to the Cape. I put the dinghy in the cockpit as a precaution.

Dixon Entrance is calm at first sight. We head for Point Marsh and Nunez Point, both of which could be mistaken for Chacon to the uninitiated. Finally the real Cape Chacon comes into view. It looks like a charter boat is fishing near Nunez Rocks. I spot a tide rip, so I give it a try just drifting. I leave the big engine running and have lunch. This is no place to discover your engine won't start. Neither of us are doing any good and the NW chop is picking up. We are not moving as we are caught between the wind and tide.

Decision time at 1349. Wind now is 15–20 SW, which means we will be quartering in a following sea. The forecast is favorable. While the ebb from the inlets will push up the waves, the tide will change and flatten them by evening, I reason. If we go to Ketchikan with the wind, we will have to buck it further tomorrow coming down the coast. So, I decide to try for Prince Rupert. If it doesn't work well after awhile, we can still change our mind. Go for it!

Soon we are doing well in four foot seas at nearly right angles to them. *Day by Day* holds her course well, a real compliment to the designer. Our former Nisqually would hit a wave and yaw way off course and throw everything around. Not this boat. She tracks. It really is amazing. We are going about the same speed as the wind. With sun glaring into the cabin, it gets very warm. I need to keep the windows closed to keep spray out. So only one choice. Run in my undershorts and no top! It still is hot, even with the aft door open. But, everything is going well as we click off each mile and continuously check the GPS for proper course. When you cannot see your destination, GPS is of great comfort, especially when no other boats are in sight. I program into the GPS Celestial Reef and Stenhouse Shoal. I want to avoid each. This way I always know where they are. We seem to follow the chart book course almost exactly. I steer for the smoother patches and avoid the higher waves. Some waves are five to six feet, but I am never scared. I feel so much more experienced on rough water now. Our speed slows, but we log half way. I do have to be careful not to broach in the bigger waves. Between the GPS and listening to two Coast Guard rescue calls, the passage is interesting. At 1749 we pass south of Hanmer Rocks in Brown

Passage to average twelve knots from Cape Chacon. The water starts to flatten.

As we enter Metlakatla Bay we pass numerous incoming fishing boats. We settle for tying up at Rushbrooke, the last basin in Prince Rupert, again outside an older yacht. Boats, mostly fishing vessels, are tied seven deep, completely filling all space between floats. Unreal! Again the boat is a mess after rough water, and yes, water got into the cabin again. This time the Customs officer comes down to the boat. After all, it is a delightful evening. He is very interested in my trip and my occupation. I gave him a business card. I explain I am a contractor and how I tried to get a house finished before I left, but my wife got stuck with doing that. He looks at the card, "She shouldn't complain, her name is on the card too!" After chores and chowder, I call it a day.

Day 16—June 22—138 naut mi to Klemtu.

We are one day and $75 ahead by not going to Ketchikan. I am slow to get going today. It is hard to clean up when I am tired and to dry out on a foggy morning. The Chevron dock here has nice showers. Some gas docks have only super unleaded gas. Chevron has regular unleaded.

The trip back to Klemtu is retracing the route north with minor exceptions. I am less enthused. I do not want to leave Alaska and there is not the excitement of the first time. Each passage is punctuated with a following breeze, a calm, light head winds and all kinds of combinations. The weather is better, but somehow I am less thrilled with waterfalls and the mountain views at each turn. We meet numerous fish boats, each with a wake to endure. By day's end it gets old. Will there be any fish left? It is hard to comprehend the impact of these fishers. Half in a daze, we suddenly come to two channels. I haven't been using a chart or the atlas. Where are we? I cannot picture coming by this spot northbound. I scan the chart and the landscape. Finally, GPS to the rescue. Ah, there we are! We are just passing Split Head toward Meyers Passage, where I spent a night on *Day by Day* returning from the Charlottes in 1996. Quickly, we turn back. Once around the head, it looks better. Within ten minutes we are back at my favorite Boat Bluff Light, which I described going north. It is prettier than ever, in the sun this time. I idle along, and south of the light I see a native and his small son jigging a hand line. After watching a few minutes I spread my arms apart in, "How many do you have?" fashion. The fisherman only grins and shakes his head negatively.

Soon we are tied to the float at Klemtu. A fuel barge is unloading, so no gas for now. Actually, we have enough capacity to skip Klemtu each way. Somehow though, it is comforting to have a full tank when you leave a major fuel port. Besides, when there is only one outlet in each town, you don't want to count on it 100 percent. I tell the attendant that I would like to gas up tonight so I can leave early in the morning. He says he only gets paid until 2100 and unloading won't be done until 2200, but he would if I am in a big hurry. We are not, but I get advice on where I can catch a halibut. Maybe next time.

Day 17—June 23—138 naut mi to Port Hardy.

I sleep well, except after midnight *Day by Day* rocks violently, knocking my shaving gear off the table. From a deep sleep, I do not know what is happening until I look out and see the culprit! It is a seiner passing by. Things are very damp inside this morning, so I run the engine and heater a couple of times to dry out. We have a kerosene radiant heater for winter use, but it would have been too bulky to take on this trip. They work great. It stores and operates behind the table leg. Be careful and check frequently to make sure nothing gets too hot near it. When starting and shutting down, open doors and windows to let out the kerosene odor. During operation, make sure to keep some ventilation, because carbon monoxide can kill. Never go to sleep with it on. But in 1998 I came up with a better idea—later!

This morning another fuel barge drops off barrels of Chevron products. These scows carry a lot more than the former coastal freighters. This one has heavy equipment, semitrailers and lumber, besides barrels. While I am waiting for fuel, I plan my strategy for crossing Queen Charlotte Sound and around Cape Scott with anticipation, in view of different forecasts of NW and SE winds. Big difference! I realize that I didn't use Chart 3605 coming north. I didn't think about it. My daily devotional for today from Psalms 23:4 reassures me of God's protection. Somehow I think today's crossing is possible. It comes to me that today and tomorrow are the days to cross Queen Charlotte and go around Cape Scott.

Ravens are big here. They are into the scow's garbage. Don't leave small things around or they will rob you! Finally, at 0930 the fuel dock opens. Now I wish I had told the attendant that I was in a hurry last night. A lot of cruising hours went by this morning. But they were pleasant, and I used my time wisely.

Entertainment for seven dock visitors is watching me fuel. Not much to do in Klemtu! A plane drops off two from Seattle to have a native guide take them fishing. Even the locals here figure out where and how to put the gas fill so it will not spill. Maybe the best idea is to have a vent on the forward end of the tank with a liquid check valve at the tank and vent overboard forward. A low long vent aft fills with fuel and either squirts out or is trapped, not allowing air to escape. A retrofit would not be easy or may not be legal.

On the wall in the gas dock office is combination salmon/halibut/lingcod gear. The attendant's uncle makes them. They have three feet of the heaviest leader I have ever seen behind a green (or red) hot spot with ball bearing swivels tied to a large halibut hook. I should have bought one since my intention to make one is still unfilled. A big husky salt and pepper cat comes down the steep ramp to check us out. Towns with cats are okay.

This time we go down Finlayson Channel to Milbanke Sound. The parade of fishing boats north seems endless. I spot three whales. When we slow, they leave. Ahead it looks like an island with palm trees on it that I cannot identify on the chart. Have I been at sea too long? It turns out to be the huge tug *Escort Protector* towing an empty log scow with huge cranes. Fishing boats cut across the chart book courses and go inside Vancouver Rock. It proves to be a good short cut for us in a calm sea. The varied boat traffic on this passage keeps my interest high.

We arrive at New Bella Bella at 1204. The gas dock is closed from 1200 to 1300, so it is lunch between luxurious bigger boats. We do look small. *Day by Day* gets a lot of looks and favorable comments on this trip. Some are impressed the way she is equipped. So am I, and very proud she carried me safely this far on my experience of a lifetime. Like so many places along the coast, small open boats are peoples' cars. When one of these land and tie up, a child pops onto the dock. She stops by *Day by Day* and says to her mother, "Yacht." I reply, "Those bigger boats are yachts, this is a toy." To which her mother quips, "Those are dreams, yours is reality!"

There is a well-stocked grocery store here. In fact, it is not necessary to carry a lot of food aboard. Stores are frequent with abundant stocks, albeit expensive in the remote areas. Elders like to sit on the dock and talk as they watch we restless ones come and go.

At 1422 we turn south at Kaiete Point into a rough SE fifteen to twenty, running against an ebb. So I slow down, get the bow high and use that sharp bottom entry to split the waves. It does a nice job throwing spray out a boat length, like a snowplow. At 1430, porpoises join us swimming at ten knots on both sides of the boat splashing us! Fun! I decide to take a look at Namu. I want to top off the tank again, but there has been no fuel here for the last six or seven years except in season for fishing. This proves you cannot trust even the latest marine atlas. Fuel became available in 1997. It is a good idea to inquire at each port where the next fuel stop is if you will need it between major ports. Namu has telltales that it was very nice in its cannery heyday.

Unlike in Puget Sound, there are no pump outs in small BC ports. So, when the head is full, overboard in open water. I hate to do that but even some shore facilities have sewers into the water. The most notable is Victoria, with millions of gallons of sewage a day going into the Strait of Juan de Fuca. There have been some American boycott efforts to make Victoria change their ways. At least it has them talking about doing something someday. The policy up here seems to be unless congested areas cause a pollution problem, it is okay to dump. In the last five years this is changing and getting better. In Washington and Nanaimo you find convenient head pump out aluminum barges, which are built in Puget Sound. New laws are coming that will restrict boat discharges in Canadian waters with some "no discharge." I am for it.

By the time we reach Kwakshua Channel, Fitz Hugh Sound is glassy. Going north I wanted to visit Pruth Bay but is was raining. Before I left, our friend, Dorothy, said the walk to the beautiful long sandy beach on the ocean side is worthwhile. Catch it going south, I thought, going north. As I head into the channel, we run into a very stiff uninviting breeze. It doesn't look friendly. Besides, Anderson said recent developments have detracted from this once pristine area. Perhaps with crossing Queen Charlotte paramount in mind, I had little interest in anything else. So I pass on Pruth Bay.

One thing that amazes me is how well everyone gets along in the remote areas of the Inside Passage. I never saw a police presence in 1994. I always did think skippers at sea and residents in the wild have a higher discipline than those in populated areas. It gives you a good feeling. As you travel this country you realize how vast it is and how it would be rare for a person to explore it all in a lifetime.

The new police catamaran moves fast in BC waters.

At 1725 we reach Safety Cove in beautiful water and weather. I take a break to program the GPS, look at charts, and listen to marine weather. It looks *go* for crossing. I remember my morning devotional on God's protection, and say, "Thank you, Father." At 1816 we leave Cape Calvert and are doing eighteen knots on a glassy ocean. I utter,

"Thanks, for directing me, Father. I listened and you calmed the sea from the forecasts." Soon we are doing twenty-one knots and all is well as we pass outside of Egg Island and head for Pine Island. I listen to radio chatter between two long liners anchored in bays behind Egg and Table islands. One place was Jones Cove. Another, they called Fredies Yacht Club which sounded like it might be a float in Takush Harbour. When I was there in 1998, I saw no float, so don't believe everything you hear on the radio.

I am joyful about my four glassy crossings of Queen Charlotte: One on the *Pursuit*; one by ferry; two on this trip. It is not always this way. I recall Dad making a harried crossing in a large yacht converted for war use when he returned from Alaska during World War II. It was so bad that December 1941 night that Dad didn't think they would make it. Water was in his makeshift stateroom on the after deck with his footlocker floating back and forth. He said at one point the lights went out and he thought that was it. But, they made it. Without radar, too.

Cape Caution is abeam at 1907. Porpoises are all over the place at Pine Island. They are the only company on this crossing as there are no other boats. Experience really helps. This coast is becoming quite familiar now. I think I can tell where Christie Pass is, as the swells suddenly became very large. We surf down them and the rpm picks up. A gentle NW follows us now at the end of the ebb. There are numerous warnings about avoiding inlet ebbs. That is good advice. Since we have mostly crossed in good water, I ignore that counsel, not by choice. When the weather is good, you take advantage of it, if the automated reports and visual checks are okay. Fortunately, on this entire trip, I do not have to alter our schedule to accommodate inlet ebb tides.

Lest you think Sandy Point to Sitka is without hazards, I remind you it is not. In 1918, the CPR *Princess Sophia* passenger steamer met a tragic end near Prince Rupert and sank with 346 people aboard. You say that was then, this is now. The water and the rocks have not changed. In spite of electronic guidance systems today, vessels get into trouble. According to a *Bellingham Herald* report, in which the above incident was related, on March 27, 1995, yet another mishap. The 60-foot fishing vessel *Anna Louise* ran aground on the rugged coast NW of Bella Bella on March 25, 1995. The skipper and crew abandoned ship. So, skippers beware! I have numerous clippings of modern boating mishaps up and down the coast where people drown on large and small vessels. Please be careful.

We arrive at God's Pocket at 2024. My kind of place! For nearly as long as I have had my Alaska dream I have heard of this place and wanted to see it. It is a hole-in-the-wall cove with very limited space, just off Christie Passage. Besides being well protected, it is easy to slip into the Pass and check on the sea and weather. Thus God's Pocket has great value for those going north from this side. On this evening, the two buoys are occupied, with two more boats at anchor. One remaining dock space at God's Pocket Resort tempts me to stay. Besides, they have hot showers. Moorage is forty cents per foot. Somehow, I feel we should go to Port Hardy for the night, get fuel and be ready for Cape Scott as early as possible tomorrow. So with my famous "I'll be back someday," thought with me since 8th grade days, we are off down Goletas Channel. Some fishermen are trying their luck off Duval Island. By 2105 we are at Port Hardy. The entrance to the marina floats at the south end of the bay is not an intuitive one. As we idle along the waterfront, I do not want to believe the narrow entrance is close to The Seven Hills peninsula shore. A grim reminder is there. A commercial fishing vessel has mistakenly gone through the kelp bed to the west of the flashing red light. It is a sad sight. After hitting the reef, the tide went out and she rolled on her side, flooding her hold. As we pass her in a rising tide at dusk, her crew pumps her hold. A jubilant crew has her afloat forty-five minutes later. There is no engine damage. Before bedtime, skipper has her running. I must admit in Victoria and Nanaimo harbors I have gone on the wrong side of two buoys without harm. It is easy to do. In a new place you are so busy looking around that these dangers are not always obvious. Every year yachtsmen hit rocks in Puget Sound, the San Juan and Gulf islands. Dangers are often close by.

Moorage is full so we tie to the Esso gas dock that doesn't open until 0600. It is good to call home. We have nothing but good news to share so that is special. The shower room is either in disrepair or in remodel. At any rate I cannot get any hot water so I take a cold shower. But then this is Port Hardy!

Day 18—June 24—128 naut mi to Battle Bay.

I sleep well but only for my usual five hours. Today is the big day to cross both Nahwitti Bar and round Cape Scott. Roger Rue (see Bibliography) will now be our guide since he has been around Vancouver Island twice. I respect his judgement and related experiences. It looks like forty miles to Cape Scott and a 2–3 hour run. The barometer continues to rise slowly, the flag at the dock is limp and the bay glassy. All good signs. I check the current table. It looks like slack is about two hours after the gas dock opens. Perfect. While it is nice to read about where you are going on land or sea, I don't want every detail. There is something to be said of discovery. Exploring new unknown horizons adds a lot to life.

A sign on the dock advertises 24-hour VHF repair. I probably should do that. Somehow I think I will not have to broadcast. Since my radio is in warranty, I prefer to have it fixed when I get home. Like Rue says, a radio isn't necessary but it could help you when you are in trouble. I decide to rely on CB, only if I must. Sometimes in out of the way places, the CB can be your best radio. Although we have had them two boats, I would not carry them as a permanent radio. If you like to chatter, then the CB is for you. I use VHF very sparingly. It should be used for safety with a minimum of social contact. *Do not talk on channel 16*, except to call for help or locate another boat.

This book is not intended to be a complete trip guide by any means. I consider my trip as God's trip. My intention is that He be exalted in my life and in this book. Hopefully, my experiences will help others both in cruising and in life. When I visit each port, I am not sure where I fit in. I am not a fancy yacht skipper, nor a sport fisherman by each port's standards, or a commercial fisherman. I like to visit with them all. I do know I have a free spirit and I am a maverick, but like us all, I am one of God's children. If that is a contradiction of terms, then may God forgive! I do know He has guided and protected me very well on this trip. And yes, I did give thanks after yesterday's passage.

At 0647 we leave Port Hardy with a report from Cape Scott, "wind three knots," with the outlook light and variable. Perfect. The trip up Goletas Channel is relaxing and scenic. I am excited again. You have to be a certain breed to make this trip and to go around Vancouver

Island. I play "Day By Day" and sing along. Tears of joy and gratitude engulf my vision as we pass seaward bound fishing boats. A rock formation on Nigei Island looks like a face—it could be the Alaska Airlines logo except he lost his left eye. More porpoises again. Cape Sutil comes into view. Soft gentle swells give us a pleasant forward rock.

We duck into Bull Harbour at 0758. It is calm, quiet and full of flipping herring. The steep rocky shore is coated with algae greens, yellows, reds, oranges and browns. A rock formation in the harbor looks like an ancient duck with a large bill that keeps watching me as we turn 180 degrees around it. I can see why this place is heralded as a refuge while you wait for favorable conditions to go around the Cape. Floats, docks and pilings are clues of past activity. For some reason, the inner harbor is littered with drift of all sorts, mostly natural, like nature likes to litter here. At least seven buildings line the head of the bay. A sign on the dock, "All nongovernment vessels must keep clear at all times," somehow lets you know you aren't welcome! After completing a counterclockwise circle around the island, we exit without sampling clams or crabs that Rue says are here.

In August 1997 I anchor overnight here and walk to the abandoned CG Station and walk on the large steep northerly beach. While here then I meet Cheryl and Bill on their 22-ft Osprey, *Bohemian*, from Bellingham. Like me, they are on a trip around Vancouver Island and our paths cross on that trip.

As we head for the bar, the swells pick up. I see a line on the water ahead, which is the bar. We are into current since we are fifty minutes behind my calculated slack, but it tends to flatten the swells. With a bar depth of as little as forty feet, I can imagine what a five and one half knot ebb would be like in large westerly swells or waves! This place is one to watch carefully. We cross the bar as do the trollers and draggers, each in a line bobbing like ducks.

Fog or low clouds obscure what must be the Cape. We pass a sloop going our way. Then I see the Cape and Cox Island as we are getting there at eighteen knots. I did program the GPS to be sure we make the turn at the right place. Birds are going nuts over bait. Do I stop

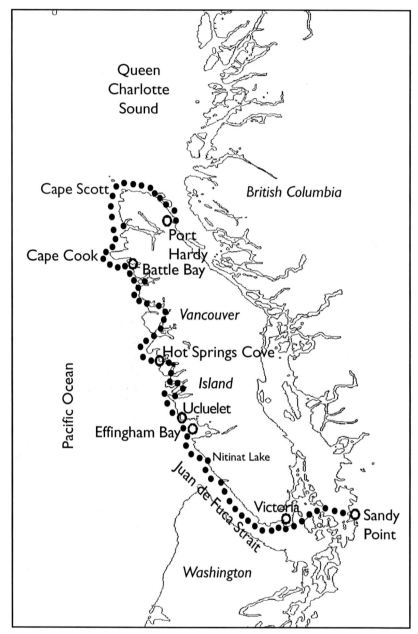

Day 18 through Day 23 route.

and fish, or go on? We go. Each day's policy is: Destination; then catch dinner. Well, I have half of it right most days. It starts misting. Just what you would expect from great capes like Scott and Flattery. Soon what I lain awake nights anticipating, will be history as we pass Cape Scott. We dance through a kelp line. This is not where most families would vacation, but it is my adventure day by day. Seaward clouds look like mountains.

A vast sandy beach is just east of the Cape. It looks like a fun place to explore. Little did I realize until I got home, when I looked on pages 20 and 21 in Watmough's *West Coast of Vancouver Island* cruising guide, that it was as awesome as it is. The guide is a gift to Cynthia after my trip so I could share some of the beauty with her. Ironically, many of the aerial pictures are more spectacular than seeing it first hand at water's view. I am surprised to learn it was the Danes who first colonized Cape Scott. A relative maybe? By the way, on page 22 of the guide you will see my description of Bull Harbour. Rue, *Sailing Directions* and Watmough all mention the danger of a Cape Scott passage, so do not let my smooth passage lull you into complacency.

In 1997 in my second time around Vancouver Island trip I follow the shore in the fog using radar to keep a proper distance. I land and walk the sandy beach at Nissen Bight. Later, I use radar to find Experiment Bight, land there and walk the narrow neck to the south side at Guise Bay. Watmough's aerial picture shows why I am ecstatic about this area and why it is a Provincial Park. On that trip Cheryl and Bill rounded Cape Scott in moonfog in *Bohemian* before daylight in calm seas. I do not advocate that. Besides you would miss too much.

Cape Scott to Sandy Point

Day 18—June 24—83 naut mi to Battle Bay.

We pass Cape Scott at 0935. My calculated slack is 0920. Not bad for an old guy, Arlen might say if he were here. The interesting thing—I did not plan my trip ahead of time to have it that way. That is just the way it worked out, as it has so many times on this trip. A twenty foot sloop motors out on the inside of us closer to the Cape than I would care to. A fishing vessel outbound is close to Cox Island. I break open a KitKat bar—number three as we pass the three-quarter mark of our trip. It's downhill all the way home now, so to speak. No soft drinks yet—not one on this trip. I brought a case of Pepsi and Orange Crush, but only drink canned juices so far. From time to time I enjoy a Tootsie Roll, though. Dorothy, and her husband John, gave them to me before I left home. They are a nice diversion in rough water but it is calm today. I must admit, feeling like I am on a race while on my cruise. In a sense, yes. The most important thing to me is to finish. Next important, is to take notes. Fishing is least important, and that is about the way it is working out. Several times I would be taking notes and, bump, we hit something. Invariably rocks were near and I thought the worse. Fortunately, my fears are unfounded. But, hitting kelp and small wood-chunks in the water is unnerving.

The mile-long, crescent-shaped sandy beach on the south side of Cape Scott is equally inviting as is the north one. Both are connected by a narrow sand neck joining Cape Scott to the rest of Vancouver Island. Someday I hope to return, as the beaches of Cape Scott will be fun to explore. I don't imagine there are many days where the ocean is as calm as it is on the day I pass by with no surf. And there are no people on these beaches either! If you do land on these beaches, use extreme care. The coastline here somewhat reminds me of the Washington coast south of Cape Flattery.

On August 19, 1997, I do return to go around Cape Scott again. As the first time, the water is calm but there is fog. But as I leave the beach at Experiment Bight the fog lifts just enough to see the Cape while the foghorn is blowing. This time I am much closer to the Cape than the first time, just idling along to get a good look. I anchor in Guise Bay on the south side of the Cape and row the dinghy to the crescent sandy beach. From there, I hike a long two kilometers to the lighthouse over the old plank road used to build it. The fog horn is a half kilometer from the light over an exciting elevated board walk, with steps and swinging bridges above water. As I get close to the foghorn, it stops and I get an incredible view toward Scott Islands and the surrounding coast. Gravelly and sand beaches nearby are my world with only a few people, in the area— none from anchored boats. The grassy areas of the narrow neck connecting Cape Scott to the mainland are laced with purple flowers that I cannot identify. The most incredible part of my two and a half hour visit is as I was motoring out of the bay, the fog drops like a curtain as if to say the show is over at this awesome place. God blessed me today. Just because I have had two calm passages around Cape Scott, it can be very dangerous with the weather changing rapidly, just like the fog did. Always have an escape plan, so you do not get trapped without an adequate escape or hiding place.

In 1997 I explore Hansen Bay and find it a lovely spot, especially the sandy beach near the entrance to the lagoon. Rare for me, I land *Day by Day* on the soft sand, being careful to not let an errant swell beach her near high tide. After accidentally dropping a beach shoe overboard in four feet of water, I have a dickens of time recovering it in the current on a drifting boat using a boat hook. But, I get it back. I am delighted to find no footprints on the beach. Hooray!

By 1019 we are inside Sea Otter Cove. The entrance is a little tricky. We follow the preferred, narrow east entrance described in *Sailing Directions*. Once inside past the light, you need to bear to starboard to avoid the shallows at low tide rather than head for one of the buoys. I do not, and not aware, I bump the wheel for the second time this trip. Again no real damage. But my publications did not warn me. Now you know. One lone US ketch is at one of eight buoys. Later, the sloop we passed at the Cape came in. Since this place is heralded for crabs, I try. Nothing, except two small females. I wave at the couple in the ketch who row by. No response. Unfriendly Americans? Maybe from their oceangoing craft perspectives, they think a small "egg shell" is inappropriate out here. Perhaps they are like Ray, who doesn't wave if you are not properly flagged for full identification. We do not have any flags flying today, only our boat name on the transom. Usually, when I am not fishing, in Canadian waters I do fly the Maple Leaf on the bow staff and the Stars and Stripes on the staff aft on the hardtop. *Chapman* shows the proper way to fly flags and yacht club burgees. In the US Power Squadron I learned that you are never to fly a nation's colors on radio antennas, something you often see today. To me it is bad manners. I also frown when boats fly windsocks and they are not properly flagged. I call them lollypop sailors. In 1997 I enter on the north entrance, anchor and enjoy the small island closest to the cove.

After lunch, we head ocean-bound once more. At 1320 I see bait, so I decide to troll. Rue indicated he caught salmon under sail out here. The ocean out of a Neah Bay used to be productive for me in June. After an hour, I conclude it isn't today. We are cruising counterclockwise around Vancouver Island. That seems to be the consensus as the best way. Fair weather northwesterlies in the summer, can give you a nice push down the coast. Ocean swells tend to be more in your favor heading this way. My experience is that it is easier to travel east in Juan de Fuca with the prevailing westerlies and swells. There is something psychological about starting around the island in the scenic protection of the inside with lots of boat traffic. You have time to hone your boating skills and make sure everything is working well before you head into more adventuresome waters. In our case, it only makes sense going outside on the way home. I could not imagine starting out on an Alaskan trip in 250 miles of ocean unless you are an oil tanker. Going around the second time in 1997 counter to the clock made sense even though we did run into southerlies.

We stop in Winter Harbour. Being well protected, I can see why Captain Vancouver spent a winter here and I spend a night in 1997. On the approach, you are sure there is no opening, until you get past Hazard Point. There is a nice float here. This place is so quiet during our visit and on two subsequent visits. It is mostly a fishing port with few pleasure boats. There are no yachts during this visit. My kind of place! While one book states that Winter Harbour is served by water only, there is now a gravel road extending from Port Hardy. We are fortunate to get gas, as the only dock is open from 1500–1800. We get here at 1530, but there is no rush to serve. One fishing vessel skipper storms away after an unproductive wait and complains that fuel is five cents per liter higher here than in Coal Harbour. I decide not to go up there as it is a long run, and I reason Cynthia and I will trailer *Day by Day* there someday to explore Quatsino Sound. We do in July 1995. Joel operates aircraft under the name of Air Cab, a boat launch and boat storage at Coal Harbour. He is very accommodating but his space is limited. Coal Harbour is a small working port with few tourist facilities, but we love it. Seaplanes come and go and climb the ramp that once was part of a whaling station. Watching the coastal freighter call and unload geoducks is entertaining and educational. Most fascinating is the unloading of large, live red snappers from a fishing vessel to a tank on a truck. They are in high demand for fresh catch of the day served at Vancouver oriental restaurant tables.

Ice is $4 at Winter Harbour. A sign on the fuel dock warns you that moorage is $85 per hour when you are not fueling! The fuel dock attendant says few pleasure boats come here. Most that do are going around the island. After he hears what I am up to, he says a woman who writes books recently sailed in here from France in her forty footer. Maybe someday he can say two boats came in here in 1994, whose skippers wrote books about it! I ask how fishing is around here. "Depends on who you talk to," says he. A boardwalk along the water, connecting houses, adds a lasting memory of Winter Harbour. This is my planned destination for night nineteen. Still there is an urge to go farther for night eighteen tonight, though it is hard to leave this peaceful port.

As you leave Matthews Island, you can see three buoys for tying up if you choose. Watmough shows these as conditional, probably in SE blows. We met the troller *Ocean Bandit* towing in a big dragger. Oops, she has her net tangled in her wheel. This is all exciting country—rugged, beautiful and unpopulated. So remote, yet close to home. In 1997 I venture into Browning Inlet. I hope to hike up the trail and look over Grant Bay, but I don't feel like making the effort on this morning.

We pass Lawn Point, which is well named for its appearance of a field looking like a lawn at sea in contrast to the miles of rocky shore. A Canadian Coast Guard cutter is sitting offshore as we pass by. Drug patrol maybe? Docks have signs requesting the reporting of suspicious activity. It is a problem along this coast. Depressed fisher-men are tempted to off-load drugs from ships at sea and smuggle them into the rugged coast, so I hear. In 1997 I do go ashore at Lawn Point and anchor at 50° 19.31'N, 127° 57.77'W and motor the dinghy, dodging kelp. I could have dropped the hook within two hundred feet of shore. Better to be cautious in out of the way places. On the beach I find footprints and the "lawn" has numerous tall grasses and weeds, some of which would be a nice fragrance in a closet.

In 1997 I explore Klaskino Inlet and Klaskish Basin without seeing another boat. Both are worthwhile but my favorite is the latter where

I creep in and plane out. This area looks like a National Park and it is a Provincial Park. *Bohemian* anchored overnight in Klaskish, as I recall Bill telling me upon meeting them later. My favorite of the day, though, is Cape Cook Lagoon. After my 1994 trip, I am intrigued by the picture of it in Watmough's guide, though unnamed. Researching I find the name after my visit. A caption in Watmough warns that usually only "adventurous kayakers" visit while larger vessels stay out. That is my challenge on a day when the conditions are perfect. With a slight flooding current near high tide I have the outdrive up and with the outboard, back *Day by Day* into the gorgeous lagoon, through the narrow opening between the sand spit and the wooded shore. We land on the soft sand on the inside of the spit and I set the hook on the beach. At the time, I think if this place has no name I will name the spit Sandy Point and the lagoon, Day by Day Bay. Well, I concede to Captain Cook.

Awesome beaches await adventurers on both sides of Cape Scott.

Here is a clue: the picture above is at Cape Cook Lagoon with the Brooks Peninsula behind. The water is light green in 1994 as we near Solander Island. We stay over a mile offshore as we pass a pussycat Cape Cook on glassy water. This part of the Brooks Peninsula extends about six miles into the ocean from the island. As such, it is greatly feared for her storms. Currents from the coast need to crowd by here and when running against a sea, that's not good for small boats. Today is pleasant, although I calculate we are bucking a two knot current. In 1997 after a calm morning with fog rising and falling on the surface, suddenly near Solander a southerly kicks up at nineteen knots with gusts to twenty-six per the continuous marine broadcast. I try not to think about what one commercial fisherman had said to me, "Remember, the devil lives at Solander." We only can make 6.7 knots near the island in 1997. With lots of spray, it is like *Day by Day* is going through baptism. At Clerke Point conditions improve as we turn the corner. I thanked God after I had asked him to sustain me in the worst conditions.

As you approach Clerke Point you think, where is land? It takes awhile before you view the Vancouver Island shore again beyond the mighty Brooks. Meanwhile, even on a nice day, I realize we are alone out here and it is a little spooky. I didn't like to even think what it would be like to have to buck wind and tide with just the eight horsepower outboard auxiliary, should the big engine quit. There is hardly any life out here. Just an occasional herring flip and a rare sea gull. One rock formation looks like a caveman with a sack, "out to get you!"

I look at the chart of Checleset Bay as we round Clerke Point. Wow, is it intimidating! Lots of rocks! The skipper of the fishing vessel *Sola* told me at the last port that it is wise to get on this side of Cape Cook and stay at, I thought, Smuggler's Cove. I scan the chart but I can't find a place with that name nor in *Sailing Directions*. Maybe, I conclude it is a local name for one of the unmarked coves or a local substitute name for one that is marked, or I heard or remember wrong. We then head for Battle Bay about which Rue writes so glowingly. Next, I program the GPS for the rocks at Sulivan Reefs, so I can give them a wide berth as we enter Ououkinsh Inlet. Once we pass safely, I religiously follow the GPS to where we turn into Battle Bay. The entrance and the bay itself have rocks so we go slowly. By 2000 I drop the hook. This place is supposed to be a great place to explore. Maybe so in a dinghy with an outboard, but it is a bit much for just rowing. It certainly is peaceful. Not a boat or soul in sight. I can only think God was watching over us as we came here past Cape Cook.

In 1997, I find the cove I was looking for in 1994—Columbia Cove, known locally as Peddlar's Cove. Yeah, that was the name, not Smuggler's Cove. I am startled when I enter the cove to find an old sunken vessel. Anyway Peddlar's is fine anchorage—very protected with a sixteen-wheeler buoy (made from sixteen inflated tires) where I tie stern first firmly with fenders on the starboard stern quarter. The steel plate on top of the tires makes a good table top to expand my small deck space. It rains hard that night so the table did not do much for me. The next day I take the dinghy to the end of the cove and walk fifteen minutes on a rugged trail through the woods to the ocean facing a sandy beach loaded with driftwood and interesting rock formations. See if you can find the one that looks like the profile of a man's head looking to the sea. This whole coast teems with history that is not that obvious today.

The sea can be cruel.

Day 19—June 25—124 naut mi to Hot Springs Cove.

During the night I awake to a noisy ripple and full moonlight. A light east wind shifted us. When I awake again at 0500 after seven hours sleep, it is calm. The forecast is for light and variable wind. Great! The GPS confirms our anchor held. I would never have explored this area without GPS. There was an military induced error for civilian use but it was eliminated in 2000. I also used radar yesterday to help keep our distance from rocks.

After breakfast and cleanup, by a tired sailor, I row the dinghy to the middle of the mile-long gravelly beach. Much to my surprise, another boat is in the bay together with their camp at the north end. A rock between us kept our privacy over night. It is tempting to make contact and find out why they are here and what they are doing. Instead, I leave them at peace. As I am ready to step onto the beach, I spot a bear! That's number three! This one is the closest— about two hundred feet. The bear browses as I watch about fifteen minutes. At one point the bear comes out of the trees onto the beach and looks my way as I take a picture. The bear's mouth moves as to utter softly, like a cat might, who is he? Soon I am ignored and the bear goes back into the woods. I bypass my plan to hike the beach, and look for the totem poles that are supposed to be here. When I get home Watmough made me appreciate why this area was popular for tribal potlatches in the past as he gives a hint of the rich history of Battle Bay. As I row further, a seal follows me curiously while an eagle patrols the beach from above. Sea gulls ignore me as I row close to their rock. As I pull anchor a kicker boat goes by. So, it is not the wilderness I thought! Still it would be fun to stay. Maybe some day. Next time I'll bring my dingy outboard. There is a lot to explore.

In 1997 I do explore beaches and islands and inlets more in and around Battle Bay. I spot a bear that trip too, that time beach comb-ing nearby where I saw the last one. With the dinghy and outboard that trip, I motor in and around Cuttle Islets among a fleet of kayaks. I am startled to find on one island in the trees a memorial to a fisher, complete with skiff, among flowers and two crosses. The wrecked Coast Guard-looking vessel and this boat gave me pause. I realize in these parts, the sea can be very cruel. I am grateful for my protection, but humbled that I am being spared disaster that can come quickly. While what I do may sometimes seem dangerous, it is never my intent to put my life or rescuers in danger. Such was not the case with two people in a sailboat in the ocean in February 1997 near La Push, Washington. At 0035 the sailboat reported they were taking on water. The United States Coast Guard dispatched a 44-ft rescue boat shortly after, only to have it capsize en route. Three crew died as a result. A Coast Guard helicopter was able to rescue the two in the sailboat, before their boat crashed into the rocks, and they survived. I say again, the sea can be cruel. You be wise.

Thanks to the kayakers, I am able to find genuine totem poles in Checleset Bay—some standing, some on the ground. If you go where I did, please treat all of these treasures with utmost respect. Also in 1997 I anchor in the Bunsby's and explore the many passages and try to absorb the history of this fascinating part. Here I meet *Bohemian* again. We have fun comparing notes on our trips from Bull Harbour. This shows that in boats our size you can have two totally different adventures even though we cruised in nearly the same time period.

At 0855 we leave with the outdrive up. We motor with the outboard at four knots with the current through high-risk Bunsby Islands passages. A sea otter (there are many here that pop up like ground hogs) seems to be fascinated by us as we pass by. I use the GPS to

Uchuck III adds charm and function to this remote coast.

tiptoe past markers M28 and M27, then mid channel toward M29. I feel like a Navy patrol feeling my way through a rocky minefield. Finally, we follow an outboard boat into Kyuquot or Walters Cove. It pays to have a large scale chart or a chart book to find your way in, although the channel is well identified with three green and two red markers. In 1994 we took a quick turn in the cove and left. In 1997 we spend a night here along with the coastal freighter *Uchuck III* which carries freight, kayaks and passengers from Gold River. Kyuquot comes as close to being a small, remote working port and

Indian village of the past that I recall. There are no cars and a diesel generator provides electricity. It is a quaint, cozy boardwalk community with essential services. Tourist influence appears to be increasing, but not to its detriment.

Next, it is up Crowther Channel, slowly I might add. "There's rocks in them waters." I ease by the east side of Surprise Island with the outboard, not seeing the rock that shows mid channel in the narrowest spot. I have lunch in Dixie Cove. As Rue indicates, it is unique. It is like going into a back room, after passing through the first room. However, the brushy shore vegetation does not appeal to me as a place to spend much time. Near the entrance is the first of many fish pens I see today. Many of the fish on the market today are Atlantic salmon grown in pens in these waters. What bothers me is they are marketed as "Atlantic king" or "Atlantic coho" salmon based on size, at least in one Utah restaurant. There are no such fish! That night I embarrass Cynthia by arguing with the waiter over the terms. They are not native Pacific salmon!

From here, it is back into a friendly ocean after seeing a guy sailing in a homemade dory, a ferry servicing fish pens and kayaks. Too much activity, I say, as we exit Kyuquot Channel. Sorry to say we pass by Rugged Point. I discover that on March 29, 1995, while looking into Watmough's picture guide. What a paradise I missed. So much for me not wanting everything spelled out for me! Now the sun is out while it rains in the deep-forested canyons on shore.

In 1997 I explore Kyuquot Sound in greater depth and land at the dock at Fair Harbour where a boat with a propane tank is getting it filled from a truck to take it to a home or business. There are two boat ramps. It is possible to trailer a boat here forty-two kilometers from Zeballos and seventy-three kilometers from the highway. I meet one person who says he and others used to do that with 19-ft boats but it is a rugged trip. Once here, they found good fishing for Kings and Silvers, but that was awhile ago. On my later trip I land on one of the three sandy beaches in a curved setting on the inside of Rugged Point. A family is camped here with women and children holding down the fort while the men are out fishing for the day. How ideal. I walk the short distance through the trees to the longer curved beach on the south side. No one is there so I walk around in complete satisfaction. At one point, standing at water's edge, I look up the beach and see a black bear coming out the woods on the same trail I had just used! I move behind a rock and watch the bear investigate the tide line. Meanwhile, I wish I had not left the camera on the boat and wonder what I should do if the bear came my way. I decide that I will head into the water with my life vest on. That is not necessary. When I relate my experience to those in camp, they say that a bear walks the beach past their camp everyday without bothering them. Their dogs get excited though.

On this trip, unlike in 1994, we stay much closer to the shore, often cruising slowly among the rocks like a kayak, but in greater comfort. Breaking swells and foam streaks give clues where there is danger. When you see upwelling, you avoid them because there is likely a rock below. I also stop at a great gravelly beach on Catala Island on Rolling Roadstead.

The journey into Esperanza Inlet is welcome and fun as we pass through the intriguing Tahsis Narrows. More fishermen now. Some trailer boaters from Washington. At last a gas stop at Tahsis where I call home. Not a bad town after not seeing one in a while. A large mill occupies the head of the bay. In 1980 Cynthia and I ride the *Uchuck III* from Gold River to Tahsis and stay overnight, then return. It is fun to see her drop supplies at camps en route. In 1997 I stay overnight at the Westview Marina in *Day by Day*. They are very accommodating with information and even offer their car so I can drive to the store, which is a mile away. River otters are active around the floats. Kids are warned not to put their hands in the water since they have sharp teeth and are used to getting fish scraps. In 1997 I try fishing in the ocean out of here but it is too stormy to get to the good spots, so no fish. Four people back home tell me about the great fishing near Esperanza Inlet. One of them, Bill, shows me his fifty-six pounder one year. The Esperanza Youth Camp is an interesting place, offering children varied recreation and Bible studies. You can look around there as I did and buy gas without the six mile round trip to Tahsis. While Bill and Cheryl were here on the *Bohemian* after my visit, they saw a cougar under a cabin porch. It tried to attack one of their dogs. Between the two dogs and Cheryl and Bill's shouts they scared the cougar off in a frantic few moments. Wow, in a Bible camp of all places! Oh, I how I would love see a cougar in the wild. After all, Cynthia and I are both Washington State University Cougars!

The closer we get home the more the MerCruiser dies when shifting in tight quarters, like landing at Tahsis. It is disgusting and embarrassing. It makes me look like a real jerk. As I am leaving Tahsis it is so bad I cannot get into reverse without the engine dying each time. After an adjustment I make it better, but not good. What irritates me is I had the carburetor and the shift worked on before I left and the warranty expired while on this trip. I thought I was stuck with a MerCruiser like the last two that never did start or shift the way they should. With that great attitude we are off. The good news is that after talking to Dave at Bellingham MerCruiser dealer, Marine Services Northwest (now Boondocks) and writing to Mercury Marine in Oklahoma, Debbie saw to it that I got a new carburetor and a new lower shift cable at no charge. That work made our 4.3 Liter be the best MerCruiser ever, finally! A year later I did need to replace the lower cable again and put on a double seal on the cable. Without it, saltwater is forced up the cable and onto the engine. Eventually salt builds up in the cable to prevent proper shifting. But, to the year 2000 the MerCruiser works just fine. While I am on engine maintenance let me share two tips that could help you. On the two and a half horsepower outboard made by Tohatsu for several brands including my Mercury, you want to be sure to close the gas cap vent when finished. Once I did not and later it would not start. The problem is, either hard rain or wash down water gets into the gas tank requiring its removal to get the water out. At the end of one of my trips I could not get the eight horsepower Mercury outboard started. The problem is the kill switch and is the most common failure on this model according to Darin, my outboard mechanic. Water and corrosion eventually get into the switch preventing the outboard from starting. Learn how to bypass the switch if this happens so you won't get stuck.

The cruise down Tahsis Inlet is pleasant. Another Trophy with twin 175 hp outboards breezes by our 155 hp bigger Bayliner. He may be faster, but no radar. She can outrun us but not in the fog. We stay to the east of Strange Island. As we pass San Miguel Islands, I can see the west wind is coming up. Instead of checking what Rue said was a reason to stop at Friendly Cove, I go headlong into a rough sea. In retrospect, for the first time on this trip, I probably erred in judgement, especially had I known the following: The early-day marine forecast is in error; it is going to be a rough passage; I pass one of the best stops on my trip. When I get home and Cynthia is looking at

Watmough's cruising guide, she asks, "Did you stop here?" With amazement I say I did not stop at Friendly Cove. I know I will go back, like I did to Princess Louisa twenty-two years later in a different season and a different boat with a different crew and seeing things I didn't see before. If I get itching enough, I'll be back!

Sure enough, in 1997 come back I did and anchored nights at Plumper Harbour, Santa Gertrudis Cove and Friendly Cove. The reason for these unplanned overnight stops is an August Pacific stormthat is wetter, windier and longer than on any boat trip I can recall. But, I make good use of my time by sight seeing and fishing. As a result, I see Nootka Sound more completely than I would have otherwise, so it is a blessing. The high points during this stay are: Queen Cove; inside Bodega Island; Boca del Infierno Bay where I enjoy dinghy rowing in and drifting out; Ewin Inlet; Spanish Pilot Group; Valdes and Galiano bays; and Gold River (no fuel there but Washington boats launch here to use these waters). The free recreation map of *Tahsis and Historic Nootka Sound* offers considerable help in understanding local names and past events. Best of all is Friendly Cove, walking to the Nootka lighthouse and seeing the colorful, historic Catholic church at Yuquot. It was well worth the $7 to see the latter and use the Government wharf, which is now Indian controlled. I anchor once below the lighthouse in the cove on a windy night. Comforting was the periodic light flashing in my cabin. I did drag anchor early in the evening so I move back and use a sentinel. One day, while in Nootka Sound, I think the wind is easing, but after a short trip toward Estevan, I decide that is not a good idea. So more sight seeing. My fishing yields very little but I do have fish dinners. Looking back on my Nootka stay, I discover while making major cruises in *Day by Day*, from Olympia to Alaska, there are only three days when I cannot go when and where I want to out of 149 days between 1993 and 1999—only 2 percent of the time.

In 1994, one of the reasons I am anxious to move on is to make an unplanned night stop at Hot Springs Cove. After reading what Rue had to say about it before my trip, I knew I want to stop there. Looking at his book more at Battle Bay and planning the next night, it seems like a good destination. My only reservation is going to a hot springs where no clothes are worn. But, I do like hot springs and I do need a bath. We have hardly left the entrance to Nootka Sound when I wonder if this is a good idea. The wind and waves are whipping up 10–20 knots westerly. We will go a ways and if it gets too bad, we can turn back. After fifteen miles of beam sea, we will then have it behind us for eleven miles. That doesn't seem so bad. The trick is to stay well offshore and avoid the many rocks, particularly near Escalente and Perez We follow the chart book courses with GPS waypoints. The GPS tells me how far off course we are and how to steer and to adjust. With GPS we stay as close to a straight line as possible regardless of wind and tide forces. Knowing our GPS predicted ETA (estimated time of arrival) at all times is good information. We keep a decent pace.

Kelp gets tangled on the outdrive twice to cause a concern over something worse. Each time after stopping and backing down, it proves to be just that, as it clears. In an hour and a quarter into rough water we have gone fourteen miles and are abeam of Estevan Point Light. This is another feared place and here we are bucking a current against six foot waves going with us! I operate with extreme care in front of the lighthouse, so as not to broach. This is our roughest water so far but there is no turning back now. Some would say we should not be out here. They may be right! I wonder if the lighthouse keeper is watching and if he or she could get a rescue going if we need help? It seems a long time before we turn to 073 degrees magnetic. When we turn, there is the light abeam again. Will we ever get out of the grasp of you, Estevan? Once past the head, I breath easier. It is still rough, but we are on our last heading before seeking refuge in Hot Springs Cove. I am one grateful and relieved skipper, once in shelter. I thank the Lord.

In 1997 we leave Friendly Cove together with Michael, solo on his sailboat *Manitou*. We agree the night before that we will travel together around Estevan, weather permitting. Two trollers are still waiting for better sea conditions as we leave. We keep in touch by VHF. This trip proves easier than in 1994 and once the water is decent near Estevan, by agreement, I go on.

At 1918 on my 1994 trip we tie to the government float, amid mostly bigger craft as usual. The wharfinger (I'll call Mr. W.) operates the most unique bed and breakfast I ever saw. He is also the Provincial Park attendant. Mr. W. built his B&B, a two-story fairy-book shingled cottage, on floats. It is called "Ark at Hot Springs Cove." In the lobby-living room you can watch fish under the house through a section of glass floor. Neat! The rates are $35 per night per person and dinners run $10–$15. Mr. W. has his plane and sailboat moored next to his green, steel-roofed B&B. By 1997, Mr. W. and his B&B are gone. Too bad.

After paying the $8.90 moorage, I am off to the famed hot springs wearing my swimming suit beneath my clothes. The trail is the most interesting since Anan Bay. For twenty minutes you are on practically all cedar puncheon that goes up and down over rolling parklike grounds. The trees are a little scruffy, but the fern, huckleberry, laurel and other lush vegetation more than make up the difference. Skippers have carved names of boats, people and dates on the puncheon. They delight you as some are very elegant artistry.

When I arrive at the spring, a native family from the village in the bay is just leaving and another family from Vancouver arrives after me. Everyone has swimsuits. That is a relief. One spring comes out of the ground and cascades down the rocks, maybe some three hundred feet to the saltwater cove. You have your choice of showers or pools depending on where you stand or sit in the creek bed. It is fantastic. I return one satisfied, relaxed, but tired skipper. In 1997 as I am about to walk to the springs in the rain, I almost freak out. A water taxi arrives with a family of four to go there, too. What should I do? As my 84-year-old mother would have done, out hike them! That I do. Improvements at the springs since my last visit include a change shelter. After the recent heavy rains the creek is dirty and mostly lukewarm, but I finally do find a hot pool and have a good bath after I clean leaves out of it. I leave just as the family arrives. I am quite a sight walking in my swimsuit and raincoat.

Day 20—June 26—63 naut mi to Ucluelet.

In the drizzle this morning, I make a short walk around the campground on shore. Then we are off. One man in a smaller boat at the dock with rather crude accommodations and another with four smokers aboard a 24-ft boat confirm I have it pretty good. I visit the hot springs at a good time too. Mr. W. says inflatable tour boats come to the cove with tourists. It can be like a zoo then. No thanks! I love Hot Springs Cove and this life of mine lately. It is heavenly! I wish it could go on forever. I shut out the world with no radio, TV or newspaper. Just calls home to my love who I wish were with me, so we could share in God's beauty and grace.

The cruise to Tofino is well protected, pleasant, and finally into the sun. I planned to stay a day in Clayoquot Sound. Somehow that doesn't appeal to me today, even though there are numerous coves and history to explore, which I do for two days in 1997. I won't bore you with all of that, but there are two highlights I must mention. One is anchoring and having my dinner in Adventure Cove, where Captain Gray built and launched the first ship on the West Coast. The cove is the most scenic spot in the sound and well protected from all winds behind Columbia Islet. Another yacht is anchored here and a tour boat makes a pass by. When I am on the beach where a stream enters, I can feel history here. The other notable is going into Matilda Inlet and to Gibson Marine Park. I anchor in the shallows and visit the mineral pool. Then I walk eighteen minutes on a very sloshy trail in mud and water up to my knees in my shorts and deck shoes. I must admit the whole experience alone was spooky but I am rewarded by the crescent shaped beach at Whitesand Cove. I would call it more like halftone white sand. Next time I will anchor on the outside and go ashore but then miss some adventure.

In 1994, I am anxious to fish and get home. The shallow water through Heynen Channel and Deadman Passage is tricky approaching Tofino past Opitsat. You will be on a sand bar, if you don't pay attention! My atlas has it well marked. Tofino hangs onto the well-protected Browning Passage. Two things do not impress me: small speeding boats that leave annoying wakes; the swift current that makes docking hard, especially if your MerCruiser dies like mine does at the wrong moment. I check out the posh facilities here, in case we decide to stay someday, in the Weigh West motel/marina. Mainly, I am trying to find a place to store fish, if my catch gets too abundant. I learn I can store fish and stay aboard for seventy-five cents per foot per night if motel guests do not need all the moorage, which they do not at this time.

At the gas dock, I ask the attendant how fishing is. "Hot," he replies. I've heard that one before! But, then there I was buying local hook-ups and anchovies at $6 per package. I've learned the hard way that it is a good idea to get local fishing advice. By 1400 I find the fleet from the gas dock attendant's accurate description. Today they are in

150 feet of water off Portland Point. The ocean could not be nicer as I lower the pink Ab and Al with bait holder and anchovy towed by the outboard. I see no action on other boats, but at the dock I learn that skippers have success stories of halibut, kings and silvers. One guy is out here in a 16-ft Lund aluminum open-boat with one outboard. Today is okay if it stays that way. Ah, there is one. Not big, but a fish. I boat a small Silver, but at least the skunk is gone. That one in five minutes and within an hour of low tide. Next I try for a Chinook. For the next two hours I zigzag among twenty-three boats and on my own head toward Ucluelet as the nor'westerly picks up. Now that I have a fish for dinner, I wonder how I can legally get a two day Canadian limit of eight fish home. Washington law says you can only land the limit at your port, which is four fish for a two day limit in the San Juans at his time. While that idea is percolating, I decide to check out Ucluelet. That way we are with the wind and I will know better what is in the area.

We enter Carolina Channel watching sport boat and troller traffic to gain confidence of where to go. Ucluelet is a boat-friendly town in an ideal setting. There are three fuel docks and three Government docks, none of which are crowded today. We choose the first float and moor on the inside. Here I meet a friendly couple, Helen and Ken, aboard the 40-foot DeFever trawler *K-Note*, which is for sale. I think, wow, that would be a nice boat for Cynthia and me to spend summers doing what I did in three weeks. Her diesel engine carries her from Puget Sound to Ketchikan without refueling. Helen and Ken show me the boat. Yes! Nice. Real comfort—two heads with showers and two staterooms and more. Still, there are lots of advan-tages to a trailerable boat. In fact, I have often thought an ideal boat would be a trailerable commercial type aluminum boat that is so popular in Alaska—tough, practical and low maintenance. Helen and Ken were pioneer boaters. They cruised to Alaska in a seventeen footer in the fifties with a fifty horsepower Johnson. Later I learn, Phil, now a Sandy Point resident, did that in an 18-ft Reinell with twin thirty-fives in 1957. Lund's book in the Bibliography tells about a later trip by Phil. The more people hear about my trip, the more I learn of other small boat trips to Alaska. Yet none are quite like mine. Going to Alaska in a small boat is like being in a movie, rather than just watching one.

Back to the real world. I call Cynthia. She isn't interested in buying the *K-Note*. Not today anyway! The stopper is, "How are you going to pay for it?" Next, I ask her if she would like to drive over and stay in the Weigh West. We can fish and she can take fish home, since transporting them by vehicle can be less restrictive than going by boat. She doesn't think so. Well, there goes my best take-fish-home idea. For the rest of the day I pursue how to take fish home and walk the town. The *Canadian Princess* Resort ship-restaurant, motel and charters and Island West Resort are highlights to view. The latter has RV and marina boat spaces. Bring your outfit over or go out on a charter. Cynthia and I bring *Day by Day* and the motor home here in July 1995. It's a real nice setup. Make reservations, though. Rich and I fish out of here on *Day by Day* in May 1998 and catch salmon and halibut.

We observe a sad experience in the Island West marina while we are here. One evening, a young couple from eastern Washington tie up their 19-ft aluminum boat in a slip near *Day by Day* and leave. That night it rains hard. Imagine our surprise when we look out the next morning to see the boat still tied to the dock but capsized! How can that be? The marina notifies the owner and we go fishing but it is rough, so we come back early after catching one seven pound Chinook. We are just in time to help the couple right their boat and load it on their trailer. It is a lot of work but, spontaneously, marina employees and customers team together to get the job done. That is the good part. Hopefully, the boat is okay after their quick trip to a repair shop. In this case, the rain falling into the outboard well caused the boat to list more, which it already was, due to more weight on one side. Water ran into the boat through a cable opening and the bilge pump did not function. Eventually the list was enough to allow seawater to enter and over she went.

Day 21—June 27—18 naut mi to Effingham Bay.

Charters, small boats and *K-Note* head to sea before us. I decide to fish the tide change, then sight see. My plan is to head where we did yesterday. As soon as we get beyond Amphitrite Point I can see this will not work. The NW wind blows early. So I decide to fish in Barkley Sound but my charts are inadequate. So back to Ucluelet to get Canadian Chart 3670 of the Broken Group. By 1230 I limit on silvers plus bottom fish bonuses. At home I can't catch a bottom fish.

Here, you can't keep them off your line. By 1300 we anchor in Effingham Bay with a couple of other boats. I spend the rest of the day eating, dressing fish and cleaning the boat. I also take a power snooze (five-minute nap) for the first time on the trip. It is good to relax—nice. I think about rowing around in the dinghy but the shore is rocky and brushy and not inviting There are few nice beach areas in the Broken Group, but those usually are occupied by kayakers or small boat campers. I would like to poke around the many islands but again you need more than oar power. I play "Day by Day" on tape. Suddenly I realize the trip will soon be over. I never want this fairy tale to end. As I look back, I can see more that I could have done on this trip; maybe taking more time. Overall, I am very satisfied and try not to, I woulda, coulda, shouda! Finally, I pray for family and the world.

Day 22—June 28—139 naut mi to Victoria.

We begin the day at 0515 by making a circuit through "the Group" around Jarvis, Jaques and Gibraltar islands. Two occupied choice beach areas are on Gilbert and Gibraltar islands. We then join a small fleet of boats fishing just south of the Broken Group at the edge of fog. Salmon come easy. I catch three and clean them by 0900. All are Silvers, except one small King. Since I didn't eat yesterday's catch, I now have my two-day limit. I know you don't want to hear this, because I have heard this kind of story, but, the big one got away! The biggest fish of the day, a king, surfaced, flipped and was gone. By 1999 limits were drastically reduced up and down the coast and vary from area to area.

Our next stop is Bamfield. *Day by Day* has been here before. Cynthia and I camp and fish out of China Creek in the fall of 1993. Boaters can launch at Port Alberni and run outside. One day we ran to Bamfield and enjoy this quaint boardwalk village some dub as the "Venice of Vancouver Island." I'm not sure about that, but it is a fun, rustic place where dock space is at a premium. On the south side of the bay, the Coast Guard Station, a store, several other businesses and homes are connected by a wooden walk and no cars. On the north side marine tourist oriented businesses and a church are reached by boat or car.

I have been to Barkley Sound six times in *Day by Day,* two by trailering with Cynthia. During those trips I have been to almost all places, but I will not write about each one. My reasoning is, that a lot of people have been here and much is written about it. Suffice to say it is fun, even in a very small craft to poke around these islands and inlets to enjoy the few sandy secluded beaches. On one trip I do see a bear on a beach. For me, salmon fishing out of, and around Barkley has been the best I have found anywhere in terms of catching fish. Nothing real large for our boat.

After two Bamfield dock stops, we are on our way home. We round Cape Beale into a calm but foggy ocean. At the time we pass Cape Beale, I do not have a clue that in December 1995 a 50-ft fishing vessel will capsize here in twenty foot seas. When I read about it, I immediately calculate the wave height to boat length ratio as .4 and wonder if there is any significance in that number? When I multiply the .4 by *Day by Day's* waterline length, I get 7.2 feet. Using our twenty-one foot nominal length I get 8.4 feet. Both numbers are less than some summer forecasts of three meter seas. Perhaps the .4 reading is a warning limit of seas your craft should navigate. The type of sea, craft, load and skipper skill are all factors that can affect the limit. After I get home I read where small boats capsized off this shore, so you can't be too careful. When Cynthia and I fish out of Ucluelet, we head seaward for her first ocean trip in an ebb against a strong northwesterly along with other boats. Suddenly, we face the largest breaking wave I ever have in a boat. *Day by Day* is six feet from the waterline to the top of the hardtop. I tell Cynthia, that we are going to take water over topside. We do—nothing but green water! This is only the second time in *Day by Day* this has happened. Cynthia is calm through it all, but when we get home she announces that she is not interested in anymore ocean fishing. Too bad. I oversold her on how great the fishing is in the ocean and how calm it can be. I chose the wrong day. We were not endangered, but again it is a hint you are approaching the limit.

Going home I get glimpses of the shore now and then. We see and hear the Pachena Point foghorn. I love these point names on the Canadian shore. When I used to fish out of Neah Bay they were just that to me—names. Now, like people, I can begin to put a face on them. In the seventies I had dreams of visiting Barkley Sound and Nitinat Lake. My dated $1 and $2 charts of places I never visited show I dream a lot. With this trip I used all of those charts, and what a good investment they are! They may not have all of the latest navigation aids, but they are in fathoms like our sounder can be. New Canadian charts read in meters but my sounder does not.

Nice beaches and a waterfall grace the shore near where I expect to see the entrance to Nitinat. Both the ocean and the weather are now perfect. In my mind, I planned to visit Nitinat many times, but only if it worked out. Everything I have read and even the chart itself gave me concern. Yet, I want to go there! Mystery? Adventure? Maybe all of that and curious for sure. The words that ring most in my ears are those I read in *Sailing Directions*, "Entry should be attempted only by those in possession of local knowledge." Add challenge to the above list of reasons to enter.

As happens most times on this trip, I do not plan for critical passages, they just work out that way. At last, I spot the entrance to Nitinat River and Narrows. You must look into the narrow slot at just the right time or you miss it, otherwise the entrance blends with the shoreline. The first time we overshoot it about a mile, thinking Clo-ose was it. Had I used the GPS or watched the chart closer that would not have happened. At 1258 we reach the bar entrance. Slack low is 1215 at 2.2 ft per the tide table yet the current is still ebbing. The low swell creates a small breaking wave. I nose into it, then get spooked, mainly because I read seven feet on the sounder. I back away, make a loop and observe some more. I think I can make it, went through my mind. I try again and this time we are in. I don't recall all the depths because I am too busy to remember and to record. The channel gets deeper inside but, surprisingly, considerable current is still ebbing. It seems like six knots—probably more like three. A mile ahead a kicker boat planes across the channel. I am struck by the beauty and tranquility of this place complete with whirlpools.

We make our way past Whyac. A small boat is tied there and several people watch us from a house deck on the hillside nearby as though we are invaders. In a sense, we are as we creep inland. I can see the rocky bottom when suddenly there is a clunk. I hit bottom on this trip for as many times as I saw a bear—three. Like the others, no impeding damage. Strange, we hit where 2.2 ft shows on the chart when we clear the entrance which shows as .5 ft. Later, studying the chart more and observing the channel, I can see I should have been closer to center channel. I must admit the chart confuses me and in the current it wasn't easy to get a good visual read on the bottom. The locals watch all this, but as I look their way, there is no clue from them as to what I should do next. At last we are in the lake. An older yacht is at anchor along the south shoreline. A few modest summer homes dot the shore and possibly an old homestead exists where the chart shows buildings. Largely, the lake is untouched with forested shores and shows little evidence of tidal action. Unless you knew, it doesn't look like a saltwater lake of dark green. In the far distance, logging is evident, but not threatening. After three miles in, we take a turn on the approximately ten mile lake which will be left to explore further another day. Leaving is easier on a current that is incoming. Now I can say I have Nitinat local knowledge! Before you try to enter Nitinat, read all you can about it. Watmough discourages you, though. It is not for everyone. It appears it would be best to enter near a slack high on the ebb. As we leave, just by my observation of some hikers, it appears that West Coast Trail users can ferry across the river. I learn later if you plan to use the trail, you need to contact the Pacific Rim National Park and pay a user fee which includes two ferry crossing charges along the trail.

Once back in the ocean at 1420 we pass Carmanah and Bonilla points. By the time we reach Port San Juan in the Juan de Fuca Strait, the west wind is picking up. To satisfy another of my curiosities, we dart into Port Renfrew. Without a float, no facilities at the dock any longer, and just ordinary scenery, there is little reason to stop.

The trip along the strait is typical of my many journeys from Neah Bay, except now I get to view the more scenic Canadian shore west of Sheringham Point. The wind and tide give us a good push, almost too good. Sooke and Becher Bay will have to wait. If I wasn't that curious after twenty-two years of passing by, another year or more won't matter. I do visit them on later trips. At Race Rocks at 1827 the VHF report says the wind is gusting to thirty knots, the highest we experience on this trip. The rough water is getting to be of less concern and a day by day event. Old displacement trollers westbound are showing keel coming off waves, then plunging and spraying the wheelhouse like the Fisherman's Friend ad on TV. I steer intensely so as not to broach. I have to ease off the throttle on the front side of the waves, so as not to bury the bow in the roughest water yet, even though the waves are only five feet. The current is with us.

Now I can see Mt. Baker and Victoria and, of course hometown Port Angeles. Our last heading to Victoria is rough, but we make it. We moor in the first Government basin on the starboard side coming in the harbor. I fix my dinner, but I wonder why. The dock fish and chips look good and inexpensive! Am I getting old or realistic? A fun, excellent place to eat in Victoria is the *Princess Mary*, a former coastal passenger vessel located near Upper Harbour. Cynthia and I have enjoyed excellent seafood there for over forty years. Call for reservations and how to get there.

The docks are nice here, overlooked by a fancy office, but no showers and only sani-cans! My next challenge is to figure out how to get my fish home legally. Flying them home is too expensive. After a call to Mother in Port Angeles, she agrees to my plan for tomorrow of my carrying half my catch to her on the ferry. That seems better than leaving them in a Canadian port and ferrying half at a time home, which I have done. This is all very dumb, to be lawful. It's discrimination! You can drive or fly your Canadian catch home, but you can't bring them in by boat most of the time, when the landing limits are different! Tonight, I enjoy watching the harbor traffic and looking at the Canadian salmon trollers at my float.

Before bedtime, let me just mention I need to tell you about the "Juan de Fuca Triangle." Never heard of it? Well, I'll tell you all about it near the end of Side Trip 1.

Day 23—June 29—47 naut mi to Sandy Point.

On a big day I awake at 0345. I am going home and I have to make those expensive fish even more expensive! By 0620 I carry half the fish in a cooler box with ice for a mile with periodic rests to catch the ferry *Coho* to Port Angeles. The wind is still blowing. I do not recall such a rolling ride on a big vessel, but then we are in the Juan de Fuca Triangle. Mother is glad to see me and plays my game of fish transfer. I return on the same ferry to Victoria by 1000.

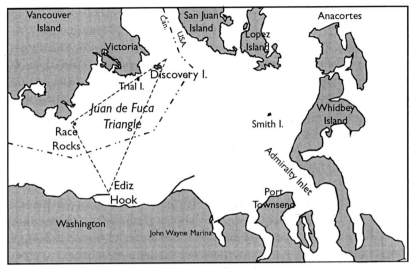

Juan de Fuca Triangle.

We start home in a very rough encounter past Trial Island against a current running into a westerly sea. A 22-ft Sea Sport follows us. By the time we reach Haro Strait, the water is fine. The VHF is busy after a 36-ft trawler hits a rock east of Sidney. We clear Customs at Roche Harbor, where there are way too many people! I eat lunch on the fly in President Channel while I play my "Day by Day" tape. As I pass Point Doughty, I cannot help recall the feelings when we were heading north near this spot a little over three weeks earlier. Even the water and weather were similar then. It is with a sadness it is over too soon, as I knew it would be at the start of the trip. I am struck with the reality that I must once again reenter civilization, as I know it. My dream trip may be over, but the memories never will be! It is wonderful! I did it! Thank you, God! Now I am anxious to see my love!

Near Sucia we join the reverse heading to Sandy Point where we began. There is Sandy Point! As we cross the southern tip of Strait of Georgia, a stiff SE wind gives us one last shot of jolts and spray. At 1400 we enter Sandy Point. It's over! There is Cynthia. She looks out the window of our house and sees us coming. We wave and holler enthusiastically until we can embrace! Such feelings! It is though I emerge from the sea of dreams. In essence, I stepped out of my everyday life for twenty-three days and acted out my thirty year dream. Now I return from that dream.

Later in the day Cynthia and I drive to Fort Casey and ride the ferry to Port Townsend. For the first time in my life, Mother meets me again at a different ferry on the same day! She gives us the salmon I brought from Victoria earlier in the day, less her salmon commission. Over dinner we replay many events. When Cynthia first hears of all this crazy fish transfer she says, "Why didn't you bring half as many fish and come home a day earlier? Besides, if we wanted fresh fish at a bargain you can buy fresh salmon for only $2.88 a pound at home!" Like I related earlier, she is the sane one!

Dad and I boat in Montana and Puget Sound before we tackle The Juan de Fuca Triangle.

Side Trips

Side Trip 1—Puget Sound

Purists might say, if you are going to cruise the Inside Passage to
Alaska you should go from Olympia to Skagway in one trip. I did
not. But I did go the full distance, if you add my separate trips in
1995 and 1999. Since we live about 140 nautical miles north of
Olympia, it did not seem to make a lot of sense to add the extra
mileage, just to say I did it as part of my 1994 Alaska trip. In 1954
Dad and I cruised the lower sound in a 16-ft plywood boat we built,
powered by a 14 hp Evinrude outboard. In the spring of 1995, *Day
by Day* and I make the side trip from Sandy Point to Olympia. Both
trips are delightful. It is appropriate to encourage others to cruise
these waters, whether part of an Alaskan voyage or not. I must

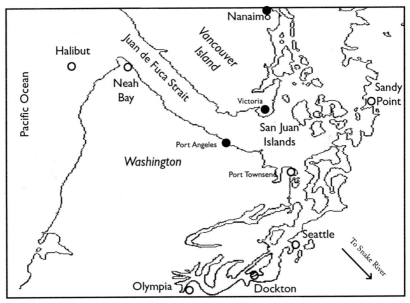

Side Trip 1—Puget Sound

confess to being in that arrogant group who feels that the San Juan Islands and north is much better cruising. In the spring of 1995 I am amazed to find hardly any boats out on the lower sound when they were already starting to crowd the northern waters. Years ago, Calhoun wondered why more boaters don't use this delightful boating area. The lower sound offers calmer, warmer waters and sometimes better fishing.

Olympia

Olympia from the water is a delight and has a great marina. On April 25 I land in Olympia at the city dock. Cherry blossoms and new-leaf green on the trees make a beautiful foreground with the State Capitol dome commanding the skyline. If you are transporting a boat from out-of-state, Olympia will be a good place to start. If you are cruising lower Puget Sound, Olympia is a good destination. Visit the Capitol and sample those famous oysters at Olympia Oyster House.

North from Olympia follow the marked channels on the chart unless you have local knowledge. At Dofflemeyer Point you can enjoy seeing a small lighthouse and the facilities at Boston Harbor. Squaxin Island and Squaxin Passage offer inviting waters and shoreline for the cruiser. I am tempted to go ashore at Coon Cove at the south and east side of the island just north of Unsal Point, which has an ideal beach. Calhoun wrote long ago this state marine park was noticed by northwest boating clubs. In 1995 it was closed since the State was unable to work out a lease from the Indians who control the land, per one report. Nearby though is Hope Island, a nice state park. Carlyon Beach has an attractive setting.

A trip in and out of Hammersley Inlet is worthwhile if you like a river-like change. The day I make the cruise is ideal—calm, lightly flooding water, sun and comfortable. It is so relaxing. I just aim *Day by Day* mid-channel without paying much attention to the chart. This works fine until I round Skookum Point. I notice the red panel just beyond at Church Point, but at twenty knots I see no problem, since boats moor on both sides of the inlet. Suddenly, I see the bottom rising rapidly. As fast as I can, I pull the throttle and shift lever to neutral. I hear a loud CRUNCH and we stop abruptly. I look aft and see a trench in the gravel through the shallow, clear water. I am afraid to look at the outdrive but I see clams laying on the gravel in the trench. Since the boat is anchored with the buried outdrive, I quickly don my swimming suit, life jacket and canvas deck shoes and jump into the knee-deep water with a bowl and pick up a dinner of clams! Next, I look at the chart. Sure enough, a shoal. A year later I discover that Calhoun advised of shoals and current to five knots in the inlet. Finally, I lift the outdrive to inspect the damage. As expected, the prop is badly distorted, requiring welding, but it is repairable and spins freely. Fortunately, no other damage, other than missing paint on the lower unit. Needless to say, this is not the way to dig clams! Furthermore, I am embarrassed, although I do not notice if anyone sees me from the neighboring houses. For a guy who made it to Alaska and back without having to change props, here I am doing just that, mid-channel near Olympia. While this type of collision did not ruin my whole day, it sure dented my ego. Although I do not tie up at Shelton, Oakland Bay does offer facilities including launching ramps for the boater.

My cruise includes Pickering and Dana passages and Case Inlet. I go ashore at the dock at Allyn. I make a pass inside Reach Island, past the gorgeous unoccupied beach and park at Stretch Island and into Jarrell Cove (Gerald Cove, on my chart dated 1939 and my 1952 *Marine Atlas*) with a marine park and marina. Calhoun calls McLane Cove beautiful and restful but avoid it at low tide. We cruise inside Herron Island where a ferry shuttles to the mainland. A person in Olympia says clams and oysters are available near McMicken Island on the east side of Hartstene Island. Vaughn Bay is fun to explore slowly where there is a nice park and boat ramp nearby. I enjoy glancing into Whitman Cove.

Drayton, Balch, and Pitt passages are my choices. Watch the rock and shoal in the latter, west of McNeil Island, site of a US penitentiary. There is a state park in Mayo Cove at Lakebay. I always wanted to see Lakebay since family neighbors at Dockton used to run by fishing boat here to visit relatives. My overnight anchorage in the cove near Sylvan on Fox Island proves peaceful. Nearby on an island is the picturesque lighthouse, connected to the three-story octagon wood and masonry building with bridges on two levels. Speaking of bridges, a cousin did the electrical work on two bridges we go under on this trip: The Narrows and Deception Pass.

Each time I pass under or over the Tacoma Narrows suspension bridge, shown on charts as The Narrows, I am filled with wonderment. It is an engineering marvel, although the original bridge dubbed "Galloping Gertie" vibrated apart in a windstorm in November 1940. Mother and I passed under the failed bridge in a train on our way from Oregon to Dockton, shortly after it happened. About that time on the train she was treating me for trench mouth, of all things. Plans are underway to allow a private company to build a second parallel toll bridge next to the existing bridge.

Be sure to stop at cozy and busy Gig Harbor. Once a small fishing port, full-time residents and tourists now occupy this picturesque stop. A visitors float is close to stores, restaurants and other facilities including a boat ramp. If it is too crowded, anchor out, but beware of shallow areas. Across from Gig Harbor is Point Defiance, home of good salmon fishing and one of the nicest parks you will find. From early childhood to this day, I always enjoy a visit there. Nearby is the ferry to Vashon Island. It is a treat for me to cruise the Tacoma waterfront in clean water. When I was in the eighth grade, my friend, Dennis, and I first cruised here from Dockton in our small outboard powered boats. The water was putrid in those days from pulp mill discharge. Tacoma and all of Puget Sound have numerous facilities to accommodate the boater. Marine atlases, the yellow pages and numerous other marine publications, many free, detail their availability.

Quartermaster Harbor

Captain Vancouver discovered Vashon Island in 1792 and named it after another Captain and his friend. Pioneering homesteads began in 1877. A trip around actually two islands, Vashon and Maury connected at Portage, is special, whether in a small kicker or a large yacht. My favorite stop is Quartermaster Harbor at Dockton. Now Dockton is not what it used to be, but it has lots of history and memories for me. My earliest recollections of my love for the sea begin at Dockton. Situated between Seattle and Tacoma, Dockton is the location of the first floating dry-dock on Puget Sound, as the drawing on the frontispiece shows. Here, protected from Pacific storms, was a community of fisherman, farmers, ship builders and dry-dock workers. In 1898 Grandma and Grandpa moved their

The Dockton house where Dad was born still stands.

Danish heritage to Dockton where their berry farm, cows, chickens and greenhouse supplied the community with needed food. This is not surprising because Grandpa came from the Island of Fyn in Denmark, which sounds like a place similar to Maury Island. (Ironically, all four of my grandparents came from areas in Europe that are very similar to the areas they settled in Oregon and Washington.) Prior to getting married, Grandpa worked on the floating dry-dock. After a days work he would row to Tacoma to go to a dance and then row home. Rowing on foggy days, he would periodically drop a wood chip over the stern to make a trail on the water so he could row straight. The family house still stands high on the bluff at the end of piano row; so named because each of the shipyard's senior personnel lived in those houses with a piano inside, our house as well. Dad was born in the Dockton house that included waterfront at the time with a gorgeous view of the harbor.

In 1995 I anchor near the park in front of Grandma and Grandpa's home where I spent many happy days. I am filled to tears with emotion. First, I try to imagine how this spot must have been in the early 1900s. To me it was ideal in 1940. I can recall when the

Concordia, the last of the Mosquito Fleet, (like the *Virginia V* still in use for excursions today) used to call twice a day on all the small ports of Rosehilla, Manzanita, Shawnee, Burton and Dockton from Tacoma with freight and passengers. In those days you did not need a car to go to town. Each port had a dock with a waiting room. It was great.

I give you my view of Dockton as I remember it between 1940 and 1950. The Dockton Park at the east end of the cove is where it is today but only with one small float at the dock. The bulkhead and buildings are logs and cedar obviously built by artisans. Now facilities are larger, newer and more complete including showers but the charm is gone. Add mahogany clad yachts from Seattle and Tacoma on holiday weekends and you get the picture of the days of wood and craftsmanship. Next to the park toward Dockton, a large hulk of a sailing ship, now found only in a maritime museum, lay on the beach. It is fun to climb aboard. Beyond the ship, next to our place, lived Yolande. He was a recluse who never met a piece of wood he did not like. After each high tide he would gather any piece of wood for his house or stove since his house was built of driftwood. I am like him because every time I see a block, timber, or smooth log on the beach I want to bring it home. But Cynthia says, "No!" Anchored in front of Yolande's, when he isn't fishing, is Nels. He lives in the double-ended troller year round with wood stove and battery lights. During the day he runs his "putt-putt-putt" generator to charge his batteries while he, too, goes to the beach to look for wood. To me, Nels had a good life. When Dad was a boy, there was a flat beach on our property. By the time I recall it, only a clay bank above the beach remains. Since Dad would be on jobs in Alaska and other remote areas, I spend quite a bit of time in Dockton growing up. In my eighth grade days I build a dock, boathouse and bulkhead, all from beach-combed materials. When I need a lift on heavier materials, Tony, Lane or Swede give a hand. Dad and I tow home a cedar log from a Burton beach from which he makes shakes. I use them for siding and the roof on the piling-constructed boathouse. I spend hours dreaming and enjoying the water from my dock. In 1995 all that remains is part of the bulkhead.

Going west is the old dock shown in the sketch. During my Dockton days, commercial fishermen tied their boats to it and stored nets and gear there. On shore is a shop building, part of the dry-dock that is falling in disrepair. Further west is the new dock which too, is gone, but in those days it is also used by Dockton fishermen. Hanging around the docks listening to sea tales helps me become a man of the sea. If I am not at the park, or on the docks, I am rowing in our boat or sometimes using the outboard. It is amazing how Dennis with his 7½ hp Martin outboard on his 14-ft Birchcraft boat and me with my 5 hp Sea King motor on our 12-ft Foldcraft boat could outrace the slow yachts of those days. We enjoy going over their wakes, too. A highlight for both of us is having a ham, pineapple and poi dinner (I don't think we really liked poi!) on the Hawaiian tug *Ono,* one Sunday. There was a dock workers strike in Puget Sound, so the tug hid her barge of pineapple in Quartermaster Harbor until she could find a place to unload. Dennis and I are like cats checking out anything new. After hanging around the tug for awhile and talking to the crew, we get invited for dinner.

Near Sandy Point the Foss super tugs *Lindsay* and *Garth* often anchor waiting to escort an oil tanker. Around them in *Day by Day* or sailing in *Fatty Knees,* I never get an invite. I guess I have lost my boyish charm! "Cheryl, can you help me get aboard?" It is not

Friends, Lindsay *and* Garth Foss *at Sandy Point.*

surprising she now works for Foss, the pioneer tugboat company (www.foss.com/history.htm) on Puget Sound. You might say that her roots began when the Foss' and Manson's may have worked and socialized together in early Puget Sound days. Pete Manson, the founder of the pile driving company with that surname today, and Grandpa were friends. They drove the first piles for the company in Quartermaster Harbor. I remember Pete telling the story at my grandparents golden wedding anniversary. Pete at one time was the dockmaster in Dockton. According to article by Blanche Caffiere, she and Garland Norin plan a book, *Past Remembered II*. Caffiere indicates from book material that Pete Manson may have been the one to name Dockton when he suggested it to his boss, Captain Warner, manager of the dry-dock, "because we dock many a ton here." In the early days Foss tugs moved Manson pile drivers from job to job. It could be that Grandpa and Grandma may have known the Foss' as well.

At Dockton, south of the new dock, is the shipyard. Chuck, of Sandy Point, who grew up at Portage, recalls the last fishing boat, *Janet G*, built there in the early 1930s. A fire destroyed a lot of the shipyard in my days at Dockton but a yellow warehouse still stands and is used by a fisherman family. The most interesting project in Dockton while I was there occurs when two brothers decide to build a floating crab cannery. They buy two Navy surplus ships. One is cleared so a major portion of the second one can be cut away and set on top of the first one. It is ingenious the way they use the dock and tides to be their hoist to get the section of one on top of the other vessel. The brothers spend months cutting and welding. When they are done, they have a two-story ship that looks top heavy to us kids, but then we are not naval architects. After they finish, canning equipment and cans are loaded on board and they head for Cordova, Alaska. Unfortunately, the ship capsizes in the Gulf of Alaska. Not all dreams come true.

The last time I was in Dockton, the school where Dad went was still standing but it needs some care. Caffiere has a picture of the five, including my Aunt Hazel (Dad's sister), who were first to graduate in 1910 from the Dockton Grade School, built in 1902. The class includes Pete Manson's daughter, Gladys. I miss by one year being able to start school here myself, after which I start first grade at Burton, where Dad graduated from high school. With these famous people attending this school, shouldn't it be a national historic site? I recall after the school closed, it being used as a place to process berries. Two churches served Dockton. The Catholic one is still in use. Mostly Scandinavian and Slavic names dominated the homes of the close-knit community that to me was the perfect place to live. The store with post office was the activity center of Dockton, operated by the personable Mr. Berry, who also grew berries. The community hall, where occasional events took place, was next to our house. The largest family in Dockton was the Plancich's. They had ten children, one of whom was in my class and were neighbors of Grandma and Grandpa. "The old man," as he was respectfully called, was the family father and skipper of the seiner, *Inventor,* and brother of my Uncle Mitch, who married Aunt Hazel. The old man was very good to me, always telling me about life on the sea and about the realities in the political world. Uncle Mitch was a wonderful man, too.

A story that still makes me cringe is the old man saying, how on a moonlit night they were run down by a US Navy ship near Neah Bay while they were at anchor. Some of the old man's crew died but he survived. Then there was Fred, one of Dad's classmates who was always drinking and working on a boat. Somehow he was fit for duty when it was his tour for engineer on a ferry. A few years ago in Dockton, I saw Lane's dad, another classmate of Dad's, almost ninety, who lives near the store which is now closed. When I ask him about various people, he says sadly, "I don't know anybody here anymore." So it is when you outlive everyone in your community. As I glance at the King County street numbers that did not used to be here, I am reminded that the good old days of Dockton are only a memory.

My trip inside the harbor to the marina at Burton, is challenged by geese on the floats and in some boats. Later I find sea lions have taken possession of the buoy at Decatur Reef. No one should pass by Blake Island though. Docks at the north end make it convenient to visit the state park. A highlight, whether you come by your own boat or on a tour, is a visit to Tillicum Village right next to the dock. An Indian longhouse fashioned after ancient dwellings provides visitors with arts, crafts, a traditional salmon dinner and a stage production. Trails crisscross the island. I thoroughly enjoy a three-mile spring walk around the shoreline.

Bremerton and Poulsbo

If you like navy ships, you will see them at the Navy yard in Bremerton in Sinclair Inlet. I find them fascinating and also find the lowest priced fuel here on my 1995 Puget Sound trip. My run into Port Washington Narrows and Dyes Inlet is pleasant. For those who need a mall within walking distance of a dock, you will find that at Silverdale. I once was taken aback while chatting with bored teenagers on a family sailboat at scenic Bamfield, BC in 1994, when I asked, "What could be better than this?" Without hesitation I was told, "A mall!" Whales inside this small inlet cause concern to environmentalists a few years ago but they delight local boaters.

As I did in 1995, you may want to go around Bainbridge Island. Port Madison, Eagle Harbor, and under Agate Pass bridge are my favorites in that circuit. Be sure to go into Liberty Bay and spend some time in the inviting Norwegian town of Poulsbo with their tasty bakeries. Visit Rose's Teahouse for their signature dishes of Black Forest soup and bread pudding. The latter is as good and as big as it gets. En route, you will go past the Keyport Naval Torpedo Station.

Lake Union

I always enjoy a slow pass of Elliott Bay and the Seattle waterfront. At the Elliott Bay Marina I see more upscale yachts than I have ever seen in one port, many with faraway port names. I scoff at any port name where you could never get the boat here by water. If you have the time it is fun to go though the Ballard Locks and go into Lake Union and Lake Washington. Regardless of the size of the boat I go in, I am awestruck by the myriad commercial and pleasure craft, houseboats and mansion-like homes along the lakeshore. One time on a Fourth of July, Dad and I found refuge in our open boat from a sudden shower by stopping in a boathouse on Lake Union. On my 1995 trip, Cheryl treats me to a waterfront meal at Latitude 47, on the lake where I tie *Day by Day*. Afterwards I find overnight moorage on a decadent float geese claim. A famous seafood restaurant has a dock for boaters on Lake Union; Ivar's saying is, "When the tide is out, the table is set." Well, it used to be that way! And it was at Dockton. Now signs say beaches are polluted. When you go through the locks make sure you follow proper procedures and you have two

50-ft lines. Use old fenders if possible next to the locks. One trip I get creosote on them that is nearly impossible to get off.

Saratoga Passage

To make a loop you can go on both sides of Whidbey Island. On the more protected side, up Saratoga Passage at the Everett marina, are two signature dining spots—Anthony's and Confetti's. Both are by the same ownership with the latter less expensive. Further north in Penn Cove you will love the petite tourist town of Coupeville. Just a short walk from the dock are several good eateries. Our favorite is the Knead and Feed hanging over the water with great soups, sandwiches and desserts. The famous Penn Cove mussels are grown nearby and are a treat if you are a seafood connoisseur.

Port Townsend

You reach Port Townsend from the north on the more exposed passage outside of Whidbey Island, which is fine in good weather. This red-brick-building, early Puget Sound town is full of history. The main street provides excellent restaurants and tourist shops close to the boat basin. Our favorite place to eat is the historic Belmont Hotel close to the visitors dock. Port Townsend is famous for the annual summer Wooden Boat Festival. Boats and RVs adjacent to Point Hudson share facilities, next to a lighthouse whose foghorn can remind you it is there.

Cruising south, going through the Port Townsend Canal between Indian Island and the Olympic Peninsula is a more scenic and protected passage than Admiralty Inlet but there can be a 4-knot current. In 1995 I anchor in Mats Mats Bay, thoroughly protected, but with a secluded shallow entrance with a reef. A stop at Port Ludlow will let you see how a former Pope and Talbot lumber mill site has been transformed into a premier retirement community, excellent restaurant, and top golf course. To the south is Port Gamble, a 1900, New England model mill-community. When I pause here in 1995, I wonder how long the Pope and Talbot lumber mill can exist. In 1996 we get the answer—it is closing. Now it is gone.

A cruise, as our family did in *Seaspell* in August 1972, to the end of Hood Canal, can be rewarding. We anchor at the end of the canal in the shallows of Lynch Cove. The warm water is delightful for swimming and water sports. Nowadays you might encounter a submarine underway or at the Navy base on the east side of the canal. Check the regulations if you want clams, oysters or shrimp in the canal. When you go under the Hood Canal floating bridge, realize, like the Tacoma Narrows, you are seeing the second one. The first one was destroyed in a vicious 1979 windstorm. These grim reminders should caution boaters to beware of northwest storms even in the protected waters of Puget Sound.

Going north again, I always find it fun to go through Deception Pass, especially if you can go with the current. The high bridge, the shear rock walls, other boats, the long gravely beach and little coves give you plenty to observe or stop and enjoy. Lottie Bay is a delightful stop NW of the bridge in the passage.

Swinomish Channel

To make a loop, go one way through Rosario Strait and the other through Swinomish Channel. Stops at Skyline Marina in Burrow's Bay and at the city floats in Anacortes are suggestions. Anacortes is a popular port for launching out-of-state boats. I meet one skipper up north in 1999 who, with a permit, tows his 28-ft Bayliner 2859 Ciera Express with his Ford pickup, from Quincy, Washington. He launches it in Anacortes. In my view this model boat was the best value at the 2000 Seattle Boat Show. It would be my choice if I were getting a larger boat. It has many good features for my kind of cruising.

Boomers in Anacortes is a great place to eat. If they again get it back in operation, you can tie your boat up on their float off Guemes Channel. Swinomish Channel is well marked but pay attention. If you get out of the channel on the north end, it gets shallow in a hurry. Watch your wake in the channel all the way through. LaConner is a fun place to walk around if you can find moorage. A favorite eatery is The Lighthouse Inn, which offers moorage while you eat. Watch the current, which changes direction twice a day. If you decide to buy a home at Shelter Bay, learn all of the implications about living on leased land on an Indian reservation.

San Juan Islands

The San Juans are a paradise story in themselves. We first visit them in the boat we built, *Happy Talk,* with a single 35 hp outboard, in 1963. After cruising in the San Juans in our six different boats, I say with authority it is wise to have auxiliary power. That is true when cruising any large body of water. There are numerous attractive places for the boater in the San Juans. My favorite port is Friday Harbor. It has great appeal to me as a place to live, but we settle for pleasant visits and eating at our favorite spot, Downriggers, at the dock. For twenty-five years we feel the San Juans are too crowded in the summer, but fall, spring and February are delightful. February 1996 I make a three day cruise and have sunshine and calm water with anchorages, beaches and trails mostly to myself. It is the crowded conditions in the San Juans that drive my desires, in part, north toward Alaska each year.

Near the San Juans, is Bellingham. It is a well-equipped port where we once moored *Nadja.* Three restaurants within walking distance of the docks we recommend are: The Marina, Bayside Cafe, and Lucci's. Get a ride down Chuckanut Drive and eat at the Oyster Creek Inn if you like oysters. You will love them. It may be possible to anchor and go ashore near there and walk up the hill, but if you do, get permission from Taylor Shellfish farms. Anthony's is coming to Bellingham, so that will be delectable. Bellingham has good marine service facilities. I can recommend Jim or Kris at Olympic Boats (Bayliner dealer), Dave at Boondocks, Dick or Darin at Clearwater Marine and Jerry at McKay's Mobile Marine Services and Repair. Tell them I sent you and it probably won't help if they are busy! If you need electronics services try Jerry at San Juan Electronics. Before we go to the Juan de Fuca Triangle, let me share with you my favorite propeller repair shop: Cap Sante Marine in Anacortes.

Our home at Sandy Point is located on the edge of the San Juans and for that reason we say the sea is our back yard—it literally is.

Juan de Fuca Triangle

Perhaps now is a good time to tell you about the "Juan de Fuca Triangle." This is my name for it—no one else's, and I will tell you why. It is that area bounded by Ediz Hook on the Washington shore and Race Rocks and Discovery Island on the Canadian shore with one leg passing though an island with the fitting name of Trial Island. Inside the Triangle a number of events have happened almost as though there is some type of spell on the area.

My first encounter is in 1951. At Port Angeles there is good fishing and bigger waters to explore. That first winter Dad and I build a 14-ft Chris Craft kit-boat powered by the first 10 hp Johnson outboard with gearshift and separate six gallon tank. With it, Dad and I can keep up with the Blackball ferry, *Chinook*, that sails between Port Angeles and Victoria. One weekend in May the Strait of Juan de Fuca is dead calm and the salmon are not biting. Seeing the *Chinook* heading out, I say to Dad, "Let's go the Victoria." I have never been to Canada and what easier way than to go over in an hour and come right back? After a discussion, I convince a reluctant Dad to go. The crossing is easy and soon we are in Victoria Harbour. Dad sends me to a gas station to get more fuel. Upon our departure, much to our surprise, the west wind has come up and the strait is rough. We decide to follow the shoreline to Race Rocks as it is calmer. Then we will have a better angle to the sea and perhaps toward evening the wind will slacken. By the time we reach the Quarantine Station we can see the strait is still rough and gas is getting low again. That early Johnson is hard starting and seems to use as much gas going slow as fast. When trolling, the pressurized system will bleed excess gas, leaving a trail behind. After more gas, we are on our way. As we cross Race Passage in heavy chop the engine starts missing. Dad removes the screws from the sparkplug cover and dries off the exposed plugs. Soon we are on our way, only to be sputtering again. About this time, a Canadian seiner comes by and the skipper asks if we are in trouble. After Dad explains our fate, the skipper says, "Come aboard." He tries towing our boat, but she is too cranky and in danger of being swamped. After the crew brings her on board we are on our way on a comfortable passage. It was fun. For Dad, I'm sure it is less so.

When we are about a mile off Ediz Hook, the skipper says he will drop us off. He wants no money. Dad gives him a $20 bill and says,

"Buy something for the crew." Since the motor will not run, I begin rowing toward the end of the spit in a now calmer sea, pushed by the westerly swells. Darkness is fast upon us when we hear something banging the bottom of the boat. With the flashlight we see something I never saw before or since. Hundreds of dogfish are swimming under our boat. My oars will even lift them out of the water as I row. Spooky! Before long we are outside the spit close to shore opposite the boat ramp. You see, we never told Mother we are going to Victoria so our fishing trip that day is longer than normal!

Meanwhile, a small crowd gathers at the spot looking out toward us including the Coast Guard from their adjacent base at the end of the Hook. Mother calls Dad's worker friend, Spike, and says we are overdue. Spike assures Mother and the Coast Guard everything is okay. He tells them Dad has been around saltwater all his life and knows how to take care of himself (and me). I am prepared to row the extra mile around the spit when the Coast Guard says they would send a boat around to tow us. No argument from me! We get first class treatment as we pull out the boat on the Coast Guard ramp for amphibians, something not normally allowed for the public. It is a good adventure day for a teenager, sunburn and all! A bad joke with Mother whenever we go fishing after that is, if the fishing's bad, we might, as they say, "Follow the birds to Victoria!"

The dogfish episode reminds me of an experience Rich and I have in the ocean off Barkley Sound. As I am standing in the cockpit of *Day by Day*, I hear a thump against the hull and see something brown out of the corner of my eye. Later it happens again but this time I get a better view. A seal is trying to jump in the boat or at least get near my hand! I am about to protect us from the sea monster when this thought occurs to me: A charter boat was probably out, and fishing is slow so they fed seals herring. This seal, seeing me, probably thought I had a hand out for him. Well, I decide to keep my hands in! The rule is you don't feed bear or seals!

While I am digressing on wild stories, one time I was commercial fishing out of Neah Bay many years ago when things were slow. A sports pole, bolted to the boat as required by commercial rules, has something on it and a curled tail is showing but there is no fight. It pulls hard without jerking. When I get it up to the boat it is a 6-ft blue shark! What would you have done? Well, I bring it aboard and show the family. The movie *Jaws* is on and I want to dump it in front of the theater. Cynthia wisely says, "Don't you dare. You will get arrested!" We should have eaten it as the meat is white and beautiful. I am sorry to say the shark goes into our compost pile. In retrospect that was a wasted resource and wrong. I would not do that today.

Back to the Triangle, like the more famous Bermuda Triangle, this one too claims its victims. Cynthia and I are pleasant prey on our first days of marriage as we cross the Triangle twice on our honeymoon. Famous English Channel swimmers try and fail to cross this Triangle. Bert Thomas finally became the first to succeed after more than one try. A monument to him is on the shore near Victoria. Sudden storms dismast sailboats, capsize boats and persons have been lost at sea in the Triangle. Arlen and I are heading seaward on our last commercial fishing trip in *Seaspell*, at 0630 on August 13, 1976, in the Triangle, when suddenly the engine revs higher and we drop off a plane. The upper gears of the MerCruiser 888 have failed. So we troll to Port Angeles with the "Little John," our 9.5 hp Johnson outboard. To our surprise we catch five Silvers in the middle of the strait, a place no one used to sport fish. After an expensive repair, two days later we are on our way to Neah Bay, to have our most productive fishing trip ever with *Seaspell*.

All my years crossing the Juan de Fuca Triangle, something will usually remind me it is there. Sometimes it is the dolphins insisting on frolicking in our wake and zipping back and forth under our bow. Maybe it is the beautiful sky and sea. More than not it will be a wave or two you will never forget! On June 21, 1976, I am returning from a commercial fishing trip to Neah Bay by myself. Being alone on this kind of trip is a first for me. Arlen stays behind to help his Uncle Rich build a summer home at Sandy Point. Arlen's last words to me, which often ring in my ears, are, "Don't do anything foolish!" On the trip home, I have a beautiful run up the strait. After Race Rocks the water is very frothy in an unpredicted 30–40 knot sudden wind. I am almost frantic as the boat pitches and rolls. It is like heaven and hell. The setting sun illuminates the snow on Mount Angeles to the south in golden glow and the wind blows froth like orange sherbert across licorice troughs. Dark clouds hover overhead. In the distance an outbound oil tanker is bearing down on us with its intimidating, cascading bow wave, with the newer ferry *Coho* not far away. In a foreboding sea, I pray as I fear for my life. I cry because I am scared and I think this is the end; yet comforted, as I see the beauty in this Juan de Fuca Triangle trial of mine in moments I can never forget. I slow down and quarter into the sea, realizing that I should not continue home. I am grateful to make it into Victoria Harbour for the night, then home the next day. That trip convinced me *Seaspell* is too small to be pounding up and down the strait. That year we bought *Nadja*.

In 1972 I am foolish enough to think I can water ski across Juan de Fuca Triangle. Cynthia tows me up and down the full length of Lake Whatcom several times and skiing twenty miles seems easy on a single ski. I can do it. On the day of the race there are small craft warnings for the Sixth Annual Race, which I had never entered before. You are required to have a full wet suit. I do not have one, but I am not disqualified. I use my short-sleeve short-legged light weight one. As I sit on the edge of the log boom to take off, I wonder what I am doing here as hot fast boats roar their chrome-stacked exhausts. Since it is rough I decide I had better use two skis. When the gun sounds we are off, but it is obvious we are the slow boat. We are left behind. As soon as most of the front runner boats leave the calm water on the inside of Ediz Hook and enter the rough water of the strait, the fast boats falter. Soon one other Bayliner and we are in the lead. Fellow worker, Dick, runs our boat and Arlen is my observer. Everything is fine, but with two skis I am getting tired, when a piece of driftwood knocks off one ski. Suddenly it feels good and I can ski better in the rough water with one ski. But what about the other ski? We have to go back and pick it up. It is so rough I cannot get started again on one ski, so back on with two. One of the difficult things is dealing with the bright sun on a moving sea with a white boat wake. After awhile I am spaced out. Two thirds of the way across, the water is getting calmer when Dick finds himself in the biggest drift of logs and other debris I ever saw boating. He cannot safely find a way through it so he stops. By the time he finds a way out I am getting cold and I cannot get up on the skis. So much so, Dick says I am coming out of the water because I am suffering from hypothermia. I need help to get into the boat. I remember how warm and nice the cabin feels. Meanwhile we cannot see any other boats in the race. We decide to head for the finish line in Victoria Harbour. When we arrive, out of seventeen boats only three finish in two classes. We are the unofficial fourth place finisher but I am disqualified for not skiing to the finish line. Had I warmed up and skied the rest of the way I would have had a trophy. The race was to be back across the strait again after a rest period, but the race is canceled at that point and has never has been held since. Meanwhile our boat is reported missing on the radio. Cynthia and her family are concerned. Actually, we are the first boat back to Port Angeles. But these things happen in the Juan de Fuca Triangle.

Three boats later, on July 10, 1993, I leave on a maiden sea voyage in *Day by Day*, to sport fish opening day in the Pacific Ocean. It is perhaps the roughest trip overall to Neah Bay. In the Triangle off Victoria I see a very sharp curler wave ahead, so I slow and try to take it as easy as possible. I can see what is going to happen. Soon, the bowsprit is in the wave and green water engulfs the windshield and hardtop! It seems an age before it all runs off. Never in all my years of boating has that happened! Not even during the 2,500 mile to Alaska and back. Only in the Juan de Fuca Triangle! But, yes it does happen once again later, remember?

Before I leave the Triangle, there is one more messy thing to mention. That is, Victoria discharges raw sewage into the Juan de Fuca Triangle. I mentioned this before, but it is worth saying again. By doing so, perhaps the sewage will be better managed in the future and that will be the beginning of the Juan de Fuca Triangle getting a better reputation in my book.

Leaving on a more positive note, I am reminded of our visit to Fisgard Lighthouse, guarding the entrance to Esquimalt Harbour. Built in 1860, it is the oldest lighthouse on the west coast of Canada. It looks over most of the water in the Juan de Fuca Triangle. Inside the lighthouse is a very fitting quotation: "He that will learn to pray, let him go to sea."

John Wayne Marina

To the SE of Juan de Fuca Triangle lies the very protected Sequim Bay and home of the small but very beautiful John Wayne Marina. It is named after the famous movie actor, who donated land so that a marina could be built here. He often used to visit here aboard his yacht *Wild Goose*, which is a converted Navy minesweeper, as I recall. Arlen and I see the *Wild Goose* once when we were at Neah Bay on

Seaspell, but John Wayne is not on board at the time. I spent one night at John Wayne Marina in *Day by Day*. From here Mother and I visit the New Dungeness Light and explore surrounding waters. If you land by boat at the lighthouse as we do, you must do so in the signed area inside the spit. Volunteers are custodians and guides for the light. On this particular week, a family from California is doing duty as they have at other lighthouses. They learn of these opportunities on the Internet.

In the Port Angeles area, nearby, is the home of salmon trollers, other fishers and *Pacific Troller* author, Francis Caldwell, who take a deep interest in the survival of salmon. More than once the *Peninsula Daily News*, carries letters to the editor on their views. A recent letter points out the sea lions are a major threat to salmon survival. To that I would add, seals and whales. When I was a kid there was a bounty on seals. One time, trolling off Neah Bay, I recall seeing seals crisscrossing under the boat. Salmon that I did pull, for a long time were bitten in half by seals. It was like being followed by a pack of vicious dogs under water.

At Neah Bay and Ucluelet, sea lions bark and splash around floats and boats like dogs. They look for handouts or help themselves. As I mention at the beginning of this book, all the problems affecting salmon decline need to be identified, if we hope to work on solutions.

Washington Coast

Puget Sound side trips for some include the Washington coast. In my earlier years, I spend considerable time chasing the Pacific salmon along the Washington coast both as a sport and commercial salmon troller. In 1974 I fish out of every port except Willapa Bay. My favorite in these days is La Push. A quick launch out the Quillayute River and you are in the ocean. Salmon are not far off shore either.

Before you cross any bar along the Washington, or any other coast, make sure you know how and when to cross. I would avoid Willapa Bay if at all possible. This might be a good time to suggest taking Power Squadron courses to improve your boating proficiency. I took classes through Advanced Piloting. If you sail off shore you should complete the Navigator course. Learn how to use a sextant in case your electronics fail. See the web address for the Power Squadron and Coast Guard Auxiliary in the Bibliography for more on classes and safety. In the future, some States and Canada will have more stringent requirements for operating boats in those waters.

A very pleasant trip in good weather is to mosey down the coast from Neah Bay to La Push and poke around the rocks. There are numerous indentations to explore. I used to anchor in a place fisherman called Skagway Rocks just south of Cape Flattery, 48° 21.8'N, 124° 43.0'W, with other salmon trollers. One night I came to know the meaning of the bitter end of the anchor line. It is dark with a SE wind. Other boats are there so I drop the hook of *Nadja* outside and windward of the fleet. We drift fast with the rode paying out quickly. Somehow, I just catch the very end in time and am able to get a wrap on the cleat before securing it. The line is not fastened in the anchor locker as it should have been. I thank God that night I was able to hang on just long enough. This anchorage is best in calm or NW winds. On a beautiful moonlight night it will give you a pleasant taste of ocean anchoring. Before I anchored again, the bitter end was tied to the boat.

An interesting place I anchor six times and where I would like to return, is just SE of Ozette Island (48° 9.3'N, 124° 44.0'W). The first time I stay here it is foggy when evening comes, and I do not know where I am, except on a more or less north-south line between two radio direction finder beacons. No GPS in those days. A Loran then is big and expensive and not found on small boats like our 31-ft. Suddenly, the troller *Sea Lion* is heading toward the beach. I hail the skipper and ask where he is going for the night. He says, "Cabbage Patch." After he grants me permission to follow, we are not too long before getting inside through the rocks on the south side. I am amazed at the protection from the swells. Not a good place to be in a storm, but in good weather it is a great spot, except for some small non-biting gnats that call the place home. I recall seeing beach fires of campers who hike to Cape Alava from Ozette. I am tempted to row my dinghy the half-mile ashore to check out the beach. Since the shore is rock studded it may be difficult to land. Now this area is a part of the Olympic Coast Marine Sanctuary, dedicated in July 1994. It is an area seaward thirty to forty miles running nearly sixty miles south from Cape Flattery.

I have anchored as far south as Destruction Island and behind it. As many trollers used to do, I would sometimes drift at night with my strobe light on, when I commercial fished. At nightfall, just shut her down and go to sleep. It is not unusual to drift ten miles and awake in the fog not knowing your exact location except by resection with two radio beacons. This is actually foolish and I would not do that again near the mouth of Juan de Fuca Strait with all of the ship traffic. They should avoid you, but they may not, as on one occasion two ships ran into each other while navigating with radar.

On one drift I recall a most remarkable experience. On August 4, 1978, at dusk, on *Nadja*, I am out on the Big Prairie out of Neah Bay, probably near the blue dot defined below. About a hundred trollers are with me tonight, with us on the leeward drift side of them. I am on the forward deck to put out my sea anchor (I never saw much value in them) when the sea is suddenly alive with leaping whales all around, some within fifty feet. I am dumbfounded—both scared and thrilled! Then, sitting on the deck I decide to enjoy the show that lasts quite a few minutes. I cannot forget the pungent odor of their breath—like that of a cow. Then as quickly as it started, the show is over. What kind of whales? I wish I knew.

Now that salmon fishing isn't what it used to be, and even sport seasons are often short and spotty, many have turned to halibut. In those earlier days, no one talked about sport halibut fishing in the ocean. Most halibut were caught in a few spots along the south side of the strait. More recently, the sport fleet has discovered you can catch the slabs in three hundred feet of water fifteen to twenty-five miles off Cape Flattery. Rich and I do this in May of 1996 and 1997. If you like to eat halibut, can reel a heavy load for a long time and don't mind rough water at times, this kind of fishing is for you. Neah Bay has a new marina that rivals many, with concrete docks complete with water and electricity—both 30 and 60 amp services. The facilities are fine for trailering boats to Neah Bay or leaving your larger vessel. Shore side restrooms are limited, but a shower house is available across the street for $2. On shore you can hear lots of fish stories and get the coordinates of the last hot bite. Rich and I find the southside of Swiftsure Bank and the blue dot (48° 17.8'N, 125° 21.3'W) areas the best. For sure you will have company. On one trip on *Day by Day*, Rich lands a fifty-eight pounder for the port high of the day. On another, Cheryl's husband, Doug, is high halibut man on our two-boat, two-day outing with a thirty-five pound halibut. No power reels should be allowed. They are not sporting and when you are reeling hard on a halibut, the noise from them on other boats is annoying.

Trip Up the Snake River

Whoa! This is not Puget Sound Side Trip stuff! Oh yes, it can be. If like me you ever signed up for Alaska literature, you will get many attractive brochures on a wide variety of Alaskan cruises. More recently, Cruise West is promoting Snake River cruises in the off-season in the fall and spring. One that caught my eye has a picture of the classic *Spirit of '98* on the cover of the pamphlet in the Snake River canyon. This is the same vessel that hit a rock in Tracy Arm in July 1999. The *Spirit of Alaska*, which I passed in my 1994 trip north, and two other Alaskan small-ship cruisers additionally offer a variety of experiences from Astoria to deep in Hells Canyon. This is of great interest to me since I cruise the Snake River in *Day by Day* in April 1999. Like me, these Seattle based boats start in Puget Sound. They go by water all the way. I trailer *Day by Day* to the Snake.

For many years I thought about cruising our boat from home, down the Washington coast and up the Columbia and Snake rivers, or the other way around. Going down the coast in the summer you should be favored by northwest winds and swells. Up the Columbia you are usually pushed by strong west winds. I would rather go with the wind in a small boat than take advantage of the current. It is also nice to end your cruise in fresh water. Since I have fished in three of our boats out of all Washington ports but one, I do not feel a need to cruise the coast. Running the free-flowing Snake above Lewiston always sounds like a good adventure to me. Calhoun's *Volume I* relates small boat Columbia and Snake river cruises before the days of jet boats dominating the river runs. Only once in *Happy Talk* did I do any Snake River rapids running before the dams flooded them.

I begin my 1999 Snake River run from Lewiston. A boat dealer tells me that in my MerCruiser I can safely go to Asotin or six miles. He also says you need three boats: a jet for the river, one for the saltwater and a lake boat. I have one and the wrong one today according to him! On this trip I see Portland based stern-wheeler cruise ship

Queen of the West three times. The day I head up the river the *Queen's* passengers are returning by jet boat. Cynthia and I have gone by jet boat up the Snake River to where we can see the Hat Point lookout in Oregon. Based on what I can recall on that trip and with higher river flow now, I reason I can go further than Asotin.

With the depth sounder alarm set on ten feet I feel my way up the murky river, sometimes following range markers. As usual we are running alone, but see some boats along the way. Water ranges from placid pools of little current to one Class III rapids. In one case *Day by Day* barely has enough power to climb through the wavy current as I make sure we have enough water under us. It is exhilarating! The lower river is tamer with increasing challenges as we go up river. At Cache Creek at the Forest Service Station I get a permit to enter the Hells Canyon National Recreation Area. This time of year you can do that but in the busy season you must get a permit in advance. I am warned that there are no other boats up the river since it is getting late in the day. If something happens, we are coming downstream, I reason!

My goal is to make it to the Salmon River. I almost do, but a few problems pop up, so I settle for a couple miles short, considering the time. But I am satisfied going up river forty miles on one of my most exciting boating days ever. In addition to the fascinating river, the scenery is magnificent. Sandy beaches and steep rocky walls give way to rolling grassy knolls, topped by timbered ridges and finally snow-capped mountains. The scene constantly changes up and down the canyon seeing more or less of all the attributes at any one time. Even idling we come down fast. Remembering where to go coming down is not always easy but you sure are committed and you came down! I am embarrassed to say this but for all of my Snake River cruise, I use a road map and a small one from a 1999 *Sunset* magazine article entitled, "Year of the Snake"! After the trip I got *The Wild and Scenic Snake River Boater's Guide.* I highly recommend it. In my log I write on April 27, "A day to remember! Thank God for a beautiful day."

The next day I take the pickup and trailer to Columbia Park Marina in Kennewick where in 1805 the Lewis and Clark Expedition observed "the multitudes of this fish (salmon) are almost inconceivable." Man's abuse, including over fishing and dams on the Columbia and Snake rivers, have been the demise of salmon. Having said that,

I do not believe removal of dams is the answer. There are other options using technology and wise management.

A bus trip and two taxis get me back to *Day by Day* at the Hells Canyon Resort Marina in Clarkston. For the next two days I have a relaxing, easy trip down stream through four reservoirs and passage through huge locks that are surprisingly very boater friendly. Most times *Day by Day* is the only boat in the locks. It is like being a flea in a bathtub! On one lockage we are with the Corps of Engineers tug, *Lassen,* with a salmon barge. She is intercepting salmon smolts at each dam and transporting them below Bonneville Dam to speed their passage to sea. If you have not been through a Columbia or Snake river dam to see from an underwater viewing room, fish go through a fish ladder, do. It is fascinating! The lock schedule is on demand by VHF radio, except it is every three hours from 0900 to 2100 from May 15 to September 15. Calm water, few pleasure boats, greening hills, roaming cattle, barge traffic, grain elevators, railroads with high bridges and beautiful parks with marinas are the hallmarks of this trip downstream. It is wonderful. So much so, that this trip competes very well with a trip to Alaska. For sure, it qualifies as a Puget Sound side trip!

Day by Day, Lassen *and salmon pass Monumental Dam on the Snake River.*

Side Trip 2—Inlets and Passages

Perhaps no place on earth has more inlets and passages exciting to a small boater than that area along the British Columbia mainland between Vancouver and Cape Caution. While points further north and outside Vancouver Island offer a few more spectacular areas, the

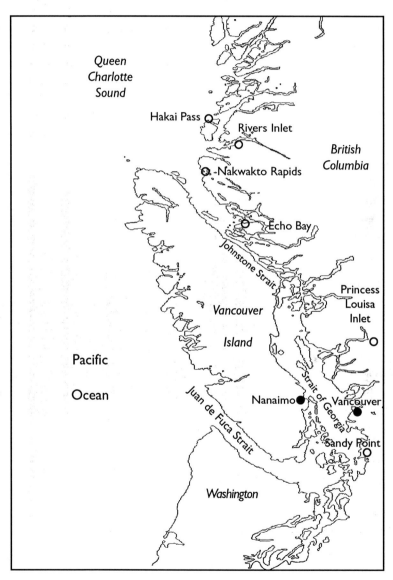

Side Trip 2—Inlets and Passages

above area could satisfy you for a lifetime. It is vast and largely uninhabited by boats or settlers except at a relatively few places. *Spillsbury's Album* of photographs and stories show what life was like in some of these areas. Spillsbury who lived in these parts at an early age will take you back—you will be there. While these areas can be crowded in midsummer, it is not hard to soon be alone if that is your desire. After being from Olympia to Skagway, if I had to choose one area to hang out on a boat, it would be that area north of Vancouver along the mainland shore inside of Vancouver Island. While much if it is the same, there is always a mystery of what is around the bend or in the next bay.

Sechelt

Howe Sound and Indian Arm give you a good introduction to inlets close to an urban area and not a long cruise from Puget Sound. One year I explore the more interesting reaches of Sechelt Inlet. I spend one August night in Storm Bay in the little cove at 49° 39.78'N, 123° 49.72'W with four other boats, each stern tied to shore. It is a good idea to have a reel of small line (I use ⅜ inch polypropylene) so you can tie to shore. Since there is room, I anchor in the middle of the cove. The next day I just had to look at the narrowest spot, Tzoonie Narrows, which is in a provincial park. Trailering to the town of Sechelt is a good bet for small boats to explore the inlet from there, or cruise on north, but you must cross one ferry. (There are boat ramps almost everywhere, some published some not, from Puget Sound to Alaska) The most fascinating place, as you might expect, is Sechelt Rapids. In 1995 Rich and I run up and back though a four knot current in *Day by Day*. I am mildly thrilled. Rich is less enthused, but he still talks about his best ever oyster burger at the Backeddy Tavern in Egmont in Skookumchuck Narrows. It is good.

One year, Cynthia and I hike to Sechelt Rapids to see them on a maximum flood at a higher tide. It is rather spell binding. Just like a dashing river. Another man, gazing at the rapids at that time, and I, agree we could probably make it through in our boats by going on the far shore. The older I get, I am not sure I will try that gamble. During my 1998 trip I enter Sechelt Rapids with a five knot current and leave the next day on an ebb. Consulting *Canadian Tide Table*

Vol. 5 for times of slack water before entering and exiting the rapids is wise.

Princess Louisa Inlet

There is a very special place near the end of Jervis Inlet—Princess Louisa. The name alone suggests it might be unique. The first two times I am there, once in July and once in February, guess what? It rains both times! This is not unusual, since Princess Louisa is nearly a landlocked four mile-long saltwater lake surrounded by shear rock walls rising to seven thousand feet. As the Pacific moisture-laden air squirms into the narrow chasm, it gets squeezed. In so doing, the air has not much choice other than to wring out the water like a sponge onto the boaters below.

Traveling up Jervis is like many BC inlets—a wide river-like channel flanked by high mountains. Suddenly you approach Malibu Rapids. As you arrive, an unlikely opening appears. You wind through an S-shaped course past rocks and a distinctive point where the inviting Malibu Club overlooks a passage capable of nine knots. Our first trip in *Seaspell* with our family of four against near maximum current is not a problem. The camp is open for visitors but not for boater services. Many a high school youth has been inspired by their stay at the Malibu Club facility.

My first ever boat log entry for Princess Louisa on July 5, 1973, reads: "Weather overcast & lt. showers didn't dampen enthusiasm for most beautiful site in NW & States…saltwater lake…waterfalls, vertical mountains, rainforest, beauty…air, snow fields & more—God's creation. Calm. Fantastic. Quiet. Like wilderness but 5 Bayliners were there…out of 15 boats…Rained all night…." The inlet lake, to me, is always calm and only the sound of the waterfall overpowers all. In February 1995, Rich and I in *Day by Day* are the only boat inside, where I record in the log: "Always beautiful. Snowing 2,000' above…Enjoyed 3 hrs @ Chatterbox Falls to ourselves…like Heaven in the Rain." After a fire on the beach in the shelter in fine facilities, at the marine park, we leave as other boats approach.

In my August 1998 trip north, I am a day ahead and the weather is nice, so I decide to make the side trip once more to Princess Louisa Inlet and see it at its best. As I enter with the current, my thoughts reflected in the log are: "I know God lives here—it's so beautiful and peaceful—that perfect." For the first time, I land at the Malibu Club float to be greeted by a volunteer yacht host, James. Then Jim, an attorney and a volunteer, gives me the complete tour. Malibu Club is run by Young Life. Christians from many denominations enroll teen guests at Malibu Club with the goal to provide them the best week of their life. Besides good food, fellowship and recreation, they listen to inspiring talks. While not a requirement, some youth commit to Christ while they are here. Malibu was built by Tom Hamilton, the inventor of the airplane variable pitch propeller. He used it as a resort for the rich, but it flopped, and the place fell into disrepair until Young Life was able to purchase it.

Malibu Club, Princess Louisa Inlet.

When we arrive at the float near Chatterbox Falls it is full, so I decide on this trip to anchor in front of the falls. From there, I row the dinghy in gleaming sunshine as close as I can to the falls, then check out all of the anchored boats. Most impressive is the large, 1930, immaculate yacht, *Taconite*, once owned by Boeing. No doubt Boeing and Hamilton knew each other and this vessel may have been to Princess Louisa so they could talk possibilities and deals while having some fun. Before I leave, a 1928 classic double-ended, fully restored, mahogany cabin yacht drops anchor between us and the falls—a perfect picture. A young couple is on board who restored her. Somehow these classic yachts fit Princess Louisa with the character it deserves. I am almost ashamed to be here in a fiberglass boat, which lowers the character of days gone by.

Taconite, a 1930 yacht, and Chatterbox Falls, Princess Louisa Inlet.

The only negative I experience on three cruises up Jervis is, for the first time, losing an anchor. Rich and I are navigating slowly in pitch black by radar in February when we decide to anchor in Vancouver Bay knowing it is not the best anchorage. We know it better now! The stay is nice but the next morning, after two hours of struggle to raise the hook, I reluctantly cut the rode and say good bye to $100.

Fish pens or logging cables on the bottom won out. Apparently, the water is too warm to raise salmon in these parts, fish became diseased and growers go bankrupt. Pens are cut loose to sink, as if deep water is a junk yard. Between the fish pens and logging cables from days of yore, many innocent coves are "criminals" for taking your hook. That proves the definition of a boat as a hole in the water into which you pour money! Being a philosopher and a calculating engineer at heart, I reason that with over thirty years of boating and only one anchor lost, that's only $3 per year! If I suspect a problem area, I use my self-tripping spare anchor. Others will find a diver to raise an anchor stuck on the bottom.

Desolation Sound

In August, 1997, I cruise two-thirds of Malaspina Inlet. On the approach, I find Desolation Sound in all her majesty, not in the dreary conditions for which she was named by Captain Vancouver in the summer of 1792. Many of today's boaters do not share that view, particularly on a nice day from May to October. On this day, I find sun, jagged snow-capped mountains, blue rippled water, green forest mantle over rocky islands and hills and ranges topped with puffy white clouds pasted on a bluest sky. The inlet does not seem crowded, but I see thirty-seven non-local boats either at cruise or anchor. Seafood farming operations dot various bays, some with Heinz 57 variety plastic floats disgracing the waterscape. My philosophy: Fish farms should be regulated in limited areas with operational guidelines that do not degrade the environment. Maybe they are, but it is not always apparent. Perhaps, like clear-cuts, not everybody will be satisfied no matter where they are. It is true we need to build houses and eat seafood. Finding the right balance is the key. Watch for rocks in this inlet. Most I see are locally marked or easily located if you are alert. Wootton Bay and Theodosia Inlet could be good anchorages. No boats are at either except one is at the entrance of Theodosia. A nice beach on the back side of Portage Cove is private and signed, "No trespassing." In Grace Harbour, a part of Desolation Sound Marine Park, several boats are at anchor in an otherwise hot and scrubby shoreline area. Frankly, I like cooler June with fewer boats and its refreshing showers. It appears new homes in the inlet are replacing logging as the biggest man-made visual impact. On this trip I anchor in Roscoe Bay with other boats and hike to Black Lake. I enjoy it. On these trips it is fun to spot boats you know.

I have not been to the ends of Toba, Bute, Loughborough, or Knight inlets. I might someday. Just be familiar with the names and read about them, or find other boaters' impressions, and maybe you will want to check out more than one of them in your lifetime. In most every case, the inlets are deep with steep rock shores offering little protection in a blow. While it is nice to see the mountains, there is a lot of sameness. You use a lot of fuel because the inlets are up to fifty miles long. So for me there are other priorities. On the other hand, there is something to be said for seeing everything for your self and being an expert because you have been there. Besides, every moment on the water can offer an unexpected surprise.

From here north I try to take either favorite passage routes, or investigate new or old ones for me. I never tire of the region to Johnstone Strait. The several rapids, inviting government wharfs, cozy coves, intriguing settlements, and bays with no one there, all attract me with each passage. If you want to fish, Campbell River is a good bet. We have done both well and poorly there, but the possibility of catching a Tyee (Chinook) over thirty pounds is certainly a reason to try. I think of Campbell as a little cousin of Nanaimo. While it is not as big, it offers the boater excellent services and their gas prices are lower.

One thing that I often think about cruising in the "inlet zone," are the large luxury yachts. They appear often at marinas and along the way. If you study boat ads in various NW boating publications, you must be amazed as I am how expensive these floating palaces are. It is also hard to imagine what life must be like living aboard, better than most of us do in our homes. Then I wonder how the owners of these "lodges" get their money. There is not enough in our several families to buy even one of the more modest large yachts. On my return trip in 1996, a gas dock attendant at Campbell River and I are discussing this subject when he comments how the superrich skippers are really nice people. "Then you have the people who think they're rich, but aren't, and they are real jerks." says he. What got me that trip, as I am cruising Strait of Georgia at a little less than twenty knots, is a sixty footer whizzes on by me in the same direction! Abusive of our future's fuel supply, I think. Cynthia and I wonder at times if our society has lost its value when we see such large yachts and big estates with ostentatious homes. One boating magazine featured a 124-foot yacht with twin 1,450 hp engines that could push the 150-ton yacht to 20 knots. Or consider this ad: "The Sunseeker Predator 80…80 feet, 50 tons at 50 mph. Think about it."

Whatever happened to the days of a rowboat or small kicker boat? Maybe we have lost our reality. I like to think that *Day by Day* combines some of the best of both large and small boat worlds. On the other hand I can be called a hypocrite because I run all over and burn a lot of gas myself. Yes, that bothers me. We sold *Nadja*, in part due to her poor one mile per gallon. We also sold our motor home due in part to its poor mileage of seven miles per gallon. We now have a car, that we drive more than our pickup, which consistently gets over thirty miles per gallon. A 36-ft sailboat uses no fuel under sail and boasts 12 mpg under power. The 26-ft diesel double-ender Allweather powerboat, made in Ferndale, Washington, claims 20 mpg. She only uses forty gallons from Bellingham to Ketchikan. Wouldn't it be nice? In "Observations" I develop an idea that could be an answer.

October 1974, Rich, Arlen and I find the waters north of Pender Harbour to Stuart Island calm, uncrowded and exciting to explore in that first expedition for us, aboard *Seaspell*. To look in the next cove or see what it is like to peek at or run through a rapids is shear delight. In this region there are numerous government docks and floats at so many little places, like it used to be in Puget Sound up until the early 1940s, during the days of the mosquito fleet.

In all of the out of the way places I always feel safe, except once. In 1974 when we peek into Owen Bay, there is an older wooden yacht anchored that is somewhat derelict looking with a crew of questionables that look about the same. We do not feel welcome. In fact from their stares, all three of us think the guns might be out any minute, so we quickly leave. This may be a silly notion on our part, but why find out?

At one time, Owen Bay had a government dock, store, marine station, sawmill and a school where dances were held occasionally on Saturday nights. Only ruins give clues of the past, although a couple of new homes are near the rapids.

During my 1997 trip around Vancouver Island, I run almost all of the rapids in the 50-degree latitude, 125–126 degree longitude region. Many, in *Day by Day*, I go near maximum flow both against and with the current. I admit you get braver. When I am alone it is easier to run rapids rather than deal with my passengers' safety and fears. Same is true in rough water. After my Snake River run, most saltwater rapids seem tame. Still, treat all rapids with respect.

Overall, I am comforted by the discipline and order found among boaters and at remote locations. In all my years cruising up north, I rarely saw a law enforcement officer, nor was one needed. Most of those were in popular fishing areas as fishery patrol officers.

In May 1979, when four of us brought the *Pursuit* from Petersburg to Bellingham, south of Wrangle Narrows we find a drifting sport fishing boat with a man slumped over in it. We pull along side and jump aboard, but we can not rouse him. He is breathing, and indicators tell the rest of the story. A loaded pistol is on the seat beside him which we presume is part of his halibut gear. The cover of his outboard motor is off, indicating he has trouble with it. On top of the motor is an empty whiskey bottle. Nothing is going right for him today, so he tries to "douse" his problems, then falls asleep. Neil, our skipper, calls the Coast Guard and tells them we will take the boat in tow to Meyers Chuck, which we do after hiding his gun in his boat. By the time we get there at dark, the fisherman understands what we have done for him. This is not a scary episode, but an example of how things are handled in the remote areas of the Inside Passage.

I do not report on every nook and cranny I visit. Other books and magazines give us interesting reading about many locations. It is often hard to say this place is more unique than the next place. Each place is special in its own way while often sharing characteristics with others. Every person places a different value on each spot making it more or less important to he or she. I do find Mansons Landing, Whaletown and Rebecca Spit of noteworthy interest. Be sure to get out of your boat at all three of these places. Enjoy! Great walking and beaches at Mansons and Rebecca. When I have time, I delight in finding a very narrow passage and flowing through it with the tide, or fighting my way back. It's fun to return with the water forces reversed. At times you may have to wait for a tide change or be patient for a more favorable tide to enter at all.

Echo and Sullivan Bays

In 1996, en route to the Charlottes in *Day by Day*, I explore areas around Echo and Sullivan bays that I have not visited before. One of those is Simoom Sound. This turns out to be more of a curiosity satisfier than a highlight, as I foolishly troll in and out of the sound in the rain. More rewarding is a cruise up Kingcome Inlet. I enjoy entering it via Shawl Bay and the shallow (4.6 ft), narrow passage inside Gregory Island. Then across Moore Bay. Watch the rocks! Entering Kingcome, I love the rain and calm with gray beauty everywhere from sea to sky and the mountains in between. Perhaps the computer gray tones were conceived here. Fascinating to me, are the lighter and darker looking splotches, on a calm surface, in the rain. It appears that there are differences in surface tensions. One theory I have is kelp exudes minute amounts of an oily substance that may cause this. On this day the snow-capped mountain tops, so near above the steep slopes from the inlet, are draped in clouds allowing only peaks to show. Into Belleisle Sound for a quick look with no one there except a seal. It smells so good, like a forest basin should. Clear-cuts in here resemble slides—effective. A lush green meadow at waterside and waterfall prompts me to think that this cove could be a national park in most states. Coming out of Belleisle you face a waterfall maybe twenty-five hundred feet high streaming down the rocks, with a lesser one nearby.

At the head of the Kingcome, loggers are at work near Anchorage Cove, at the mouth of the Kingcome River, that looks like Grandma Petersen's tea—she liked her cream. Without a river chart I make my way slowly up current to the community of Kingcome Inlet, alternately using the big engine or outboard depending upon the depth. It is a little unnerving when you cannot see the bottom. Rather than stop to explore the village or beyond to Kingcome, I drift downstream two miles. Loggers and Indians with supplies go buy me in work boats and skiffs but no one waves. You might say this is not tourist country and I do not blame them for not being friendly. Calhoun describes a more detailed visit to this area.

I spend considerable time on my 1996 trip doing six knots in this region to prove I can get better fuel mileage by going slowly, so when I get to the Charlottes I can extend my cruising range. It doesn't work out that way. On a sixty-seven mile loop, six knot cruise in

Puget Sound, *Day by Day* gets 3.5 mpg versus a normal 2.4 mpg with a lot of favorable tides. On the way north exploring inlets, she only got 2.1 and 2.4 mpg on separate six knot cruise sections, after encountering unfavorable winds and or tides. So, like another skipper said, it does not pay to run displacement on planning hull boats. I do feel for the sake of future generations, thought needs to be given how to improve fuel economy on boats. For gunkholing in these parts, a boat with basic amenities aboard and a two foot draft is desirable. Our 21-ft Bayliner fits that bill nicely even though mileage is not that great. Baronet Passage is an example where *Day by Day* feels comfortable while I explore. In fact, there are a wealth of small inlets and passages to check out between here and Broughton Island. I have seen many.

Robson Bight, SW of West Cracroft Island is reported to be one of the worlds busiest known orca crossroads. Lots of ship and barge traffic pass this way too. I have heard that playing flutes to orca in Johnstone Strait will bring them out. Too bad Cheryl didn't do that when she used to play and boat with us. Surprisingly, on all my passages, I pass here only once and at night in a seiner. In our boats I always go through the smaller, more intimate passages further north. Well, in 1998 on the way south, I finally did it. Somehow I learn that boats are not to go into the bight and that you are to stay one-half

Mighty loads pass through the Inside Passage.

mile off shore. Radar is handy for this. On the day I arrive from the north I am amused by all of the tents pitched on shore, south of Cracroft Point, with observers using telescopes. An orange inflatable is cruising the area to encourage boats not to go too close. On my visit it is easy. I motor slowly between two whale watching tour boats and I find the people aboard more entertaining than the orca. The most amusing of all though, is that the whales are not in the protected bight but in the area outside where the boats are to be!

Greenway Sound is worth a stop. The marina, all on floats, is plain vanilla but is very clean. They have a water view restaurant. If the rest of the food is as good as their pizza, it's great. When I land in 1996 going north, I meet present and past Sandy Point couples in boats heading south. They share some pizza—tasty. The night before at Echo Bay I meet Harry and Marylou from Sandy Point on the *Cat's Meow* and they share crab with me. If you have a shrimp pot with lots of line, you can catch your own dinner in these waters, though I have not tried. At times you can buy fresh shrimp off a commercial boat along the coast.

On July 20, 1996, I have a captivating run through Carter Passage. I arrive at the east end shortly after 0500 on a damp morning. I hope to be there a little earlier, closer to high tide. I do not have Chart 3547, which you should have, but I use my 1978 cruising guide with its large scale chart of the passage. While clearly marked not for navigational purposes, it works fine. At the East end of Carter, a sailboat is anchored. I slip by unnoticed. Carter Passage is a series of narrows and small wider lake-like bodies, all with a wilderness touch. On that trip, Carter Passage is the most scenic. You pass through a thick forest of varying widths like going from room to room. Trees overhang steep rock walls to the water's edge. A favorite on first pass. The glassy calm experience reminds me of the thoroughfare to upper Priest Lake in Idaho. Traveling with the current east to west on the ebb is nice but at high risk. At times I have the outdrive kicked up and use the outboard to keep us straight in channel. At one spot I think there is kelp in the channel. It is a rock! So beware at the narrow spot near 50° 50.2'N, 126° 50.3'W. At this point, on the north side of the rock it seems there is only about a boat width of clearance in three feet of water, an hour after a 13.4 high. With the ebb and a light east wind it is easy travel. Through the west end we are doing about four knots in about twenty feet of water. It is fun but

I am grateful to be scar free. The close call is a bit much but I give thanks. My philosophy is to protect my outdrive. If I ding up the fiberglass, it can be repaired when I get home.

The run through Stuart Narrows, Drury Inlet and a dinghy ride into Actaeon Sound is all worthwhile. The narrows is the most scenic part with the rest lesser quality, with the scrubby trees and hills on a rocky shore. Actaeon looks more like a reservoir as the tide receded. It is possible to go in another seven miles beyond where I do, but my curiosity is satisfied. My preference for this area is Grappler Sound to Kenneth Passage and all of its inlets. You can anchor and explore basins, lagoons, coves and tidal falls. While I regret not going up Mackenzie Sound this trip for lack of time, I do go a year later. Mackenzie is beautiful. Apparently at the resort in Nimmo Bay is where President Bush, et al, complete with helicopters, visit at one time. Anyway, if you make Sullivan Bay or Greenway Sound your base, you will have a lot of fun exploring this area, particularly if it is your first trip. Even after my first trip to Sullivan Bay the area is a mystery to me with a magnetic pull to return. I do return and I feel more satisfied. I still would like to go back and spend more time near the tidal falls and into the lagoons off Kenneth Passage. Several other boats are in the area, on my visit.

Along the west side of Broughton Strait you will find interesting places which I have visited more than once. Most notable is Tele-graph Cove which is cozy and has a blend of a logging days and tourist look. One year Cynthia and I launch *Day by Day* at Alder Bay and stay in our RV, where all spots have a water view. Facilities are nicer in Port McNeil for just the boater. Some day we want to return to Sointula and not just pass by. It is an old Finish community that to this day retains some of its character.

Nakwakto Rapids

My nature is to find out what is out there. When I first read about Nakwakto Rapids, the fastest in North America, at sixteen knots, I want to see that. At the same time, just the thought of being around such a powerful surge sends a chill of intimidation through my veins. The stern warnings in *Sailing Directions* catch your attention and give you pause. I recall some years ago reading a story about a woman, long ago, with an old slow boat with several children going through. This woman anchors her boat in a cove near the rapids and goes ashore to a vantage point. When she sees the rapids near slack, she hurries back to her vessel and makes it through. We have the advantage of accurate current tables and if the sea is not adverse at the entrance, this side trip can be rewarding as it is for me. Prior to my visiting Nakwakto, I decide to check out Blunden and Allison harbors. In 1996 I spend a night at Blunden. There are several other boats anchored and exploring. I find it is a great dinghy area, although I do not have time to check out every spot nor the tidal falls into Bradley Lagoon, which extends two miles beyond the falls. Still, I have a good feel for the place and I would have no hesitancy to use Blunden as a safe port if needed. Indicators that this is still an Indian encampment adds interest and credibility to a protected harbor. At one spot clam shell deposits, through perhaps hundreds of years, have built an impressive beach and uplands.

A visit to Allison Harbour is totally different. I am cautious passing by islands and rocks near the Southgate Group. Once into Allison, you discover it is a single long inlet. Nothing or no one is in there, although it is scenic. At one time there is a float and post office, but no longer. After gaining confidence on the bottom, I plane out the inlet and into Schooner Channel. I meet no boats on this July 21 perfect weather and sea day. I feel privileged to have such ideal conditions as I approach a fearsome rapids. Even sea conditions on the approaches are a matter of concern on all but the best days. I arrive at the rapids near slack. It looks innocent. Only *Day by Day* and I and a log with six sea gulls are in slow circular motion in the rapids as we drift at one knot. Soon we are part of all of the flotsam. It is fascinating to watch the changing relative positions of logs and kelp in a bumper car-like race in the swirling patterns. Turret Rock sits in the eastern part of the narrows. I pass it on the narrow side on my port hand. The rock is a misnomer above water in that it is fully clothed with trees and thick vegetation. I am taken with the numerous signs showing who's been here. Nice idea but a little tricky to land on it, so I settle for a picture.

We run up Seymour Inlet far enough to look into the three lagoons at its southern or lower arm. Next we pass a logging camp; all is quiet on this Sunday morning. Even with logging, Seymour is a lovely quiet place and an escape from boats in mid-July. My only concern is fuel so I limit my travel. If you make Sullivan your fuel base, then many boats will have no problem cruising this area and seeing it fully. *Sailing Directions* states there are no anchorages in Seymour. I do not share that opinion.

My trip up Belize Inlet is limited to Village Cove and Strachan Bay. As I pass by Nakwakto on the way it is steaming at 9.5 knots on the ebb so I give it a fairly wide berth. My interest in seeing it up close is tempered by my caution. In Belize Inlet a small boat is underway to a fishing spot. Probably a logger enjoying the weekend good life. I do see one large yacht in Belize as I am leaving. The glassy water, many mountains and lack of boats makes this area a best-kept secret wilderness. There are no beaches—maybe some, but marginal. There are old clear-cuts but they have been re-carpeted with trees. This part reminds me at high tide of Swift and Yale reservoirs in Washington. There are two floating cabins in Strachan Bay near the creek discharging from Pack Lake. There is a good anchorage in Village Cove and an ideal protected one in the SW cove of Strachan Bay. A coned peak near Village Cove is distinctive and keeps my attention. If I had a disappointment, it is that I do not get to check out Eclipse Narrows and the restricted entrance into Schwartzenberg Lagoon. I may go back and see more. I want to find a nice perch and try to observe Nakwakto for a full cycle during a maximum flow period. I still give these rapids a lot of respect even though *Day by Day* and I ran Class III rapids in the Snake River.

On my southerly passage in August 1998, we duck into Miles Inlet at 0749 after crossing Queen Charlotte. A sailboat is anchored at the tee and has a crab pot out. I explore the area as much as possible at a lower tide. It will take a high tide and a dinghy to check it all out. I am impressed that this is a good anchorage and a place to keep an eye on sea conditions.

Smith Sound

In 1998 I run into Smith Sound where I find only two other pleasure boats anchored. Commercial fishing at times and some logging are the main things going on here. This is a place of easy access and a chance to get away from it all if you don't expect any shore side facilities. I anchor alone, stern first, with my trip anchor one night in

McBride Bay, on the west side, near the rock at 51° 18.25'N, 127° 32.73'W. Watch for boulders. At the head of the bay is a gypo logger operation with a tug and a shack on logs. McBride Bay is alive with small fish, with huge schools periodically swimming under us. A natural and largely unused body of water would express my impression of Smith Sound. I go nearly as far as possible into Broad Reach. With more time I would have taken the dinghy through the narrowest pass into Takush Harbour where I do take a turn in *Day by Day*. My entry through Ahclakerho is gorgeous at sunrise with wisps of fog overhead against the timbered slopes. The water is so calm and smooth we move slowly almost with a motionless feel among the many scenic islets. The only blight is logging debris, which has not been adequately cleaned up from the water. I let *Day by Day* drift (not a good practice) near the narrows into Wyclees Lagoon. I row the dinghy into the ebbing current to the rapids that appears to drop four feet, two hours before Egg Island low. It is fun to row hard then drift downstream. Two yachts, maybe a charter tour, are anchored in Hickey Cove so I do not bother going near. People are ashore on a rocky, grassy beach. We run into Finis Nook where the water is brown and smells like decaying fish. There is an old cabin, two hulls, floats and log booms. This is a well protected place to spend the night without dropping anchor. On a small building is a sign, "Explosives. Stay away. Stay in 1 piece." While I enjoy my visit in the sun on this calm day to this "haunted cove," if "Finis" means "The End," stuff in here is that way. There are sandy beaches at Dsulish Bay but I do not go ashore. I look into Milbrook Cove but do not go in. Other publications speak of this as a good anchorage but watch those rocks! We run inside of Shield and Tie islands, near where fishing boats are at anchor, then inside of Spur Rocks.

Open Bight

It takes me several trips by this place before I discover Open Bight. In 1996, passing by on my Queen Charlottes cruise, I see a sailboat anchor here. When I get home I read about it and realize what I missed. On August 19, 1998, I anchor at 51° 22.13'N, 127° 46.52'W and later a little further north. It is gorgeous to say the least. A half-mile long sandy beach to myself on a day of great weather is almost unbelievable. A short walk across an isthmus and I am looking at a smaller bay where I anchor going South that same trip on a perfect night. I do not anchor in Open Bight that time since the NW wind is blowing and Open Bight is exposed. In addition to exploring beaches here I climb along the rocky shore. Most unusual and striking is the very bright white shell midden. Once you see it, like a magnet, you will be drawn ashore.

Rivers Inlet

Rivers Inlet is best known for its big fish. I meet several who many years ago venture up there in small outboard boats to catch the big ones. Today the boats are much larger, but I don't think the fish are. I do know it takes a lot of hours to catch a fish here, but when you get one, it is big. My favorite base areas are Duncanby and Dawsons landings. Each has fuel, a store and moorage, the former with electricity. Duncanby has a pub and eatery, while Dawsons has cabins on floats and a more complete store. At both places you will find a lot of help for whatever your need. At each, it is like a step back in time when commercial fisherman and loggers dominate these parts. Duncanby has lots of charm. Maybe its because every time I stop here the sun is shining on the white buildings on piling, with their red and blue roofs. It just looks and feels historic. Ken and Judy make you feel at home and Jessie will entertain you by fetching anything overboard. One trip I meander in an out of most coves and see today's fishing lodges and in some cases traces of the salmon canneries of days gone by. The Goose Bay, one time cannery, is the most intriguing and should be preserved.

Draney Narrows is particularly fun to run in and out on a 5–6 knot ebb—like a river run without fear of rocks or big waves—just a smooth flow with some turbulence. It is pretty inside. In Johnston Bay it is a thrill to see a twin engine sea plane land and take off, changing guests at West Coast Resorts. Wow, the spray! Just stay out of the way. A trip up through Nelson Narrows, past the big logging camp up Moses Inlet, in 1998, proves very interesting in a real fjord. A helicopter relays logs from a natural looking clear-cut steep slope to the inlet carrying three logs at a time. The exciting part is watching the logs be cut loose above the water, splash below the surface and recoil from the deep. Quickly a tractor tug captures them to a boom area. It takes about five minutes per turn. Periodically the 'copter returns chokers back up to the ground crew. I have a fantastic view of the operation in *Day by Day* as the only spectator. Reluctantly we leave.

At the head of Rivers Inlet on both my trips there, many other boats from dinghies to big ones are patiently waiting for a jerk on the line. In four fishing days in two years I do not succeed, nor do most others. For the few that do, rewards are big. There are many fishing techniques to learn at Rivers Inlet as I did at my barbershop back home after my last trip! On both trips I anchor overnight in the NW corner of Kilbella Bay. You will have company. If it is too crowded it is best to anchor next to shore and tie a line to a tree. Funny things happen here. Like the skipper whose winch fails and several of us struggle to help him pull his hook and chain on board by hand. One night "cowboys" from Idaho keep some of us awake and on edge while they anchor too close to other boats about dark and then tie their two boats stern to stern. It finally works. One day I enjoy maneuvering through Magee Channel and take the dinghy as far as the outflow of Geetla Inlet, since I am late on the tide to go inside. Darby Channel is the more protected and scenic passage to Rivers Inlet. The rocks are of no concern if you have Chart 3934 and you pay attention.

Hakai Pass—Spider Island

The area around Hakai Pass and Spider Island is loaded with islands, inlets, passes and coves. A look at Chart 3784 will show you what I mean. A good place to start is in Pruth Bay at the Hakai Beach Resort. It is a first-class facility in the wild where guests fly in to fish in small boats. My one stop in 1996 is greeted with friendliness as I am allowed to tie up at their dock while I look around. The treat is walking to a breathtaking white-sand curved-beach facing west. Here again I enjoy it all alone in July. Unreal! Anchored in the bay is a huge space-age yacht tended by a couple whose job it is to take it to wherever the California owner wants it next. Tough duty! One night I anchor in Gulfstream Harbour with Dick and his new 33-ft Bayliner. He is most helpful to me when I meet him at Dawsons Landing suggesting anchorages and fishing spots in this area. One thrill is catching a salmon in the same spot as I did three years earlier on the same date. I anchor three nights in a small unnamed cove off Spitfire Channel that I call Bayliner Bay. That's because Dick told me about it; we stay there and I tell another Bayliner skipper about it. Fishing in this vicinity is not too bad. Lodge boats comb the area but yachts and boats our size are rare, at least when we are there. One fascinating place to me is the NE side of Triquet Island. We are fortunate to be able to anchor in the shallows on a rising tide. It is a fun place to explore with sandy beaches and rocky coves loaded with logs from Pacific storms. The area north to Bella Bella offers an alternative scenic route to the main traveled Inside Passage.

In April 2000 I discover Douglass has suggested the name of "Spitfire East Cove" for the one I call "Bayliner Bay." His follows some World War II names in the area already. Mine is contemporary. Canadians may not appreciate Americans doing this. In time an official body deals with these kind of situations to decide what name will be on maps and charts from common usage names. Checking the coordinates in Douglass' book, the ones I recorded on my GPS and the ones I pick off the chart are all different! So beware of others' coordinates including mine!

Other passages and inlets further north are elsewhere in this book. Suffice to say there are many places to go. Even in this busy world you can easily be alone if that is your choice. One reason I don't like National Parks, Wilderness Areas, Marine Sanctuaries and other governmental designations is that they are like an international magnet, sometimes drawing huge numbers of visitors. I am not against all parks, but they do have a down side. Large numbers of visitors can destroy the qualities the designation was intended to preserve. It also leads to restrictions of use. We should be concerned about UN Heritage Sites in the US and Canada. What we don't need is a World Government telling sovereign nations how to run their affairs. Most of us find governments doing weird things at times. It is a lot easier to influence a local school board than our national government. But if you have a super government in charge, that makes our influence on local sites that much harder. But, you say, there is no management change in these sites. No, not yet.

In the areas discussed in this book you will find much private room to roam in the comfort of your boat. As I get older I am more grateful everyday, especially since overcoming cancer. I try to "savor every moment one by one, day by day."

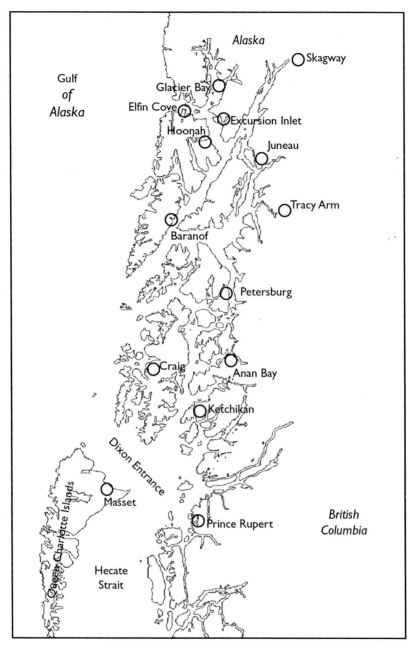

Side Trip 3—Skagway and Glacier Bay

Side Trip 3—Skagway and Glacier Bay

Originally, I had no desire to take *Day by Day* to Skagway. Cynthia and I have been there and to Juneau. Neither of us had been to Glacier Bay, but we had in mind both us of going there together someday. That changes early in 1999. I am looking for a different place to cruise. I always wanted to go to Elfin Cove. My reports were saying the best chinook fishing that summer is going to be in that area. I also want to ride the train at Skagway, so soon plans are in the making. I do not want to make the long boat run, which I have done twice, from home to Prince Rupert. I have trailered from home to Prince Rupert twice. That is my choice. In two days I can drive what would take four days by boat. Driving I use only 90 gallons of gas one way, rather than 250 gallons by boat. So the choice is easy this time. Both ways are a delight. If you have the time and have not done so, do go by boat. A trailerable boat makes a satisfactory camping trailer while on the road. Driving, you follow the Fraser, Thompson and Skeena rivers. Each river is edged by mountains. Lakes dot the route. I have seen bear—once three at one time, at road's edge. It is quite a sight one trip to see a moose cross a four-lane highway in Prince George during rush hour! Just make sure your trailer tires, bearings, and brakes are in top shape and the frame is solid and not rusted out.

Prince Rupert

I arrive in Prince Rupert early enough on May 27, 1999, to explore the backside of town up Fern Passage to Butze Rapids, after buying Chart 3958. By the way, if you have this chart, cruising into Prince Rupert will be very easy—I never had it on my previous trips. My intent is to go up the rapids and look around Morse Basin. The current is ebbing strong when I arrive. With all of the rocks I think it will be a poor idea to try and dodge them and risk putting the rest of my trip in jeopardy. So, I settle for drifting around the area while I eat dinner. I thoroughly enjoy this and watching the rapids. I opt not to wait to go through the rapids at or near slack. Be aware *Sailing Directions* states that Butze Rapids while spectacular can be danger-ous. This night I stay at the Prince Rupert Rowing and Yacht Club float at Cow Bay. This is the posh place to stay in Prince Rupert, about a buck a foot for our boat, plus it is closest to town. There is a first class launching ramp near Rushbrooke. As I am launching, many small fish swim at the ramp showing promise for the future. I store my trailer and pickup nearby at IGC Propane dealer in a secured area for $30 per week. During the summer you may need reservations.

One place Rich and I enjoy visiting in 1997 is the North Pacific Cannery Village Museum being restored in Port Edward. We drive there from Prince Rupert, but by using Chart 3958, you should be

Trailering to Prince Rupert you see Hudson Bay Mountain.

able to anchor in Inverness Passage. Someday I hope to land here by boat, then go through Wainwright and Morse basins into Prince Rupert the back way. To understand how abundant salmon was and what early canneries were like, visit the old cannery museum at Steveston near Vancouver, BC. You can get there by car or boat at the mouth of the Fraser River.

This trip north, we run inside Tugwell Island along with bigger boats outbound, then choose to hug the shore along inviting beaches. We duck inside Finlayson Island to take a peak at Port Simpson. It is an

Indian village in a setting like Port Ludlow. A red-roofed steepled church stands out. A fish processing plant and a Coast Guard-looking building with a mountain-sea mural on the side at the government dock dominate the waterfront on the inside. Our crossing of Portland Inlet from Inskip Pass to Tongass Passage is pleasant and calm. Overall this is a more protected route, if an east wind blows. I stop briefly at Eagle Point Lodge near 54° 47'N, 130° 33'W in Pearse Canal on Wales Island, mainly to take a picture for Rich of the place out of which Gary Cooper fishes on his TV show. On this day he is not here, but a guide and the mostly Canadian guests are friendly. In fact, I am told I can follow their five boats heading to the north end of Dundas Island where they have caught fish. I thank them, but on this day I have other plans. After passing a tug and barge, we slowly motor up the narrow, scenic, rock-studded Edward Passage against a current one and one-half hours after a low tide. *Coast Pilot* says this passage is "foul, and only navigable by small craft and local knowledge." That's me! Wispy low clouds let me peek at the snow covered mountains to the northwest which are "very Alaska." Lots of small fish are flipping here.

We take a turn inside Very Inlet at Foggy Bay on a flood. No boats are inside but it would be a good place to spend the night if you have cleared Customs or call them and ask for permission to do so. It would be fun to dinghy around in here, but today I want to move on. The trees show a hard life with mistletoe and spike tops. There are a few small beaches visible at low tide.

Ketchikan

Eagles are everywhere. Boat traffic picks up considerably as we near Ketchikan. It is surprising to me how many big pleasure boat skippers give themselves away as amateurs by their radio words and actions. My advice—don't! Learn the ropes before going to sea. Take a boating class. In Ketchikan I visit our Sandy Point neighbors Roz and Jerry on their boat *Softrock*. It is a somber time for them. Coming north they befriended an older solo skipper on a 26-ft sloop. Shortly after they left him his boat was found adrift with him not on board. On my way up, I hear CG reports of the missing skipper. Later his body is found. Speculation is he fell overboard while anchoring. Roz is in the process of writing the family of the lost one. I see his boat tied at the USCG dock. So, as on my last visit here, a recent boating fatality. In 1994 just before my visit, someone crossing in the dark in an unlighted skiff was run down by a big boat. You have to be careful!

Cheryl sends us an e-mail one day, upset, explaining that young people drown near her office when a tug, other than Foss', swamps their canoe. They are not wearing life jackets. Cheryl, who wore a lifejacket at nine months, said after that incident, "I am going to wear a life jacket every time I go out in a boat." Some docks have a good program called, "Kids don't Float." Near the sign, regulations tell the importance of kids wearing life jackets. Best of all, a rack has kids life jackets ready to go. The program, maintained by volunteers, allows a child who goes boating and does not have a life jacket, to borrow one, and return it when done.

At Ketchikan we moor in Thomas Basin in a large slip per instructions by radio from the harbor office. Big events for me are changing oil in the rain, watching nearby cruise ships come and go and chatting with a resident, who is living full-time year-round on a 1970s, 20-ft Reinell, with his cat. He plans to put a pellet stove in it! I think he is lonely—he really likes to talk. He also knows history a lot better than I. While people on the cruise ships are escaping reality for a week, some who move to Alaska are trying to escape reality for a lifetime. Me? Someplace in between! I find some nice gifts at the Tongass Trading Company, expanded since my last visit. In fact, the whole town seems more tourist oriented than before, but mostly nicely done. I want to come back some day and spend more time here. One original is along Creek Street, "where men and salmon came to spawn." After you arrive at a Ketchikan dock, a port patrol checks you in electronically and bills your home. Be sure to enter in your log when you arrive and leave. Arriving home I get a bill for twice as long as my stay here. Thanks to my detailed log entries I am able to convince the authorities that I am right after two responses to their bills. Do not neglect paying. According to a Petersburg authority, if you don't pay, a federal statue can allow Federal Marshals to confiscate your boat! He said they do not have much trouble getting paid.

Going through Tongass Narrows north of Ketchikan this time is a no brainer. I follow the main channel and not the north shore like last trip in 1994. It also helps to have Chart 17428 this time. Clarence Strait is calm this day and sunny. A lot kinder than last time. We pass cruise ships *Veendam* and *Sun Princess,* appropriately near Ship Island, near where I saw a bear last time. The sun on the ship and the bow wave of the *Veendam* deserve a picture that I do not get. For the first time I duck into Thorne Bay and walk around. Very quiet on a Saturday morning. Nice dock facilities and no visiting yachts. A salmon derby is going on but you would never know it. Upon leaving I hear a suspect radio report that bear are at Anan Bay. They were not! The same report said there were big crabs in Sunny Bay. I do not try. My experiences on trips to Meyers Chuck and Anan Bay are included in my 1994 cruise.

On May 30, 1999, as I leave Petersburg, I spot my first iceberg in *Day by Day.* By the time I reach Cape Fanshaw, ready to head up Stephens Passage, I am at last in new territory. In all modesty, in all of my cruising, I see no one else covering so much ground in a small boat. Everywhere I am known as the one who travels fast, sometimes getting advice to "slow down." I would like to if I had months like many do. Even Mother sees me as a risk taker who needs her prayers. Thank you, Mother! For my Sunday morning service I play *Godspell.* And I thank God for safe passage. I do believe that you need to be prepared for all emergencies and to meet thy God—it's all the same. It requires an abiding faith. I take a turn in Fanshaw Bay to observe the unused beaches near where a troller is anchored. At Steamboat Bay there is a nice beach. I want to get out but it is raining and the water is good for cruising. It also looks like one of those places bear come out looking for snacks on the beach! Up north, there are miles of untouched shoreline and no boats. While some believe there is gray sameness up here, I see it as a constant changing canvass of mountains, bays, water and sky—a kaleidoscope. Better than a museum.

Being able to see bear on Admiralty Island would be a big attraction for me. The island reportedly has the highest concentration of them of any place in the world, with one every square mile! I never see one, but then I do not try hard. While I am up north, one skipper said they saw bear in Gambier Bay when they were anchored. I do not go there.

We run inside Hobart Bay to take a look. There is a logging camp and a tug is moving logs. Near Thistle Ledge a troller lies at anchor. One way to get paid for being up north is to have a troller. That always has been in my dreams. Art at Sandy Point used to be a troller. He says it is an easy way to make $20,000. I used to troll the Washington coast with sport boats *Seaspell* and *Nadja*. So did Rich before me in his 18-ft Olympic. We used to be known as kelpers because we stayed close to shore. Cynthia's Grandpa used to troll in Washington with a real troller. That industry is now dead. Too bad. It is a good life; the quality of the salmon caught is the very best. Rich and I also believe it is the best way to selectively catch targeted species commercially. In Alaska you can still troll. Anyway, today there are porpoises.

Tracy Arm

Once I decide to come this far north, I read about the attraction of Tracy Arm; now here I am. What a boating experience. Like none other. Near the entrance this May day at Harbor Island, we are

Tracy Arm is awesome.

greeted by big icebergs. One has an eagle sitting on the leading edge as though, I am the skipper of this ice boat! In Williams Cove north of Holkam Bay, a schooner lies at anchor. Nearby an iceberg is stuck on the beach. Now imagine cruising for the next twenty-five miles up a mile wide waterway aligned with snow capped mountains with lots of waterfalls. Fog at the base and clouds above hide most of them, but now and then you get a glimpse. It reminds me of driving a level road over a mountain pass.

But the most exciting part is the many icebergs you dodge. Each has a different size and a distinctive shape. It is fun to imagine what they represent. Small chunks of ice in your path bear watching as well. Hitting them is softer than rocks but harder than wood. There are three types of ice: blue; white; clear. The biggest are blue. Remember too, ninety percent of the iceberg is under water. The nice thing about Tracy Arm is that the National Park Service is not here (Dad was a Park Service engineer at Olympic National Park. That makes me a Park Service brat!) So, no permits and not a lot of rules to follow *yet*. The main rule here is: "Be very careful and not hit a big chunk of ice or a berg." The small ones that hit our hull sound very hard.

On the way in, we pass several tour boats of various sizes running from Juneau. At the head of the arm you get views of two glaciers. I first look at South Sawyer, seeing North Sawyer as I go by. As we arrive, a tour boat, *Spirit of Columbia,* is slowly edging closer to the glacier. For awhile I follow in her ice-free wake until I am within a half-mile of the calving ice. I choose not to get close to the ship, to give her maneuvering room and to keep my distance from icebergs. I do not want to get too close between two of them and have one of the twenty-five foot waves catch us. That can happen according to *Coast Pilot.* On this day, only small waves generate.

When I arrive at North Sawyer Glacier, a large tour boat is very close to the glacier. I again keep my distance. Up here is the tour boat *Spirit of Discovery,* that cruises the Snake River, and the smaller *Yorktown Clipper.* I was proud to be the smallest boat here and the only non-local one. When I get home I read that the 192-ft *Spirit of '98* hit a rock in Tracy Arm on July 27. The skipper beached the vessel so she would not sink and ninety-three passengers are rescued without harm. So be careful! Even a $12 million ship can have trouble. I rate Tracy Arm as just awesome, up there with Prideaux Haven and Princess Louisa in its own right. It is scintillating!

Before I leave the Arm, we run to Fords Terror and anchor inside before the narrows in forty degree water. At that point, I take the dinghy with the outboard through the curved narrows, with a mild flooding current, among ice cubes and small whirlpools. I am fortunate to get in and out after a look at the Jasper National Park-like quality dome and bowl scenery. It reminds me of a small Princess Louisa. The entry is thrilling and spectacular but it can become a shallow creek bed running at fifteen knots. Someday I would like to spend the night inside. Fords Terror is a mini Tracy Arm without a glacier. Just outside the entrance is the largest iceberg of the day— one as big as a house, that came from Dawes Glacier. Nearby a long-liner is at work. As we leave Tracy Arm we pass the first yacht of the day, *Aurora*, from Juneau, and a troller. A troller is also anchored in Limestone Inlet.

I spend the night in Taku Harbor tied to a State float along with other Juneau boats out for the Memorial Day weekend in the rain. Other boats are anchored in the harbor. With my rain gear and boots I walk the shore looking at all of the traces of history of this one time bustling port. Most noteworthy are many pilings. A converted World War II lifeboat, *Blue Empress*, from Shelby, MT, lies stricken between piling as a failed dream. On shore a tree has fallen, splitting open a person's workshop behind their cabin. Alaska is harsh. Two skippers say Taku was once a Hudson's Bay Company settlement. Today only a few cabins and a fish hatchery operation at the head of the bay remain. A skipper on an adjoining boat, *Top Dog*, brought in three large crab from the harbor. One skipper in a slicker rows to shore in the rain so he can "water" his dog. The vented stove-top heater I designed works very well on this first major trip. It chases the dampness away and makes the cabin cozy as well as heats my hot cider I sip.

Juneau

The next morning I have a hard time keeping the MerCruiser running. It floods badly and is belching black smoke. When I look in the engine compartment, I discover the cold outdrive oil is one-half inch above normal level—not a good sign. Means water in the lower unit and a failed prop shaft seal like on our first MerCruiser in *Seaspell*, I reason. When I check the engine oil I notice that it keeps rising. Why? So, I have three problems: outdrive; engine oil and carburetor. I decide I had better head for Juneau with the outboard at three knots, against the current. Thankfully, it is calm. Just the rain. No one else I am sure is under auxiliary power today and using their laptop to update investments! A whale passes by. Closer to Juneau, boat traffic picks up. I enjoy passing a beautiful beach on the south or west side of Gastineau Channel. As a first time cell phone carrier, I locate a marine mechanic who can help me. Karl does not seem too concerned since my outdrive oil isn't the color of a milkshake. He agrees to try to get me hauled out tomorrow though, and take a look. I am impressed at Juneau with the cruise ship activity and the tram running up Mount Roberts, off the main street. The layout and landscape of the town is similar to Ketchikan. I spend a restful time in Juneau at their big marina, together with ravens the size of small chickens. Lots of fingerlings around the docks.

When I wake the next morning it dawns on me I am in "Juneau in June" on this first day of the month! This morning Karl is unable to locate a trailer to haul us out. I call Kris at my Olympic Boat Center Bayliner dealer in Bellingham. He said the MerCruiser High Performance outdrive oil I use is so forgiving, that he does not see a big problem. He does agree that if I plan to cross Dixon Entrance it would be good peace of mind to haul out if I can. So, with that bit of information I decide to be off. As much as I want to go through the small boat passage to Auke Bay, I decide to go the extra miles around Douglas Island rather then wait a good part of the day for a high tide. The day is cloudless and it is tempting to go up the tram. At the last minute I say to myself, I will if I can moor on the dock at the foot of the tram. I do find a spot at the end of the float with permission to stay awhile. *Day by Day* is dwarfed by three cruise ships, and especially the stern of nearby *Sea Princess*. We would be a very small dinghy hanging on her transom. The trip up the tram, new in 1997, is a real treat—a birds eye view of town, surrounding mountains and water—awesome! On the eighteen hundred foot ascent, a Tlingit gives a quick history of their people as Eagles and Ravens. In the Chilkat Theater we get a perspective on Alaskan Native culture. Natives also hold other tourist industry jobs here—the way it should be. I am impressed with the cruise ship visitors—well dressed, orderly, polite, all ages, all nationalities. I am the ratty looking one! The $19.75 that got me up here to walk around in the snow was really worth it. I am told that this is the first nice day like this in three weeks. And I am here because of my outdrive problem. Thank you, God! I have a fabulous stay in Juneau.

I glance at Oliver Inlet but a low tide does not let me enter. The setting reminds me of Jackson Hole or Yellowstone—like a river in the forest with a majestic mountain range behind, plus nice beach to the north. In November 1999 I learn from my *Marine Atlas* you can portage a skiff on a hand-pushed railroad cart along a scenic trail to Seymour Canal. Within Seymour at Windfall Harbor is a Forest Service trail to a bear viewing platform. Next time!

Approaching Auke Bay, seeing Mendenhall Glacier is impressive. In the run from Juneau, the outdrive oil rose an unusual two inches—never before. To make a long story short, by agreeing to pay time and one half, Willie's Marine hauled us out, pressure and vacuum tested the lower unit and put us back in the water in four hours and $400 later. There is nothing wrong! I have peace of mind and never have unusual oil fluctuations again. You figure it out! Lately, the engine is running fine, too, without doing any work on it. Before I leave Auke Bay I use their excellent head dumping station—it is a model.

The evening run to Skagway, up Lynn Canal is so pleasant. Calm water most of the way, so I fix my spaghetti dinner at full cruise. I stop and drift in Bridget Cove while I eat, since it is so pretty, with a curved gravel beach with no development. It could have been in Payette Lake. I want to go ashore, but then a man and a boy come out of the woods to go fishing. Time to move on! I am surprised to see a highway nearby but I never see any traffic. Cabins now and then are along the shore all the way to Berners Bay. The snowy ridges to the north and the pinnacles on the south side of Lynn Canal catch my eye. Near Point Sherman a whale spouts. Just north of Point Sherman on the east side, it looks like a massive highway project going into a tunnel. A new highway to Skagway? It is not until I see an article in the September 5, 1999, Spokane *Spokesman Review,* that reveals that this project is a new controversial gold mine by Coeur d' Alene Mines Corp. The troubling part is the mine wants to dump three thousand tons of tailings into the canal daily. Not a good plan. Especially, when salmon is a $14 million business in the canal, plus halibut and crab in the Point Sherman area is considered very productive.

Skagway

The octagon lighthouse at Eldred Rock is unusual and distinctive. A sign I can barely make out reads "USLS 1905" meaning it was built then for the US Lighthouse Service, I gather. Houses appear at Flat Bay—one is a distinctive three-story. A cruise ship is tied at Haines. Making the turn into Taiya Inlet we meet the outbound cruise ship, *Princess Dawn,* turning to port, making a nasty, most dangerous vessel-leaving breaking-wave I have ever seen. I decide to run full throttle parallel to it toward the beach to cross it at an easier place. Even then as I slow to cross, our clean boat gets the first spray of the day on a glassy sea and a jolt for the memories. We reach Skagway at 2200 in daylight. Now *Day by Day* has cruised Olympia to Skagway—the Inside Passage. I moor in a very nice marina just below where Cynthia and I stay in our motor home in 1993. It is on that trip we buy our brand new 1991 Trophy in Salcha, Alaska. I won't

Day by Day and skipper complete Inside Passage to Skagway.

relate the details, but if you ask, I will tell you all about it. It is quite amazing and is just another example how God has worked in my life.

Skagway is a fun place to recall the gold seeking past before statehood. My primary goal here is to ride the narrow gage railway to the summit, over trestles on the historic White Pass and Yukon Route. In May 1993 we get here a week before it opens, so we miss. Today in good weather, I relish the ride and narrative about those who endured hardships of the past in these parts. Even on bad days we have it easy. On the train I meet Ron and Rose, who in their 55-ft trawler, *Wildidi III*, have been to the Charlottes and around Vancouver Island. Ron, hearing of my plans to cross Dixon Entrance to the Charlottes, calls it "foolhardy." Just so you know, Bayliner will not publish any stories of my *Day by Day* journeys, (or the way I dig clams) because they do not want to promote "safaris" such as mine. Let these be warnings to you if you try to follow my sea paths! While I am in Skagway, the Alaska ferry leaves and cruise ships arrive, including the *Sea Princess* I saw in Juneau and later in Haines. I do not recall seeing any cruising yachts here other than *Wildidi III*. Quite a change here from the days when Rich served in the Army in the Alaska Communication System (ACS), prior to a ferry or highway connecting Skagway with the world. No cruise ships then. While in Skagway talking to a number of folks, it is clear I meet a lot of nice people along the way be they come by boat, ship, plane or RV. The boat ramp in Skagway provides a viable option to trailer north and boat from here, if you have a trailer and tow rig that can endure the rigors of such a journey.

Haines

Going to Haines into a heavy chop is a rough ride. Running slowly past us is the water taxi that shuttles between Skagway and Haines. It pays to be bigger when the waves get that way. Before checking into Haines, I enter Taiyasanka Harbor. I see this as an anchorage. Across Lutak Inlet is the ferry dock for Haines, about two miles from town. Arriving at Haines on a nice day in early June you are impressed with the snow clad massive mountains behind historic Fort William Seward. In May, when Cynthia and I visit in the rain in a different year, our reaction is, what mountains? What a difference a day can make. Cynthia and I will be back to look the Fort and museum over someday. I take Ron and Rose's suggestion and eat a halibut dinner at The Lighthouse in Haines, in the best seat overlooking the inlet, boat harbor and the unmatched mountains watching over Haines. The Lighthouse is famous all the way to Australia for their buttermilk pie. On this day, I have the good fortune to get the last piece. People pay $32 round trip on the water taxi from Skagway just to have pie! The waitress says even those on cruise ships come in to eat some real Alaska cooking. With a SE breeze at sixteen knots we pound our way up the canal, with the ferry *Malaspina* passing us along the way. I am glad to enter William Henry Bay before dark and anchor in calm water together with a Canadian yacht.

The next day's run to Glacier Bay is easy with calm water. A highlight is ducking into Boat Harbor riding in on a current near high tide. The entrance reminds me of that into Nitinat Lake, but wider and shorter. Inside it looks like an Alaskan lake with some meadow shoreline and wintry mountains to the SW. This would seem a great anchorage, but *Coast Pilot* warns about a rock in the entrance and SW winds. Beware! Porpoises run with us several times today. A humpback whale greets us as we turn into Icy Strait. I almost overshoot Excursion Inlet, but boats fishing along supposedly a good spot, called Homeshore, make me stop. After checking the chart we run to the end of the inlet to see a not-so-old cannery, people working around the area who show no interest in us, and sport fishing boats to trawlers all geared for fishing at several floats. A state float is mainly for sea plane landings. I see no fuel dock like my atlas shows. On my return trip I try fishing along Homeshore with a few others, to no avail.

Glacier Bay

We run on the inside of Pleasant Island past the dock and sandy beach at Gustavus without stopping. Right on time, I call in by radio to Bartlett Cove to get permission to enter Glacier Bay as my permit requires. Visitors must have a permit between June 1 and August 31 and attend an orientation to learn of the many rules and restrictions. Request a permit application from Glacier Bay National Park and Reserve. You can apply for a permit up to sixty days before you arrive. Twenty-five vessels are allowed each day in 1999, including up to: three local Icy Strait area; twenty-two non-local (that's us); plus two cruise ships; six charters; six tour boats. On the June 3 I enter, there are only eleven private boats in the bay, while all slots were already filled for July. I am the only boat to arrive and go through the orientation when I do. You are given a colored map that shows numerous closed or restricted areas. The lodge at Bartlett Cove with white table cloths in the dining room is impressive. Rooms are $128 per couple. Those without boats can fly in here and take a tour or charter boat, if you make arrangements.

Going into Glacier Bay, several other private boats are leaving. After that, I only see a tour boat, one other private boat and a cruise ship heading out. That is it. From then on, cruising to Tarr Inlet I see no boats. In some areas boats are required to travel away from shore and between 10–20 knots so as not to disturb humpback whales. I do see one spout and am happy to see puffins. Most unbelievable is the Fairweather Mountain Range like a sleeping giant. It is one continuous white coated mountain after another. Some, including Mount Fairweather at 15,320 ft are like having several Mount McKinleys

Glacier Bay lets you visit snow country in your boat in June.

lined up shoulder to shoulder. The water is a pretty blue-green and gets calmer the closer to the end of the inlet we get. Snow and glaciers to the waters edge make me think I am driving on top of the world. I have never seen so much snow so close to the water in a boat. Closer to the end of Tarr Inlet I slow so as to not hit the increasing chunks of ice. There are no large icebergs though, but a few small ones. At 59° 02.45'N, 137° 02.31'W I just drift alone, at the end of the inlet, one-half mile each from Margerie and Grand Pacific glaciers, in the calm water for two hours. It is so quiet—true wilderness. Periodically, calving ice will break the silence. If you do not see it fall it is too late by the time you hear the rumble, but you see a small wave. Margerie is white. Grand Pacific is dirty and looks more like a rock bluff. One of the chunks of ice from it looks like a floating rock. It is amazing to me that the water is up to 157 fathoms or nearly one thousand feet deep very close to a glacier. Looking at the Park Service Glacier Bay map, I find it unbelievable that in 1780 ice covered all of Glacier Bay, clear to the entrance at Icy Strait. In the next hundred years ice melted one half the bay. Since 1907, when Dad was born, there has been little melting. All of this suggests most of the melting took place before the earth was heavily industrialized. This place is so captivating—just an ultimate experience, especially when you can enjoy it alone with our God. Before leaving, I scoop up enough ice with my salmon net to fill my fish box for icebox use. Now if I could just get salmon and ice together!

We just look into Johns Hopkins Inlet. Between there and Reid Inlet close to shore it is literally a minefield with small chunks of ice in the water. It would be nice to anchor in Reid, but I want to sleep well tonight. I can imagine a cold downdraft from the snow and chunks of ice bothering me so I move on. Plus, it is a calm evening to travel in the sun. No doubt about it, this place is the Alps of the sea. Oh, I guess we see similar in Prince William Sound but this is more spectacular and in reach by Puget Sound boaters.

On this night I anchor in Berg Bay, mainly because Ron and Rose saw five bear here. As I drop the hook at 58° 31.08'N, 136° 11.21'W I am thrilled to see a grizzly grazing, maybe 150 yards away. I watch the bear for a half hour in the twilight, mostly through my 7x50 binoculars. How exciting—my first grizzly in the wild since I was a kid in Montana. When I first get here, two Canadian geese are flying wildly overhead and making an awful noise. At one point one goose lands near the bear. I suspect the bear may have gotten into eggs or goslings. Such is life in the wild. At one point I see a v-wave coming toward the boat when suddenly a seal pops up close by in the still water. This place is alive! Snow still lay at waters edge on about a third of the north shore. Such an awesome place and day.

Elfin Cove and Pelican

I really enjoy my night's stays at Pelican and Elfin Cove. Both are elevated boardwalk communities with homes and limited businesses along the way, that are among the most intriguing villages in SE Alaska. Pelican has the most moorage space and is where I find quite a few large yachts. While I am there I see the largest halibut ever caught off the fish processing dock inside the boat basin, at 318 pounds, caught that day. Wow! I am told salmon are being caught close by. Well, not for me! Pelican reminds me what it was like in Dockton over fifty years ago. It is refreshing to talk to commercial fishermen while they are working on their wooden boats and doing beautiful shipwright work from local native spruce.

Elfin Cove has more charm with its circular board walk around a knob fronting two coves. It is more touristy but still holds the flavor of yesterday. Lloyd, who handles the mail for incoming planes, has lived at Elfin Cove year round since 1947. He is very pleasant and can give you lots of history of the area. Commenting on the sea otters in the area, Lloyd says they only eat the best and freshest clams, oysters, crabs, abalone, etc. From Elfin Cove, you look right into the massive Brady Icefield, which almost looks like a cloud. As I recall, Lloyd says when you can see Brady at night, the next day will be nice. It is! I am taken with the excitement of Doug, a young man from New York City who has never seen an eagle before. He admits he is a product of the media and Discovery Channel. How thrilled he is on this day to see twenty eagles in one tree. This is Alaska!

I make a cruise out Lisianski Strait and into a calm ocean for a turn. One day I try fishing in the strait, after an Anchorage couple flies into Pelican and does well out of a boat they charter. Nothing for me. I enjoy poking around the George Islands group, the Sucia of this area, hiking beaches, over rocks with wild flowers and through the woods. Of course I have it all to myself after an anchored yacht leaves.

Returning south you have two choices. Visit Pelican and go on the outside of Chichagof Island. Go inside and visit Hoonah and colorful Tenakee Springs. The latter has the bonus of a hot sulfur bath. Weather and your feeling about open water might help you make your choice. Rather than tell you more about where I have not been, I suggest you get some charts and ask around about other boater's experience on which way you might want to go. Also read all you can. Each author has his or her bias and special interests. On this trip I meet a pleasure skipper who plans to cruise to Yakutat this summer, about 140 miles up the coast. Sounds like fun when all of the other ventures run out. At Elfin Cove, fueling with me is a diesel-powered steel boat, looking like a miniature Coast Guard vessel. This skipper has just come from Yakutat. I fail to ask what the trip was like, what is there and do they have fuel? Francis, author of *Pacific Troller* said he and his wife, Donna, were at Yakutat one time when about a 30-ft pleasure boat came by and asks if he had gas. "No, only diesel," he replies. Later he hears on the radio that the same boat calls the Coast Guard and that he is out of gas down the coast. Don't let it happen! We all get crazy sometime. Usually when I am sailing in *Fatty Knees* I think what it would be like to sail and motor to Alaska in that 9-ft dinghy. Then some mornings as I roll out of our king size bed with arthritis pain, I think that might not be a comfortable idea!

June 6, on a perfect morning, I leave Elfin Cove at 0415 while the MerCruiser smokes and runs very rich at the start. Then we have a tough time planing. It sounds like an engine miss with the tachometer jumping all around and showing a higher rpm than it really is. Also, I have a new vibration after accidentally going through a kelp patch yesterday that may have been near a rock that I barely hit. At any rate, the boat's performance does not match the beauty of the day. Although Sunday, my mood is not as upbeat as it should be. Along the way in calm water I clean the rotor and distributor cap. It may have helped some but *Day by Day* runs with hesitation into Hoonah, where I find a large marina on a calm sunny day. I tie behind an older Seattle boat, *Joyce B*, with a couple, each perhaps eighty, on board. The skipper says they have been coming to Hoonah every summer for fifteen years. I think, how neat they keep on boating. I hope I can at that age. While here, I change a slightly damaged prop, and do other tune-up tasks. By talking to dock folks I learn about Carl, a mechanic. When I find him, he is painting a house and does not want to stop because it is sunny. He does say if I need help, he can see my boat at 1800. When I give Carl my engine history, he is emphatic that my problem is not ignition.

So, on this gorgeous calm day I run along sometimes good, sometimes bad. I run from 1,000 to 4,400 rpm in increments of 500 and record how the engine is acting. By the time I reach Chatham Strait, I decide I must go back to Auke Bay and have my engine checked at Willie's Marine. After running about an hour, seventeen miles out of my way, the engine is running fine—nothing is wrong. I am very grateful of course, but a little puzzled as I turn 180 degrees and head South near Point Howard. I think, I cannot go back to Willie's and have them find nothing wrong again. They will think I am nuts! Besides, it is not cheap to find that out!

Going by False Bay I notice it is parklike at its head and there is a nice beach to the south. Each cove and every mile of shoreline offers various surprises, large and small. At 57° 48.61'N, 134° 57.2'W, we anchor between East Point and Wachusett Cove and I go ashore. Perhaps no beach walk is so enjoyable with as much variety. From the gravelly beach, to an ideal spruce forest interface to the myriad rocks. Watch for the sloping gray marble-like rocks, the animal tracks, the wild flowers, the snowy mountains to the East, the trollers in Chatham Strait. Is that enough? No human footprints. This is the only beach in Alaska I can recall none. Where I land there are many dear tracks and a fresh one of a bear with claws! I carry my whistle, a stick and flares for close range defense or to summon a boat if need be. Before I haul anchor, I reflect on my June 6, 1999, *Daily Word* for the day on the subject "Guidance." In it are these lines on how I may be taken "down winding pathways through new and unexpected territory." Wow, that fit me today! It went on, "If a detour appears out of nowhere, God could be telling me that it is time to change direction," and reminded me that "God is with me, so I never travel alone at any time." These words are based upon Isaiah 42:16. So you see, this is why I say we have an awesome God. He is as awesome as the Alaska scenery appears to me. And that is very special. When I am writing this in December and looking at the atlas, I cannot believe that I did not check out Pavlof Harbor and the waterfall. Next time!

Tenakee Springs

Tenakee Springs looks neat from the water, not far from the cannery ruins near Cannery Point. We moor in the marina east of town. It just might be the most genuine original town that is still going. Some businesses and many small cabins are of the early vintage variety. Together with a narrow street with no cars, you get the feel of days gone by. Cabins once used for cannery worker homes are becoming vacation resting spots. It is too bad that some new buildings are starting to change the town's character, that at one time provided a winter haven for the miners up north during the gold rush. Standing tall and yellow near the dock is the Snyder Mercantile, since 1899. Except for today's products, you get a good old-time feeling when you buy at this store, which is still in operation. Cabins are available through the store. And of course, now the Internet can tell you what is out here in remote places better than many of the books. Highlight near the store is the hot springs bath house. Hours round the clock are designated for either men's or women's separate bathing times. I enjoy my free bath at 2200 alone. Oh, how good it feels. Now I know why miners came here! You undress in a frame built room then descend into a masonry cellar where the old, but very clean heated pool is in a dungeon-like setting. Very nice and a special thanks to the volunteers who keep it up. As I leave, the town Postmaster came in for his dip and bath after giving me a few historical glimpses. It pays to come to Alaska with a job, if you plan to live here. It can be tough to find work if you just show up, like in Tenakee. In the marina, one man lives on a barge he probably built. He collects water from his roof and uses other innovations to keep costs low and make it functional.

Before leaving Tenakee Springs I gas up at the dock, which has no float, so for the first time I tie to piling like big boats do. With big tides you climb up a long ladder to reach the dock at lower tides. I am glad to get fuel. Leaving the inlet in calm water we meet the inbound Alaska ferry, *LeConte,* coming for freight and passengers. The store keeper at Tenakee states what Rich has told me and that is the canneries in Alaska met their fate after the dams on the Columbia River were built. It could be the efficient fish traps every where also did their part to reduce the big runs. Even in Bellingham at one time there were fish traps and the largest salmon cannery on the west coast.

Baranof

Each bay, cove, falls and endless shoreline, some with great beaches, keep my interest today. I check out Chatham where some cannery remains still exist. Today, in a nice setting, are boats and a fuel dock for private use. *Coast Pilot* states that this cove freezes and at one time an ice breaker used to call here. We anchor at 57° 28.95'N, 134° 50.01'W and I go ashore near Point Hayes. The setting is similar to my landing yesterday but not as scenic. Here you can see into Peril Strait. I find footprints of man, dog, deer and bear. Unlike 1994, Chatham Strait is calm a second day in a row and my trip south is

The mountains at Baranof, Warm Spring Bay.

smooth. I enjoy exploring the coves in Kasnyku and Takatz bays and find several fishing boats at anchor. My thrill is as great as ever as we enter Warm Spring Bay. It does look cold with snow on the peaks above and some to the water's edge. I see some changes. We tie to the float at Baranof, like last time but with five other powerboats, including another Trophy from Juneau with a baby aboard. I meet Bob and Sue on a West Bay, who on their way north run into others from Sandy Point whom I know. The old store is now gone. A new expresso stand with limited items is in the old powerhouse. This time

I hike up the trail and look for the plank walk to the two man-made hot springs pools near the falls. It is wonderful, and once again I enjoy it all alone. There are new owners of the home with the hot water tank on their deck, so "no vacancy" there this time. At the dock I reflect on the heaven I enjoy here. Warm sun. Cool air. Hot water baths. Snow capped peaks. Calm bay. Water falls. Just enough boardwalk houses to give it contrast and community. I understand one owner is trying to put in a pelton water wheel for power but he ran afoul of the law by not following permit requirements. Yes, up here.

After my seafood dinner I row the dinghy into the SW thumb of the bay, with the current maybe at five to six knots, through the narrows downhill. What a thrill. I have no idea how I am going to get out but I figure the tide has to change sometime! Inside it is like a high mountain lake surrounded 180 degrees by snow capped peaks. After hiking around I row back as far as the current will allow. I stand on the shore and watch the water slowly rise in the basin. Suddenly in about two to three feet of water a large fish swims past me in the narrows and out the inlet. Wow! Large salmon or a steelhead? I cannot get out of the inlet, yet I can see *Day by Day* through the notch. The shore is too steep and the woods too thick to walk out so I relax. Later the same looking big fish darts back into the basin. A while later the fish goes out again. Forget something? What a thrill. While in here I see an eagle, otter and seal. As I write this, I wonder how I would have dealt with a bear. I could not get out and I was not prepared for that event. Suggest you be if you come here. After maybe two hours I am able to row out the opening pulling as hard and as fast as I can and barely making it. Next I row as close to the falls, as much as the current will allow before being whisked back toward the float as I row. Meanwhile *Peppermint*, maybe an eighty foot, shiny new yacht from Bellevue, rolls in. Later I talk to a passenger aboard. "Microsoft money?" I ask. "No, Seattle car dealers." Hmm, a lot of people paid too much for their cars! "You must be a top salesman to get to come." "No, just good connections—unusual for me." One man on his brother's bigger boat is intrigued by my traveling alone in a smaller boat. He seems to think I have the right idea since his wife won't go on a boat. Two others are here from Washington in a 24-ft Olympic and are on a run from Prince Rupert to Sitka to fish. At one time I hear that Baranof may one day be a ferry terminal with a road to Sitka. Say it isn't so. Can't we leave any perfect spot alone?

The next day we run to Murder Cove on calm water, although the MerCruiser isn't running as good as it should. Not much evidence of the former cannery, but it looks like cabins and a lodge underway is looking for a change in these parts. No grizzlies, though. I want to go to Port Alexander, but with the engine less than the best and a fog report there, I decide that can wait. After I get home, a July 1999 article on the waters around Port Alexander in *Alaska Magazine* make that a destination for me one day. So what is the big attraction before I read the article? The stories and pictures from the thirties and forties in *Pacific Troller* set up an intrigue of the past that I must satisfy before it changes too much.

Keku Pass

After looking over the waterfront at Kake I head for Keku Pass. This passage is the one that books and people I talked to said not to take because the navigation aids have been destroyed by ice. The previous winter, I bought Chart 17372. After studying it, I am convinced I can make it through, aids or no. I am determined, and have allowed a full day, if necessary, to traverse it. Well, much to my delight the channel markers are back and it is very easy for us to pass this way. My chart book says, "The Summit Not Recommended without Local Knowledge." Both The Summit and Devils Elbow are dredged sections and we go through both slowly with the current near a higher tide as you are supposed to. Now you know there is a short cut for going north or south if you wish, at least in a small boat, and I have local knowledge of yet another passage. By the way, we meet no other boats in Keku Pass, although another Trophy came from that way as we head for the north end. Only one plane passes overhead; lots of rocks along the way.

Point Baker and Port Protection

Running to Point Baker the water is good but the engine acts like it needs a tune up. At Point Baker there are two visiting yachts. It also appears a number of boats end their careers here. There is a store, gas dock, B&B, post office and restaurant, all on floats. One older gentleman came by to check on the derelict boats, and they are here! I am amused at one young bearded chap working on one of them that needed an overwhelming amount of work. He is spray painting the stack black with a spray can. She may not be able to head to sea, but she will have a shiny stack! I ask if there is a marine mechanic around. "In Craig," says one gent. The faint smell of gas now and then tells me the MerCruiser tends to flood at times. Now I think I have a carburetor problem. Gas mileage has dropped about 25 percent as of late.

Around the horn into Port Protection I find a very pleasant community with homes and nice looking trollers—no junk. This port, well protected from the sea has the Silver Lining Seafood Co., a dock with fuel but no space during my visit. It would be my kind of place to live though.

Craig

My trip to Craig is like in 1994, except I temporarily get lost for a little bit by not paying as much attention as I did last time. I think I know the way, but there are many similar islets and passages. It seems I saw more last trip. I do see a bear but at different spot than last time. This bear is beach combing at 55° 49.17'N, 133° 19.51'W on a very short beach, until our boat's presence causes him to dart into the woods. I do better going through San Christoval Channel this time but neither my chart book nor Chart 17400 matches the actual buoys and markers, so I sketch them in my chart book. For bigger vessels I recommend having Chart 17405 which I do not have. At Craig, I tie to the public dock below Ruth Ann's Restaurant where I have a great steak, a rarity for me. While there, I chat with a Forest Service employee from dry eastern Oregon who is here to help the Alaska planners plan. Craig is a true working fishing port that does not appear to be distracted with tourists. Craig supports logging as well.

After dinner I go to the store to inquire about a mechanic. Todd, a customer with maybe a few too many, says he is a mechanic. He immediately wants to go to work on it in the rain and darkening evening, no less. I say, "No," where upon he tells me to change the fuel filter and put a water absorbing additive in the gas tank. Makes sense. "If that doesn't work, go to Joneses Marina. That's where I work." He does not think it is ignition.

The next morning I am anxious to try my new fixes. I change the fuel filter with the spare I have on board and add three bottles of fuel treatment from the gas dock. I also tighten the alternator, which is loose and put on a new distributor cap. My test run to Klawock is not revealing but it seems like she runs better. Klawock has a fish packing plant, a log dump and sports fishing boats—no yachts. Strictly a functional community. When I return to Craig I walk the short walk to Joneses Marina from the north moorage area. Surprisingly, no Todd works here. Describing my engine's problem, I am told no one can work on it for two or three days. I do not want to wait and Joneses policy is to treat all alike—no bumping the line for more money. I mention the whole story and how I accidentally put in twenty gallons of diesel in the tank in January for a twenty-six percent mix with no adverse affects until this trip. I am assured if I go on, the engine will not die. That is my main concern since I plan to cross Dixon Entrance tomorrow. Further I am told if I run at cruise and choke the engine to near a stall and let it run again and do this twice, all of the crud in the carburetor, including from diesel, would be "sucked out" and that should do it. With that advice I go on with confidence.

Leaving Craig in a chop, I do not feel confident giving the engine the choke treatment since I am alone. At times the boat runs well and at times it seems the prop is spinning out of the hub. We go on to Hydaburg by way of South Pass. The water is good, the scenery is attractive and other boats are out along the way. Graves and a totem pole park are at Hydaburg. Running down Sukkwan Strait the water is beautiful and the engine is running like old times. I am relieved. My plan is to anchor in Elbow Bay, which is less attractive on the water than on the chart, due to logging. At 1615 I pass Elbow but it is so calm. With reported light NW wind and a flood tide, why not cross Dixon tonight?—conditions are ideal. So out we go. At Round Island we meet a fishing vessel as I calculate a 1921 ETA at Masset. With the engine problem behind me, everything is perfect. By 1707 we are between capes and doing well with forty-two miles to go to Masset. A little later that hub spinning feel starts again, the engine hesitates and we were are down to seven knots as the NW chop picks up. I do a quick assessment. We can go back, or turn toward Ketchikan around Cape Chacon. None of that appeals to me, though they may be safer choices. I reason at seven knots I can still cross before dark. I am driven to go forward. At last we are planing fast in a beam sea from the WSW. It is a rough moderate sea but *Day by Day* is good in this kind of water. We are moving and I am confident without fear. Only one other time do we bog down to seven knots again due to engine and prop antics. The rest of the time we are "bombing" through the troughs. I watch the GPS intently click down the miles to our destination. At 1813 with twenty-six miles to go I can barely make out land on Graham Island as the north capes disappear. No other boats. Just us and the sea and our Maker and Protector. With a relieved and grateful heart we enter the familiar Masset boat harbor at 1936. Our SMG was 16.9 knots. I am very happy. *Day by Day* and the MerCruiser mastered Dixon Entrance at her widest.

Masset

At the far end of the float, forward of a large dragger, I find a rare dock opening. I call the Customs officer to clear. Thanks to Customs for suggesting I get a CANPASS before leaving home, clearing was easy. When I open the icebox I find my soup spilled inside. I accidentally open tomato sauce for stewed tomatoes and the fishing vessel next to us starts spewing, as they say, licorice (soot) all over us. So while the crossing is easy, the initiation here is hard. Yet I marvel and say, "Thank you, Lord God of heaven and earth and sea—you cared for me." It is persistence, and commitment to carry out a mission that pays off.

The next day I run to Langara to fish and stay two days. More on that in the Charlottes side trip. While here I visit my Port Angeles high school classmate, Ted, and wife, Irene who come here every year in June and who I have seen here before. Fishing is not good for him and he is a good fisherman. On the day I plan to go back to Prince Rupert it blows a gale, with rain of course. This is only the third day in five years of long range cruising that I cannot go to my destination, and the first day I never move *Day by Day* while I am on a cruise. Ted invites me to go razor clam digging on the beach near Tow Hill. I go with Ted, Irene, their daughter, Colene, and son-in-law Charles. The five of us dig two hundred razors in about an hour and a half, but the limit is seventy-five per person! I have never seen such easy digging and so few people. The long sandy beach on this north shore is attractive. I do manage to become a casualty, cutting my finger and nail on a clam. Later, Ted says the proper way, after you dig a couple of quick clam shovels full of sand to make a hole, is to go to your elbow in the watery sand sweeping your hand from the water side to the clam, grabbing the neck and pulling slow and hard to surface the clam. The clams always have the hinge or smooth side toward the water. Avoid coming down on top of them like I do and getting cut by the razor edge. Back at the campground we all laboriously clean the clams. Hint—dumping them briefly in boiling water then cold water makes the shells come off easier. As one person says, "Zip, zip." Well, maybe not that easy! That evening Irene fixes us a most delicious razor clam dinner. Ted has the right idea. He tows his boat up here and brings a freezer. His goal in about two weeks is to go home with limits of salmon, halibut, bottom fish, crabs and clams. It is a good goal. Lots of work, but fun. I am appalled to learn that there is a commercial season for razor clams where most of them are used for crab bait! When you consider Oregon and Washington restaurants have a hard time getting razors, it is criminal. I talk to Bornstein Seafoods in Bellingham about importing clams since they did buy fish from Masset. For some reason importing clams is not easy.

Rose Spit and Home

On June 14, the forecast is for gales again, although it is calm at 0400. From the automated reports, conditions sound good to me. At 0445 we are off into fog but on a calm Dixon. I am delighted to have the fog lift as I approach Tow Hill, after seeing something big on the radar. Surprise! It is a big ship anchored close to the beach. We run close to Rose Spit to get the best view possible near low tide. I can see small breakers on the south side, but considering all of the previous wind, the sea is smooth. On this day there are not the dangerous overfalls that I imagine and that are noted on the chart. How wonderful to cross Hecate Strait, one of the more notorious bodies of water in the world, on a calm day with gales forecast. Thank you, God!

My engine runs fine today but only at 16.7 knots at 3,800 rpm which is not right. At times it seems to "catch fire" and do better. By the time I reach Prince Rupert Harbour I finally do the "Craig procedure." Running at cruise I aim the boat and go back to the engine to choke it to near stall, let it recover and do it again. This is a dangerous act, I might add, as you leave the helm and have your head in the engine compartment while your vessel charges aggressively with no eyes forward. I am careful that no boats or drift are ahead of me during the maybe 15–20 second procedure. I do not recommend it if you are alone.

Postscript

Did the above procedure help? I think so. It seems the engine runs better. When I get home and before my next trip to Rivers Inlet, I run the boat in the lake and everything seems just fine. Of course I did change the prop and am lightly loaded. On my August 1999 trip north, everything seems fine until I reach Lund. From that point on the MerCruiser alternately ran great and poor. Several times I do the Craig procedure—sometimes helping—sometimes not. Upon leaving Rivers Inlet, the engine ran so poorly I could not plane the boat. I change one sparkplug with great difficulty (not much room) after deciding #1 plug is the culprit. It does not help. Rather than wait for, or try to get a mechanic to help me, I leave Duncanby Landing at 1545 in a semi-displacement mode. Once I reach the open water beyond Dugout Rocks, I am able to plane the boat with the help of a NW breeze and NW swells. That night I make it to Sullivan Bay. You recall earlier Pat solved the problem for me—a bad spark plug wire! When I get home, I replace all of the spark plug wires. After that, I think I have a new engine and decide to delay the idea of repowering with more horsepower. Then I remember what Dick on the new 33-ft Bayliner told me on that August trip. He said in a 25-ft Bayliner he once had, he wandered all around one summer with his engine getting sicker. It turned out to be spark plug wires. Now I carry one long spare wire and now you know what mechanics may not!

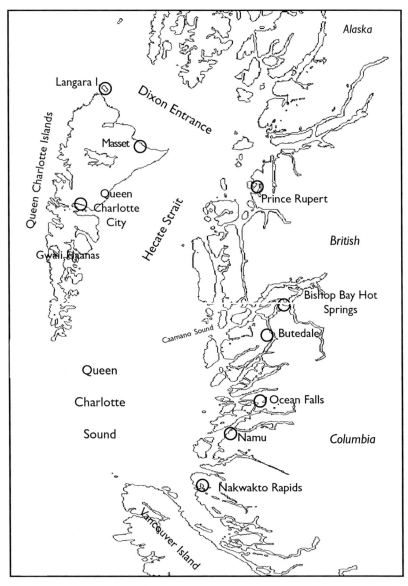

Side Trip 4—Queen Charlotte Islands/Haida Gwaii

Side Trip 4—Queen Charlotte Islands/Haida Gwaii

En route to the Queen Charlotte Islands/Haida Gwaii from Sandy
Point, in my 1996 *Day by Day* boat trip, there are several notables:
Nakwakto Rapids covered in Side Trip 2; Namu; Ocean Falls;
Butedale; Bishop Bay Hot Springs; an unplanned anchorage off
Grenville Channel and two long crossings. Beyond that, Haida
Gwaii is the best-kept secret in British Columbia.

Namu

On my first visit ashore here in 1998, I enjoy the boardwalk hike to
Namu Lake and along the waterfront that once connected a busy
cannery community. Many abandoned company houses are vacant,
just waiting for new owners to give them heat and attention; maybe
someday? Other buildings like the hotel and gymnasium may be torn
down. There appears to be a struggle to make something grow here,
and not let this place die. Let's hope Namu lives. The BC ferry stops
here.

Ocean Falls

Now this is an interesting place. If you want to see a modern ghost
town, this is it, but that is changing. A sign says "Welcome to the
Rain Festival." Once a thriving Crown Zellerbach mill town, it has
been shut down for years. Walking the town is spooky—lots of
buildings but no life except the street lights are on day and night and
water runs all the time at the dock! Seeing so many vacant homes
and businesses, including a hotel seems very strange. I hike to the top
of the dam, which is like a miniature Grand Coulee spilling water, so
I can see Link Lake and a view of town. Vacant houses are for sale in
1996 for $15,000 to $50,000—all need work. People were buying
them for vacation homes. Moorage for us is $8.71, Canadian. As
usual we are the small boat. Numerous boats have cats aboard and
some come to visit. Next to us is the 66-ft *Dodge Buoy*. When I ask
skipper if he credits his boat to Iacocca, he did say he is a former
Dodge dealer and he does have a bottle of wine aboard from Iacocca's
Italian vineyard. I saw the *Dodge Buoy* in 1999 in Prideaux Haven. I
forget to ask skipper if he still has the wine, now that the German's

run Chrysler. Jim, who runs Jim Walls Fishing Lodge at Ocean Falls, moved here because it got too crowded at Gold River. He claims good trout fishing in the lake and by running to the right spot you can catch kings to sixty-three pounds, halibut to 120 pounds and silvers to twenty-five pounds. Jim has lots of ideas on why salmon fishing has gone down and what can be done about it. This is another BC ferry stop now.

Butedale

In 1996 it looks like Butedale, the former cannery, might come to life if volunteers with my idealism succeed. When I stop by, I get a VIP tour and a glimpse of what I hope turns out to be a useful memorable destination for many visitors who like to fish and reflect on the past. Until improvements are in place, there are hazards for boats and people who visit there, so be careful. At this time they need more volunteers like an electrician to get the water powered lights going again. It would be nice to see Butedale look like its former self and provide visitors with services to enjoy in this remote area.

Bishop Bay

My recall of Bishop Bay is a majestic calm bay, in a park-like setting, with some semblance of Wallowa Lake in Oregon or Princess Louisa with mountains all around. Eleven boats are anchored or at the dock, including two American. I anchor at 53° 27.63'N, 128° 50.3'W. A unique, small bath house with hot springs water that feels so good, is maintained by the Kitimat Yacht Club, so for that I say, Thanks! The posted rules are: 1. Wash in the tub outside; 2. Respect the privacy of others; 3. Don't bathe alone (I had no choice); 4. Half hour limit; 5. Carry garbage aboard. The next day at 0500 I awake in silence broken only by a waterfall one-half mile away. I have to take another dip in the twelve foot square, three foot deep pool, where you can swing in the water with the hanging ropes before anyone else is up. Reluctantly I leave this great place, but I am rewarded at Riordan Point where a bear looks at me as if I am passing in review. Cynthia thinks bear and cats are related (they are not) and if you talk gently to them, they may not hurt you. I was close enough in the boat so I say softly, "Such a pretty bear." The bear starts to walk off after I stop talking, so I say it again. The bear stops and looks at me again, then walks off for good. When I ask the Park Ranger in the Charlottes about what he thought the bear was thinking, without hesitation he says, "Probably, 'Your crazy!'"

Just around the corner up Ursula Channel at 53° 27.7'N, 128° 56.4'W, in a small bight is such a nice sandy beach and the weather is perfect that I just have to go ashore. I anointed it "My Beach" as I am alone, and it reminds me of a beach we visited in *Vikings IV* at Payette Lake years ago. There are signs that at one time others thought this was a great place too. I can see why.

In the afternoon, after passing by Hartley Bay and Stewart Narrows, I find an increasingly strong NW wind as we move up Grenville Channel. By the time we reach Nabannah Bay the wind is up to thirty knots and it is rough. I want to anchor in Ship Anchorage but I am concerned about gas supply if we go ten miles out of the way and we have to fight wind and current to Prince Rupert. Going into Nabannah Bay does not seem attractive with a rock reef barrier to get behind and with the boat sideslipping badly as I try to explore an opening into the bay. Each time I run up quickly to the opening with the depth sounder alarm preset on decreasing depths, then quickly back off. With each approach a little closer in, finally I am confident we can make it. On my final assault with the sounder set on 10 feet and the outboard running just in case, I make a quick dart in, south of the obvious drying reef between kelp. We are in at last. After surveying the bay's bottom, we anchor at 53° 40.45'N, 129° 45.41'W, using a kellet. We swing and rock wildly as the wind swirls around the bay. On shore, I explore four of seven beaches separated by rocks. Impressive is a six inch by three foot, fifty foot long old growth timber once used in a dock. The dinghy ride is easier to shore than the trip back. It is fun watching a variety of seven craft, from a sailboat to a cruise ship, pass our window in over three hours.

Prince Rupert

At 0400 the next day I decide to head out even though it is still blowing, but less so, after seeing a tug and scow going my way in the early light. It takes us forty minutes to catch the 7.5 knot outfit by the time I haul anchor and work my way up to her. By then the wind and waves are lighter so we go on our way to find fog and gillnets on our approach to Prince Rupert. But, we make it with thirteen gallons of gas to spare.

Getting to the Queen Charlotte Islands

Finally, on July 26, 1996, I am ready to leave Prince Rupert for the Charlottes for the first time. After a couple of days of NW winds offshore, the forecast is less foreboding. In the early light, winds are calm as I head out through Venn Passage. Ideally, I want to do a figure eight around the Charlottes as Carey (see Bibliography) suggests. Since that is not attractive for me this trip, with fishing closed at Langara, I decide to head for Queen Charlotte City. At Rivers Inlet a skipper, who has cruised the islands in a 27-ft power-boat previously, suggests that if a NW wind blew, cross directly to south of Rose Spit and ride in the lee, southward. That is my plan, but by the time I reach Brown Passage, the NW wind is here and rollers are bouncing my craft uncomfortably. On my trip from Alaska I came through this area in rougher following seas, but the ride was easier. I decide to keep going as long as I do not take a wave over the deck and hardtop as I have on two previous occasions. Remember when? That never happens this time. Once passed Triple Islands, I head directly for Skidegate Inlet, a shortest distance of seventy miles and my longest ever open water passage. I am not proud to set a new open water record, but it seems proper. From pot floats, the current is going the way we want, and the beam sea makes easier going. In reflection, it is better to go the way the ferry does through Edye Passage.

During the crossing I see only two boats, both commercial fishing vessels, as spray drenches *Day by Day*. I am well prepared with VHF, radar, GPS, an inflatable dinghy, survival suit, flares, mirror and an EPIRB. My philosophy this trip, as always, is to be prepared, and if all else fails, try to drift toward a shore and survive with my water-proofed survival kit. Thankfully, the closer I get to Skidegate Inlet, the calmer the water, until about eight miles off, I spot a bright orange substance on the surface of the water, like paint, that appears everywhere. Later, I learn it is one of sixteen varieties of red tide. If it doesn't stick to your boat, most likely it is not paint.

172

In 1997 and 1998 I tow *Day by Day* to Prince Rupert and ferry to the Charlottes. This is the safer way in a small boat. Haida Gwaii, or the Queen Charlotte Islands, located an average sixty nautical miles west of the British Columbia coast, is a place most Northwest boaters avoid. Open, and often rough, water intimidates many as it almost did me in 1996. Yet, it is one of the few wilderness treasures within cruising range, even in a small boat, as I proved. By boat it is not a trip for the weak-kneed. Most fly or ferry to the Charlottes, but there is less adventure going that way.

"Side Trip 3" shares my experience going to the Charlottes in 1999 a fourth time in *Day by Day* and a second time by water. Like going around Vancouver Island twice, a second time to the Charlottes I prove you can do it solo in a small boat. It is much more hazardous going to the Charlottes because of more open water and fewer boats around. On the other hand, it is less risky than taking a 23-ft rowboat solo across the Atlantic, as Tori Murden did in 1999—a first for an American and a woman. In 1976 Pat Quesnel became the first person to row from Washington State to Hawaii. He did it solo in a 21-ft rowboat after attempts to make the trip with others failed. So you see, my cruises are less adventuresome than some. But, if you make a trip like mine, be sure you have backup plans and are well equipped. Associated Press articles on the two solo rowers appeared in the December 3 and 4, 1999, issues of the *Bellingham Herald*.

To me, the 160 islands and islets of the Charlottes is a wilderness, even if it does not met a true US Forest Service definition. They are a group of islands capturing some of the best of Alaska and British Columbia. You will find sheltered fjord-like inlets, and forested mountains that compress five thousand feet of Oregon or Washington forest regimes in half that height, all visible from your boat. Add a wave-battered coastline with a largely undiscovered land of abandoned Haida villages and you have a wilderness in every sense of the word. When you add some of the best salmon fishing in the world, with small towns that can fill your basic needs, you have a land that extends over 150 miles north and south that can satisfy a wide variety of outdoor seekers.

Haida Gwaii means "Out of concealment islands" or today, "Home of the Haida." The Haida are the Indian original inhabitants and occupy the Queen Charlotte Islands along with settlers since 1870.

Two large islands are the most notable on small scale mainland British Columbia maps and charts. Graham Island lies to the north and Moresby lies to the south. Gwaii Haanas National Park Reserve is the prime protectorate of the southern part of Moresby. Gwaii Haanas means "Place of Wonder." With that introduction, it should be obvious why the Queen Charlotte Islands are a unique, special place. It is a challenge to get here. While it is a wilderness by many counts that can test your survival skills, basic services are in the area. The Haida are friendly people who want to preserve their culture, yet share it with the world. It is place where you can enjoy unspoiled beauty with few other boats. For more history read Carey's book or the notes on the listed Haida Gwaii map in the Bibliography.

Queen Charlotte City

Skidegate Inlet is enjoyable for me in 1996. Essentials can be purchased within walking distance of the government wharf at Queen Charlotte City where moorage is tight, but available, sometimes by rafting. During my stay I find only two other American boats here, both much larger. A motel with available showers is near the wharf. The local residents are friendly with both Haida and others eager to visit. Chief entertainment for summer youth is jumping and diving off a dock about twenty feet above the tide level. I admit they are braver than I. One fuel dock serves the inlet and islands south. It is only open five days a week, located two miles east, next to the ferry docks. The owner remarks, as I am fueling, that I am in the smallest boat he ever saw coming from the US by water. There is a nice large marina at Sandspit with lots of moorage in 1997, but there is no fuel.

The most pleasant moments for me in Skidegate are those spent on two islands adjacent to Queen Charlotte City. In both cases, they are unoccupied and are decked with gravelly beaches. Locals seem not to know their names and I will keep them incognito as well, as one person is reluctant to have me share all of their secrets. On one island, I anoint what I call "Perfect Beach." Imagine calm water, where you can take your boat right next to shore to the most perfect gravel beach at all tides. I find tranquility, swimming, hiking and just "soaking up heaven" all as if it were my own. It amazes me on a summer afternoon, on a weekend in July, no one is here, even though you can row a boat from town. A more challenging venture nearby is

The author enjoys Perfect Beach.

the cruise through Skidegate Channel to the west side. I follow the channel markers near a high tide, with one finger on the chart, and one hand on the wheel as I skim by visible boulders in the river-like ebbing stream. You cannot pass through at lower tides. I hope to see the Pacific Ocean from the West side, but a fog bank and a NW chop satisfy my longing to the main inlet, and a run up Armentieres Channel to marvel at the visible alpine sub-zone so near the water. The trip back is easier with the wind and tide, and following another boat our size, turning precisely up the slalom-like course.

Gwaii Haanas

My 1996 trip south in the islands begins with a fifty mile run around Sandspit, crossing the shallows very carefully, and into Cumshewa Inlet. Much of the area of northern Moresby, and the smaller islands, have been logged. It is this southerly encroachment of logging that prompted protests that led to the creation of Gwaii Haanas National

Park Reserve. Prior to visiting Gwaii Haanas, visitors must attend an hour-long orientation covering safety and cultural protection. I find it worthwhile. Starting in 1997, visitors to the park need reservations or chance being one of five walk-in visitors allowed each day, which I am in 1998. The park visitor center in Queen Charlotte City, and the Haida museum in Skidegate offer valuable enrichment before visiting Gwaii Haanas. Shops in the area sell Haida made crafts for gifts or souvenirs. Haida Watchmen (men, women and teens) serve as contacts on VHF Channel 6 for visitor assistance. Groups of 2–4 Haida Watchmen (including at least one Elder) occupy five heritage settlements to serve as visitor guides, as you tour sites of former dwellings and existing totem poles. Gwaii Haanas is co-managed by the Haida and Parks Canada. Five cultural sites which you may visit each have Haida names: K'una (Skedans); T'anuu (Tanu); Hlk' yaah (Windy Bay); Gandla K'in (Hotspring Island); Sgan Gwaii (Anthony Island). I have been to all but Hlk' yaah, since I mistakenly explore a long, beautiful adjacent beach. Each site is unique. My favorite is Hotspring Island. I have been there four times, two with Rich. Here, under Haida supervision, you can be in hot baths in one of three natural pools at water's edge. How nice to enjoy uncrowded hot water without sulfur smell, a seashore and mountains all at once. Clearly, of four hot springs I visit on my boat trips north in two separate years, this one is the best. K'una may be the most perfectly located site from my perspective, on a peninsula with two lovely beaches, together with original totem poles or mortuary columns. The most historic from my point of view is Sgan Gwaii at the village of Ninstints on a beautiful sheltered cove. Most remarkable are the outstanding memorial and mortuary poles. This village is a designated United Nations World Heritage Site.

A rule in Gwaii Haanas that makes a lot of sense is the one that says that no more than twelve visitors are to be visible on shore at anyone time. This protects the wilderness values and makes you feel more like you are a privileged visitor. As a practical matter, I see very few boats in Gwaii Haanas. Most of the time you see no boats and no people. In 1996, in three days in the park I see about two dozen vessels ranging from kayaks, inflatables, fishing vessels and sailboats. I see no large power yachts nor boats the size of *Day by Day* except one large one at anchor. Each night, I anchor alone, although one night two boats are anchored on a far shore. Shore areas are limited, but I am always alone on shore in 1996 except at the hot springs, where I meet Watchmen and a few visitors. Being alone, I never felt lonely—only at peace in a busy world.

I always love narrow passages and small bays to discover. You have that in the Charlottes. My favorite is Dolomite Narrows in Burnaby Strait also known as Burnaby Narrows in Gwaii Haanas. While the narrows are accessible at higher water, I am late in 1996, so I anchor next to a sloop on the north end in the forested narrow channel. I am taken with a gravelly beach, with an earlier settler's cabin, thinking what an ideal place to live. Young people who settled here thought so thirty years ago, but they learned idealism isn't always permanent. Tempting as it is to go ashore here, rules prohibit it so as not to interfere with abundant wildlife. So, off I go in my 6-ft inflatable with the 2½ hp motor moving slowly against the current in the shallow water. I thrill to the schools of small fish and seaweed dancing rhythmically in the current—truly my own aquarium. Along the shore there is more evidence of earlier settlers, deer looking at me and raccoons eating. On the trip back through the narrows I merely drift, soaking it all up as fast as my mind will fathom it. Another landmark I will not forget is Helmet Island. It is well named and distinctive—it etches in your mind.

In 1997 Rich and I trailer *Day by Day* and ferry across Skidegate Inlet on our way to Moresby Camp. En route to launching we see a bear cross the road. That is the only one I see in the Charlottes. One crew says they enjoy a bear show in Echo Harbour, but seeing two boats anchored here one evening in 1996, I chose to anchor alone in Anna Inlet. I try to respect others' privacy as well as keep my own as much as possible. By trailering you save one hundred water miles round trip from Queen Charlotte City. Thus in 1997 we were able to go to Anthony Island, while I did not have enough fuel to go by water on the 1996 trip, even when I travel a lot at six knots. Sgan Gwaii is magnetic, complete with small curved bays and still standing totem poles as I mention above. Rich and I are fortunate to get a grand tour and lots of history by a Haida.

If you plan to tow your boat to Moresby Camp, be sure you have a 4-wheel drive rig to make some of the steep hills and to launch your boat, preferably at high tide on the gravelly beach. You travel logging roads used by the largest off-highway log trucks I ever saw. Find out when you arrive what the local rules are for traveling the roads. One rule is, in active logging areas you wait until a truck comes by, then follow it. When Rich and I follow one we feel like we are running a football behind the biggest blocker we have ever seen! Along the way we see some of the smallest deer ever. One tiny fawn, who is temporarily separated from his mom, runs beside our slow moving pickup looking up at Rich as if to say, hey, Mom are you in there!

West Side Charlottes

Three times I have been to the ocean through Skidegate Inlet. Fishing is slow for us except a halibut for Rich in 1997. I enjoy immensely my solo 1998 cruise to Blue Heron Bay in Gwaii Haanas and to have it to myself. It is an awesome experience to stay overnight and hike over rocks through sparse vegetation to the highest dome, over four hundred feet high, where I pray and give thanks, looking down on my anchorage. If I had to die in the Charlottes this would be the place—heaven at sea. We go as far south as Sunday Inlet before turning back and looking into Tasu Sound, Kootenay and Bottle inlets and Security Cove. I am fortunate to have forgiving Gulf of Alaska winds going and coming. The western shore drops precipitously, so it is fascinating to cruise in close, often among the rocks to get a kayakers perspective, which they do on this coast. Less you think I am totally irresponsible, I am on alert how I will deal with a breakdown in these parts. Access through Tasu Sound would have been my choice if I cannot get towed or make it on my own. This would be an expensive and difficult journey that tourists should not count on.

One adventure is going through Canoe Pass in Buck Channel with not quite enough water. Scenic and a short cut, yes. I need the boat hook to dodge rocks and even use my hip boots to walk through portions, leading the boat when the flooding tide allows. But we make it. There is a good boat launch east of Queen Charlotte City which I find to be safe for overnight parking.

The west coast of Graham Island is building as an unexplored area I must visit someday. In 1996 this is on my ideal itinerary. A good excuse to go is, I already have the charts! The plan would be this: Launch my boat at Masset; take my tow rig and trailer to Skidegate Inlet; get a ride back to Masset. Head to Langara and get the skunk off at a familiar fishing spot. Next run down the coast, in good sea conditions of course, to Port Louis where The West Coast Fishing Club maintains The Outpost Fishing Lodge.

In the spring of 2000, I tell, Lisa, the manager of the lodge, that *Day by Day* may bring me by someday. She said to stop and say hi if I do. Her stories about what her guests enjoy here make you want to get a reservation or go the adventurous way as I cruise. Here I would try to validate that fishing is as good as Lisa says.

At Masset I meet a fisherman, who with his troller, takes two men and their kayaks to this lonely coast to camp and explore. Further down the coast I would enter Kano Inlet where the Oak Bay Marine Group *MV Salmon Seeker* anchors as part of their fishing resorts from Ucluelet to Langara. Articles about finding trophy fish, glass balls and plastic heads meant for Mattel's Tommy Pickles dolls from a lost cargo ship are reasons for me to go! More than that, once you have been to the Charlottes you just want to go back again and again. I would end this trip by going back through Skidegate Inlet.

To make the above trip you need a fuel supply to last 150 miles plus whatever fishing and exploring you do. Keep in mind you cannot carry more than three portable fuel containers, full or empty, on the ferry, including the boat and your tow vehicle.

Ice is another tough one. You need to find enough to last and ice your fish. Then you need more ice when you land. This can be difficult and expensive in the Charlottes because there aren't a lot of mainlanders over here in small boats wanting ice. Rich and I bought $20 of flake ice, when we found the person to come down to the ice plant one evening at Queen Charlotte City. In Craig, I was able to fill my ice storage for a donation to the donut fund. Sometimes you can get fish boat flake ice free in season at fish docks but don't count on it. Near the ferry dock at Prince Rupert, on two occasions I scoop up surplus ice in a pile near the fish packer dock. It pays to be innovative when you are homeless! I always plan to be home in seven days from the time I catch my first fish. Fish cleaned right after it is caught and kept in ice with the water drained off now and then is like fresh fish when I get home. Big boats with freezers have an advantage. Don't exceed your limit! We know of cases where fishers are arrested for too many fish. In the future I may get filleted fish vacuum packed and frozen. Keeping it covered with ice at all times should extend travel time.

Part of small boat traveling involves planning and execution of details that lodge fishers never worry about. It is worth it. Oil rich salmon from the cold northern waters is the best there is—it just tastes better!

Fishing

I knew of one party who tow a 19-foot boat into Rennell Sound and find good fishing but it takes two of their 4-wheel drive pickups to get out of the very steep, wet and muddy road. I drive our 4x4 down there and find nice camping spots and a calm bay but I would never take our boat down that road. A sign warns you of the danger.

In 1997 and 1998 I trailer to Masset so I can fish at Langara Island. It is the most beautiful place I ever salmon fish. In some ways it reminds me the way Neah Bay used to be in the 1950s. Most fishing is by small boat from fishing lodges or mother ships. No matter which way the wind blows it is possible to fish some place, although you may have to move to the other side of the island, as we did, if you get a wind shift in the night. With Rich in 1997, I catch my largest salmon ever—a thirty-six pound King. Rich is a good coach, or I might not have made it. In *Day by Day* we are usually the "big boat" of the fleet at Langara. In 1998 I bring home eighty-one pounds of salmon and a small halibut, my first while sport salmon fishing alone. In 1999 I get skunked here, but wind limited my fishing to letting one get away. My sick engine and running low on gas that trip make me want to cut my losses and head home after I explore Naden Harbour and Wiah Point, both decent places to port your vessel in a storm. Other than mooring buoys, there are no facilities for the boater at Langara. One year, two others in a boat our size pitch a tent on shore. Some Haida are unhappy that fishing lodges bring all outside help and supplies without benefiting them. On the other hand, The West Coast Fishing Club and other Queen Charlotte lodges are using fascinating methods to preserve and increase salmon production in addition to providing lasting experi-

A happy day for me at Langara Island, 1997.

ences for guests. There are also Haida who run charter operations in the Charlottes. The most interesting thing for me in 1999 is listening to the Langara Lighthouse keeper explain on VHF to a fishing lodge boat what life is like on a remote lighthouse. That story could be a book in itself. I do consider using VHF for this purpose an abuse though. In 1998 after a limit, I circumnavigate the rockbound coast of Langara in a lumpy but enjoyable sea.

Masset has an excellent boat ramp and a safe place to park while you are gone. There is a motel near the boat ramp and the campground is not far away. Twice I enjoy excellent salmon at the Cafe Gallery. The folks in TLC Automotive are very helpful and fix my boat trailer brakes. The Masset web site and their published, "Welcome to the Village of Masset," offers much information.

On my return boat trip home in 1996 I plan to go to Prince Rupert, but with NW winds forecast the day I leave, I decide to go with the flow and go straight from Skidegate to Caamano Sound, nearly one hundred miles of open water, with no other boats. This is not a spur-of-the-moment act, but one of much study. The trip is flawless and comfortable, even though the seas are at times quite mountainous. I save fuel and time, and increase my sea credentials. The rest of the trip home is pleasant and productive with limits of salmon at Hakai Pass.

Let me tell you one more story that has a lesson. Rich knows I am paranoid about salt on my boat trailer after use. Returning from Langara in 1997 to catch the ferry back to Prince Rupert, we stop at Mayer Lake to use the freshwater boat ramp. After we are salt-free, my then two-wheel drive pickup will not pull the trailer out. Unknown to us is that the trailer mires in a soft bottom at the lower end of the boat ramp. So, we unhook and rig my cable come-along (purchased in eastern Oregon days to pull out our pickup if it ever got stuck. Never had to use it). To our surprise, it is easy to pump the lever on the come-along but the boat trailer will not move. Instead all four wheels of the pickup are sliding toward the lake! Soon we have another two-wheel drive pickup chained to mine but both pickups cannot pull the trailer out. With the two pickups chained together so that eight wheels are holding on the ground, we place boards I carry in front of the trailer wheels so that the trailer will climb onto a bigger footprint. With the come-along, three of us take turns pumping the handle until the boat trailer is on a firm part of the ramp. Ironically, I brought the come-along and boards in case we had to use them at Moresby Camp. We did not. The lesson? First, before you use a boat ramp, check out the ramp conditions. If you suspect a problem in an out-of-the-way place, take two chains, a come-along and four wheel-boards, each at least 4-ft long with you. Doing so for me saved a wrecker bill. By the following season we have a 4x4 pickup.

If you take your boat to the Charlottes on the ferry, a good schedule is to take the day trip going over. Coming back, take the night ferry and sleep aboard in a stateroom. Then you will be rested and ready for the road when you get to Prince Rupert. Get the highest deck stateroom you can. They are cooler, quieter and have their own bath. One time we slept on the lowest deck and it was hot and noisy. You cannot sleep in your vehicle or boat on the ferry. Be sure you get reservations both ways and know the exact overall length of your outfit. BC Ferries service is excellent and so is their website for seeking information, making reservations and payment.

Dreams and Reflections

Dreams and Plans

When I began this book in 1994 it did not seem that dreams were popular. Now everyone is talking about them. That is good. My view is, all desirable things begin with a dream, a thought or prayer. I am reminded of that each day when I look out the window and see our neighbor's boat, *Dream,* tied to her dock. On June 26, 1996, Rev. Robert Schuller on TV preached about "The Power of a Dream." His twenty point sermon could be summed up in the words of Henry David Thoreau, "Go confidently in the direction of your dreams. Live the life you've imagined." Thomas Jefferson, our third President, a man of vision, and one responsible for the Lewis and Clark Expedition, spoke these words: "I like dreams of the future better than the history of the past." Like Jefferson, I too like dreams. For over thirty years I dream of taking a small boat to Alaska. In 1994, I do! Many I talk to along the way admire my undertaking. As Joyce tells me in her gift shop in Sitka, "Everyone should follow their dreams. Few do." A friend says I was crazy to make such a trip! Well, some thought Columbus was crazy too, remember?

Many times I dream about an Alaskan boat trip. Dreams are easy. Just enjoy them. No other effort required. Dreams pose challenges of how will you do something, like, how will I cross Queen Charlotte Sound? Then the details get muddled and you wonder if you really can, especially if a few doubting Thomases suggest failures or fill you with horror stories. In spite of all that, if it is a right idea for you to follow, eventually the details will unfold, or you will be led to others who can help you define a clear vision of what it is you are trying to do. If you want a major boating adventure, I submit that the dreams first will help you make it a reality, as it has for me. For my Alaska trip, dreams over and over, step by step were a big help. A TV documentary said to the effect, "Alaska is a place for the adventurer and for those who are a little restless." Hey, that's me! A May 23, 1999, *Bellingham Herald* article on adventure stated, "Oceans and mountains offer exploration for the spirited." Without bragging, I think I was a little like President Theodore Roosevelt in carrying out my Alaska dreams. He was courageous, determined, energetic, did not bow to critics and he wanted to get as much out of life as possible.

One phenomenon that I have observed over the years in connection with boating dreams goes like this: You have the dream. You take the adventure. Then you have the memories after. So often, the dream before, and the memories after are actually more enjoyable than the adventure itself. Have you ever experienced that? Yet you can never experience the memories without the adventure. This may be because dreams are ideal. Often the adventure is not, nor by definition is it guaranteed. The memories can be a fun reflection on the adventures, be they good or bad. The adventure often requires a lot of energy, money and good decision making. Dreams and memories do not. Still I like to do all three.

For my Alaska trip, the dreams are long and many. I am not sure when and how they began. I do know that in 1941, when Dad boards an Alaska Steamship for Alaska in Seattle, I am intrigued. Beyond being sad and tearful to see Dad off to battle the mosquitos and other elements in getting new roads built in Alaska, there is a mystique even to a 5-year old. The steamship itself is the way ships should be. They have big smokestacks that put out real smoke. Hulls are tall, sharp and narrow. Dad's ship is painted black, white and dull orange. The Alaska Steamship logo stands proud on the stack. It is all so nautical; not like the streamline, practical ferries or cruise ships of today. Dad used to write detailed letters about his Alaskan and Yukon experiences. They are vivid and still stick with me today. When Dad would return home for the winter, he would tell stories of the big pancakes in camp or how he built a boat so the survey crew could get to the job easier. Dad would bring home Viewmaster picture reels of what it is like in Alaska. I am sure these early impressions have some bearing on my later passion to boat to Alaska. Two books of my youth that championed adventure may have influenced me: *Jet's Adventures* and *Two Boys of the Ohio Valley*. Later I read *We Live In Alaska* to learn about Alaska adventure.

Maybe my passion to explore is in my genes. My four grandparents emigrated from Europe two centuries ago. Grandpa Petersen once gillnet fished the mouth of the Columbia River under sail power. His greatest fear was being washed to sea across the bar. Grandpa Kruml once swam across the Columbia River. He also got "pinched" for catching salmon with a pitchfork near his farm in the Willamette Valley! Dad worked on some of the most challenging roads in Montana and Alaska. Mother shut the door of an outhouse on a cub bear in Montana, after throwing butter in the outhouse, after the bear robbed the neighbor's food cooler. I watched it all, as I was the first to see the bear! It was sad when the Sheriff came to shoot the cub. I attended eighteen different schools growing up. Cynthia and I have lived and worked coast to coast.

Rich, who is like a real brother to me, worked and lived in Alaska. His stories of fishing, hunting, berry picking and the local people intrigued me more about Alaska. In 1966 when reading *Family Ark*, I put myself mentally on board with the skipper and his son as they head for Alaska in their 17-ft boat. I make the trip and suffer though their trials and enjoy the pleasures. By then, our family of four has *Happy Talk*, our first boat. It is more realistic dreaming when we have a real boat. I know I dream about an Alaskan boat trip with all of our six boats, fourteen to thirty-one feet.

After reading *Me-and-er To Alaska*, I am intrigued how two rather different people got along well on their slow cruise north because they both had that same yearning. The skipper wants to live each day to the limit. Me too! In the late seventies, I thought for sure I would take a trip north in *Nadja*. That boat had all of the amenities for a long cruise, but it never did work out. In 1978, Cynthia and I have a great week-long trip in *Nadja* from Bellingham to Echo Bay and back via Desolation Sound. As nice as that trip is, it just whet my appetite to go further north.

My expectations of going to Alaska seem very real for the first time in 1993. We purchase our 21-ft Bayliner, *Day by Day* in Alaska, in part, with that in mind. My vision is that Rich and I will probably make the trip without thinking of the boat's limited cabin space. One owner of a boat like ours, told us about their family-of-four cruises and his fishing trips to Rivers Inlet with three men. At the time, it all sounds plausible. After all, literature and salespeople tell us that our boat can sleep four. While Rich and I have cruised on *Day by Day*, a long trip is a bit much for two.

By fall 1993, I am certain I will be going to Alaska in June 1994. On New Year's Day 1994, I write in my diary, "God willing, this is the year I go to Alaska in *Day by Day*." Rich and I talk about his going, too, in his 21-ft Olympic, *Harland Bell*, but soon that idea fades. You recall it is Cynthia who came up with the idea that I go alone. It's true I have been the happiest when I go alone, as it is the least complicated way to go. Traveling with others gives you less flexibility in the things you want to do and when you do them. Soon it became apparent that I will need to get "dream specific" and fix the details of my trip well in mind. Five months is not too much time to plan a trip of twenty-five hundred miles. Traveling alone has the advantage of making it easier to communicate with God. There are fewer distractions and you are the only decision maker.

Getting ready for a small boat voyage to Alaska is not unlike getting ready for an Atomic Demolition Munitions mission in the Army. As a lieutenant team leader, I have to see to it that a detailed list of items is assembled before each mission. Next, I make sure every detailed step is accomplished en route to the mission site and the mission itself is accomplished by a highly trained team. My Alaska trip preparation is also similar to a football coach getting ready for Saturday's game, then playing it. In my case, I am team leader, coach, quarterback and grunt to get it all done! I must now lead my dreams to waking action! In 1996, during his presidential campaign, Steve Forbes, Jr. said in effect, "Life is too short to dream. Act out those dreams."

I do a more complete job of planning and preparation for my Alaska trip than for any other in my life. It pays off. Fortunately, I do not use all the preparations. It is like life insurance; you hope you won't need it. When you are well prepared, you don't need everything. But when you are not, what happens? You need what you don't have! Thankfully, I am well prepared. Two lists I make are essential: what needs to get done; what to take along. It seems like I am always adding to my lists rather than crossing out.

By the time of the 1994 Seattle Boat Show, I am convinced I need a Loran or GPS. Rich and I attend a GPS seminar and see all the electronic displays at the show. At one point when discussing the merits of GPS with a salesman, he points out that a GPS will not keep you from being rundown by a Washington State ferry in the fog! That impresses me. Suddenly, I am looking at radars. Soon, it becomes clear I will not leave the show without a Furuno model 1621 radar. Buying was easy. Explaining to Cynthia "why," is more difficult, especially, after I have her sold on GPS or Loran. I think I cannot justify buying both. Last minute before the trip though, I do buy a Magellan GPS. Mary and Jerry, at San Juan Electronics have just put on a presentation at the Sandy Point Yacht Club on GPS, Loran and radar. Jerry says you really need GPS in SE Alaska, an area where Loran will not work. He is right!

It is amazing how different you feel about your small boat when you have radar and GPS. You now realize that darkness and fog does not force you to use sailing ship techniques that are like wandering around in the dark. In all my commercial trolling days I long for radar and Loran. Now I have the best of both. I realize how far I have come beyond my eighth grade boat dream expectations of someday owning a 16-ft wooden Reinell with a 33hp Evinrude. I shake my head in disbelief and gratitude.

In the Army we had a saying, "Prior Planning Prevents Poor Performance." Actually they used another "P" word as well, but we don't need it here! If followed, this slogan can help a lot. I plan every detail. In considering what I need, I will think, what is the worst that can happen? I plan accordingly. I set realistic goals, with alternatives in case my main mission did not work out.

My dreams eventually get translated into specific plans, then into action. I don't know how many times I think about a particular location, like Queen Charlotte Sound. The tales I read and hear make me lie awake and wonder can I make it? Well, of course! My May 1979 *Pursuit* trip, Cynthia and my summer 1984 BC ferry trip and both of my 1994 crossings in *Day by Day* are glassy calm. So is Dad's first crossing in 1941. This shows that you do not want to take all of your fears too seriously. In eight trips, Queen Charlotte has never stopped *Day by Day* crossing when she wants.

How many times have you jumped into your car or boat and just taken off on the spur of the moment? I have done that and it can be fun. Going to Alaska is not like that. Before my 1994 trip, a young couple was picked up by the Alaska ferry, after being attracted by a distress signal. In this case, a burning shirt soaked in gasoline, was their only flare aboard the 18-ft boat. They set out without even a life jacket. That is not the way to go to Alaska!

Perhaps the best way I can demonstrate my preparation is to list everything that I took. In "Reflections" are listed all the items that made up the *Day by Day* cruise vessel and my evaluation of them after extensive cruises.

Reflections

Today is full of blessings. I really believe that. God has helped me throughout my life and on my voyages. Indeed, I feel my 1994 Alaska cruise is a blessing. It is a lifetime adventure! Nothing in my life, short of religion and family, compare to it. Yet, I enjoyed a thirty-two year engineering career, visited all fifty States, including Alaska three times before, Canada, Mexico and Europe twice. Still the Alaska small boat trip alone takes all. And my sequel trips rate high as well.

Thinking back on all of the places I have been and the things I have done in *Day by Day*, I have a very satisfied feeling. To me it is amazing. Certainly, since 1994 I have had a much wider boating experience than all of my other fifty years of boating coast to coast. That is what retirement is all about. Most certainly, I did not do it alone. God is at the front and center of all of my accomplishments, and I thank Him. So did many others help me. Though I travel alone, I cannot count the number of people before me who did things and those along the way that are helpful, that contribute to my success and pleasure. The early explorers to the West Coast did not have the many advantages we have, but what they did helps us today. I am reminded of a saying on the A-1 Builders sign in Bellingham, Washington, a few years back: "Be humble, great things were done before you were born!"

Discipline, Planning, Persistence

In all of my cruising if I had to sum up what made me successful as a result of my own efforts, I would have to say it was discipline, planning and persistence in that order. You might want to look up in the dictionary what each of these words mean. To get started on a venture, to get beyond the dream stage, you have to be motivated to a sense of order, and to force your self to be obedient to your own desires as well as "learning the game" of what it takes to make the dream to come true. That is discipline. I cannot overemphasize planning. This involves making a "to do" list of all of the details that must be done before you embark on a long boat trip, that when accomplished will allow you to achieve an end result. That is planning. Before and after you are underway there will be many deterrents to keep you from your goal, but if you press on in spite of obstacles, but you are not foolish, you have a chance to succeed. That is persistence. Each of these attributes is what it takes in many aspects of life from football to making a living to writing a book. Where did I get these qualities? My parents got me started right, and the US Army reinforced them.

Evaluation of Boat, Equipment and Me!

Admittedly I am not *Consumer Reports* or some Government testing lab. But, my experiences should be of help to anyone who desires to make a boat trip of any kind to Alaska or anywhere else. It may help anyone in buying any number of products the author found useful in rather harsh circumstances. Perhaps it is the engineer in me, or as a former researcher, I like to evaluate things. Not for the sake of testing, but to gain feedback or information as to how things perform and how one person reacts under various conditions. Used properly, this kind of test data can help others and ourselves have a better life. Although my trip was somewhat selfish, I would like to share in a way that is useful.

If I had all the money and time in the world, no, I would not have taken such a fast trip in the boat I did. But I would I not have taken a cruise ship. For me, that is too artificial, easy, and with little sense of adventure. That is not to say cruise ships aren't a good way to travel and Cynthia and I may do that someday.

An ideal boat for me to take on this trip would be about a 40–60-ft motor-sailor or trawler. She would be diesel, have a pilot house and have at least a thousand mile cruising range. She would have two staterooms, each with full baths. The boat would have all modern household appliances and a high-speed inflatable dinghy. Crew members can join and leave me on a summer long cruise as we agree. Ideally, Cynthia will be with me all of the time. Since I do not experience an ideal world, the above is not in my immediate dreams. I recall, too, what one skipper says at Refuge Cove during a discussion on boat sizes: "It's not the size of the boat that counts. It is the character of the skipper that does."

The boat—Bayliner Trophy 2159

So how did I happen to make my trip in a 21-ft Bayliner that is no longer built? Reality is that Cynthia and I have had a long, happy marriage, and it gets better. During forty-three years of marriage we have owned six boats 14- to 31-ft for thirty-three of those years which averages 20-ft in length. After owning a 31-ft, then a 17-ft boat for an average of 24-ft for the last two boats, we concluded a 20- to 24-ft boat was the ideal compromise for us. It still is. Several other people we have known have moved from bigger boats to a 21-ft. Rich has had a bigger boat. Now he owns a 21-ft. Cynthia says not to get too comfortable of a boat, or I may not want to come home!

When you consider all the possibilities, I can think of no other boat that can do so much and still fit in our garage. The fact we bought a new Bayliner in 1972 and 1993 makes a statement. Owning a 22-ft Bayliner before influenced us. The bottom line is this: The Bayliner 2159 Trophy is a great boat and I prove it is excellent for cruising to Alaska and back. I agree that a 2359 Trophy or other brands in the twenty-one to twenty-four foot range will work.

The design of our 2159 is outstanding. It is a good rough water boat with a hull made to take "mean water." The cabin and hull look sharp and are functional. Some strengths of the 2159 are:

❀ Hardtop with an Alaskan bulkhead (in other words a closed cabin)
❀ Dinette table for two
❀ Sink and thirteen gallon water tank
❀ V- and quarter berths
❀ Visa portable head
❀ Origo alcohol stove
❀ Icebox
❀ Fish well
❀ Fuse-wiring access
❀ Storage space
❀ Self-draining fiberglass decks
❀ Bow pulpit-railing
❀ Compass and controls
❀ AM/FM/cassette radio
❀ Adjustable helm seat
❀ Opening hatch and windows

and wiper

❀ Pole holders

❀ Built-in tackle box and live bait tank

❀ Trim tabs

❀ 4.3 Liter 155 hp V-6 Chevrolet engine and

MerCruiser Alpha drive with power assist steering

❀ 86 gal. gas tank

❀ Two bilge pumps

❀ Swim step and outboard motor bracket and of course running lights and horn

The dealer added San Juan fresh water cooling and a Red Dot engine hot water heater and an Impluse Model 2801 depth sounder which also measures water temperature and low speeds.

I added:

❀ Fire extinguisher

❀ Furuno 1621 16-mile radar

❀ Magellan GPS

❀ Danforth D-750 anchor with 26 feet ¼-inch galvanized chain and 263 feet of ⅜-inch nylon line

❀ Water separating fuel filter

❀ Second battery with three-way marine switch

❀ Outdrive oil monitoring reservoir

❀ Eight horsepower Mercury outboard with three and six gallon fuel tanks (stacked— lower with extended vent)

❀ Insulation of fish well and more around ice box

❀ Access ports to storage space

❀ Vented stove-top heater I designed (first use 1999)

❀ Second 12-volt outlet

❀ Cockpit fender holders with four fenders

In addition I carry a 6½ ft Bombard inflatable dinghy with hard transom, oars and 2½ hp Mercury outboard with extension arm (plastic pipe); second self-tripping anchor with chain and line; third lower bilge pump; Racor fuel/air separator check valve in fuel vent line; survival suits; life jackets; life vests; life cushions including one throwable with line attached; mounted radar reflector; flares; boat hook.

Overall, I would rate this boat Excellent or "B+." In spite of its shortcomings of being underpowered and getting poor gas mileage, having a poor gas fill and cabin water leaks (not serious), it has overwhelming favorable characteristics. One Bayliner dealer thinks if the factory would take just a little more time in assembly, they could eliminate water leaks. The ultimate passing test for our boat was the way it carried me comfortably and safely for 23 consecutive days and 2,500 miles in June, 1994 including in 350 miles of open ocean. Since that time, in extended open water cruising, with over 1,200 engine hours equivalent to over 60,000 miles on a car, the outfit runs and looks like new. The engine never has needed oil between changes. Except for the gas filling problem, most items have been fixed or tolerated. Considering the price and features, the 2159 offers the best value on the market for this size boat in used boats, since this model is no longer built.

The bigger 2359 with a 350 V-8 would be a good choice. Sea Sport and Osprey and others make similar boats or used to. In 2000, Bayliner has a new 23-ft hardtop which is similar to the older hardtop Trophy's. I calculate that from a factory delivered dry boat to being fully loaded, I added about two thousand pounds. Good thing I went alone! Although *Day by Day* was sold as a 21-ft boat, she is only 18-ft at the waterline. This means when she is fully loaded she sits over four inches deeper in the water at rest. This weight requires more horsepower to plane the boat. If this same load of cargo is added to a longer boat, she will sit higher in the water and have a longer planning surface that should be more efficient. This was the case with our 22-ft Nisqually. Higher, more economical horsepower in *Day by Day* should also be more efficient to push her at a higher speed that the present engine cannot do.

Our MerCruiser and V-6 perform superbly, except for minor prob-lems. It now is the best starting and shifting of three new MerCruisers we have owned. It took persistence by me, Dave at Marine Services Northwest, now Boondocks, in Bellingham, and a supportive MerCruiser corporation warranty program to make it happen. For the first time, I would want to buy another MerCruiser if it had fuel injection like the 210 hp 4.3 Liter but I would want multi-port which they do not yet have. My thanks also to Gordon of Gray Marine in Ketchikan, who with Richard from Port Angeles, got me going with MerCruiser repairs while on my 1994 trip. Thanks to several others in 1999 who helped me along the way or reassured me my power unit was okay. I can't forget Pat at Sullivan Bay who gave me a used spark plug wire and made my engine run like new again after he quickly determined what was wrong. We bought our then unnamed Bayliner in an unusual way while on a

Alaska motor home trip, by getting a brand new 1991 boat in 1993. It was Cynthia who found it. At that time we had no home Bayliner dealer. But thanks to the help of Gary of Salcha Marine near Fairbanks, Alaska and Ken of Bayliner in Arlington, Washington, I was able to fix boat and trailer warranty items.

Accessory Items and Supplies:

Below is a list of items taken to Alaska, or on other long cruises, and my opinion of their value:

Essential:

- All of the items listed as part of the boat above
- Spare propeller and nut and locking washer
- Dinghy patches
- Safety harness and line
- Spare fuel filter
- Engine belts (bought at Wrangle)
- Charts and publications (see later lists)
- Inflatable pump
- First aid kit
- Cortaid lotion
- Two propane lighters
- Second GPS
- Hatchet & knives
- WD-40
- Duct tape
- 8 x 8 ft plastic tarp
- Tools and flashlight
- Multimeter
- Boat log
- Electrical splice kit
- Kellet gear
- Spare batteries and fuses for everything on board
- Outdrive and outboard
- flushing adapters (two)
- Small stuff (twine)
- FWC zincs (change them!)
- Sleeping bag and pillow
- Waste basket
- Plastic bags
- Polarized sun glasses and strap
- Oil absorbent pads
- Foil and plastic wrap
- Boat license
- Dishes, pots and pans
- Duffle bag and clothes
- Cash and credit cards
- Ice
- Soap
- Biodegradable detergent
- Handi Wipes
- Dishpan
- Outboard lock
- Paper towels and toilet tissue
- Head (toilet) chemical
- Rain gear
- Squeegee, sponge and chamois
- Binoculars
- Bag Balm
- Deck key for gas and water

fills on a float
- Hand operated bilge pump
- Survival kit items: EPIRB; Emergency signal dye and mirror; Smoke signal, Waterproof matches; Wax lighters; Emergency rations; Strobe light for life jacket; Water
- Survival suit
- Gallon of stove alcohol

- Marine-Tex (epoxy)
- Rubber gloves (heavy and throwaway)
- Oil and fuel filter wrenches
- Food
- Personal needs
- Lifting back brace
- Bible
- Boat Log
- Pen and pencil

Useful:

- Hand-held compass
- EZ steer to connect MerCruiser
- Second spare propeller and floating prop wrench
- Sea anchor
- Four spare gas cans with 12.5 gallon total of gas (only for out of the way places)
- Cassette tapes
- Rainex and window anti-fog cloth and or liquid
- 12-volt spot and trouble lights
- 12-volt vacuum cleaner
- GE portable CB radio
- USGC Auxiliary Courtesy Marine Examination sticker
- BC and Alaska fishing licenses
- Diary
- Camera, tripod and film
- Plastic stacking storage bins (7)
- Portable electrical heater and cord

- 30 amp dock power adapter
- Two down riggers and lead balls
- Three fishing poles and salmon lures
- Salmon net
- Crab ring
- Insect repellant
- Sun screen
- Solar shower
- Swim suit
- Water jugs and water
- Office and charting tools
- Sewing and shaving kits
- Remington battery travel razor
- Halibut line hook (bought at Port Hardy)
- Snacks and beverages
- CANPASS and US Customs PIN
- Salt water soap
- Mirror
- Gasoline hand siphon hose
- Insect repellant
- Candles

- ❋ Spare oil filter, oil and oil removing pump
- ❋ Halibut spear
- ❋ Pole belt
- ❋ Cellular phone
- ❋ Laptop computer
- ❋ One or two ice chests
- ❋ Gaff hook
- ❋ Sharpening stones
- ❋ Spare towing line
- ❋ Shore line on spool
- ❋ Phone cards (BC and Alaska)
- ❋ Bilge cleaner
- ❋ Spare oil: outdrive, power steering and trim tabs
- ❋ Rags
- ❋ Stoppers to place in deck scuppers in rough water with heavy loads when fishing (chair leg caps)
- ❋ Wet suit
- ❋ Waterproof box for current and expired flares
- ❋ Carbon Monoxide detector. (People can get very ill on boats due to carbon monoxide poisoning from gasoline engines when underway. So these detectors are useful for more than just when you sleep. Exhaust fumes often are pulled back into the boat unless you have proper ventilation.)
- ❋ Float coat

Desirable (but did not have)

Fuel injection engine; Auto pilot; Microwave; Inverter; Forced air furnace; Hot water heater; Shrimp pot; Electronic charts; 4-cycle 9.9 hp auxiliary outboard; 110/12 volt refrigerator; second depth sounder (added in 2000); Differential GPS.

What was Best?

As you can see, I took a lot of stuff in a small boat. The GPS was among the most used item on all my trips. You should not leave home without one! My original Magellan Merdian ($400) gave out on a 1999 trip after one previous $100 repair. Fortunately, I bought a Magellan Blazer 12 ($100) GPS as a backup. It worked so well it is now my primary GPS and I bought a second one for backup and hiking. I am impressed with the Furuno 1621 radar. (New models have replaced the numbers above.) While not foolproof to "see" every thing, the radar works very well and I would not go to Alaska or in the ocean without one. The same is true in inland Washington and BC waters, if you go out in the fog. While I did not have it until 1999, my vented stove-top aluminum heater (like a shoe-box lid over the burners that vents out the window) is the most useful item of comfort in damp weather, when not underway. I wonder how I got along without it. It works as well as a kerosene heater I used to use but without the odor or bulk.

Small things make a big difference on a small boat; like the Handi Wipes for keeping clean without using a lot of water. They are a good substitute for soap and water, even for grease if you have been around the engine. Most have aloe and lanolin and work well for that spit bath before and after bedtime. Make sure you get a brand that feeds well out of the plastic container. When you are on a fast trip you don't want to be always trying to find and thread the loose end! Oh yes, waterless hand cleaner is good for real dirty hands and for getting grease and creosote out of clothes and off fenders. This may sound strange, but I need to mention the best paper towel I have ever seen—So-Dri by Fort James Corp. I first got them in a discount grocery at a very low price. Never had heard of them before, but they do not dissolve like some name brands.

Bag Balm, in the same can Grandpa used on the cows, is for sale in a local drug store. Roofers in our area use it. While it says on the can, "For Veterinary Use Only," I find it extremely useful on my hands for dryness and cuts as trollers used to do for their hook-nicked hands. If it can be that close to our Nation's milk supply, I will take the risk. It is also valuable for putting a thin coat on deck hardware when you know you are going to take on a lot of spray. When I made my three week, 1994 boat trip, without bottom paint, *Day by Day* grew tiny barnacles on her transom. Putting Bag Balm on all transom components prevents that without leaving an oil sheen. Marine-Tex can be a Godsend. In 1994 a stick jammed behind one of the trim tab cylinders. When I pulled it out, I broke the plastic hose fitting off the cylinder. Marine Tex to the rescue. In 1999, during the Auke Bay haul out, the depth sounder bracket got broken. I fixed it with Marine-Tex. Both are holding just like new.

I don't want to sound like a boating commercial, but I would be remiss if I did not mention MerCruiser (formerly Quicksilver) 4-cycle engine oil. Few dealers carry it and they seem to think it is no better than any other motor oil. I disagree. Here is why I think it is a must for any marine automotive gas engine. It is a 25-40W oil with additives to protect your engine when running hard or in storage. When our V-6 is cruising at 3,500 rpm, it is like towing a heavy trailer up hill at over 80 mph in a car hour after hour. It has done that for seven seasons. I have owned five automotive marine engines in boats and thirteen engines in cars and trucks. Two of our boat engines and three vehicle engines had internal failures using the same leading brand oil, which has been faithful in our other engines. Only five of all of the engines we owned have not used oil between changes—two of those are the last two Chevrolet MerCruisers where their 4-cycle oil was used. No engine failures and no added oil between changes in our engines with the toughest duty only happened when using MerCruiser 4-cycle engine oil. That is why I believe in this oil. I change oil and filter every fifty hours or equivalent to 2,500 miles and not every hundred hours like my MerCruiser book says nor every twenty hours like it says on the oil container.

EPIRBs or Emergency Position Indicating Radio Beacons send out signals for rescue services. I carry the low-cost Mini Class B unit on *Day by Day* which operates on 121.5/243 MHz. In an emergency, when it is activated, the signal could be picked up by satellite and heard on a ship or aircraft to begin a rescue within a twelve mile radius. It would be better to have a 406 MHz unit, which enables a vessel to be located within one mile and relays your NOAA/SARSAT registration number to the USCG, telling them what kind of vessel is in trouble. Better yet, is the new Rapid Fix 406 which can interface with a GPS to send rescuers to your exact location. Like most electronics, they get better and less expensive. It is planned to phase out satellites equipped to receive the 121.5/243 MHz signals by 2010.

A dinghy is essential to get ashore and to serve as a life raft in an emergency. It also makes a good top carrier when right side up on the hardtop. An inflatable is the only choice. Mine weighs thirty pounds and carries two adults. This 6 ½-ft model fits nicely on the swim step, in the cockpit and in the cabin when inflated. For one person it works fine. No question a bigger inflatable is better for safer and more comfortable passage with more people. But then comes the trade-off, how are you going to haul it as well?

A forced air diesel furnace would be extremely desirable from a comfort standpoint when not running and you are in the cold and rain. On a small boat it is difficult to find a place to install one. They also are expensive and they drain your battery. A next best solution might be the Wallas Safeflame 95 diesel stove. This is a countertop unit with an enclosed flame. It can be used for cooking or with an optional blower unit for forced air heat. Battery drain and handling smelly diesel fuel are drawbacks. It is also expensive and you have to find a way to vent the stove. After years of using open flame alcohol and propane cook tops, and kerosene and propane portable heaters on three boats, I came up with a compromise idea. Thus my alcohol stove-top heater was born. As the picture shows, like a shoe-box lid, it fits over either a gas or alcohol open flame cook top and vents outside. For $100 I had Lynden Sheet Metal, Inc. in Lynden, Washington, build it. They did a splendid job and helped me select the proper materials. My unit fits the Origo 4000 alcohol stove, but other sizes are possible to fit other stoves.

My vented stove-top heater design works great.

The specs are for this stove and my boat are: 9 inches wide by 18 inches long by 2 inches high of nearly ⅛ inch thick aluminum; in the upper right hand corner, as close as possible to the corner, is a 1⅜ inch vent hole with 1⅜ inch high nipple; 3 inch by 6 inch by ½ inch high cleats are on all four corners to keep pots and pans on the stove; a separate vent pipe, ⅛ inch thick, is 21½ inches long with a 6 inch long (make it 7 inch) 90 degree elbow with one end cut back 45 degrees. The result is a heater that uses an existing cook stove that sets up in seconds. It heats like a cozy old wood stove in the corner using clean fuel and venting moisture outside. When it is cold or rainy, I put a small piece of Plexiglas in the open window below the vent, since the vent pipe goes out an open window just wide enough to accommodate the vent pipe. The main variable in other boats is the vent pipe, which needs to be configured accordingly. Mike, at Pacific Marine Exchange in Bellingham, Washington has and thinks a heater flexible pipe may work just fine. Mike and I thought about making and selling stoves like mine. I tried to get Origo interested in making them, but there may be regulations in some countries that require all heaters to be enclosed flame and vent to outside. Which brings up a good point—*Never go to sleep with any kind of unvented or open flame heater on.*

During my first stove sea trial, in January 1999, I am impressed. It is 37 degrees outside and gets too warm in the cabin with two burners going. The windows are water vapor free when the cabin is warmed. You can cook and boil water on this stove-top heater. Keep in mind, as with all non-forced air systems, moisture will go to the colder areas of the boat. For that reason, it is good to air out the boat daily and when underway operate the hot-water engine heater with some windows open.

Overall, the selected items taken above on my Alaska cruise is Outstanding or "A-." With the above items, *Day by Day* was commissioned in a manner to make her an extended cruiser.

The Skipper

How did I do? Perhaps the reader can judge. Maybe my friends and relatives have an opinion about my mariner skills. I never ask and they never say. Frankly, I do extremely well when it comes to the planning, purchasing and executing my dream. Not perfect, of course. But I would rate myself maybe Excellent or "B+". I completed the 1994 trip in less time than planned. I did it safely without any mishaps or damage, except minor prop dings, which did not affect top rpm performance. Essentially I was within budget. I did less of some things and I did more of others than planned. I certainly overestimated my ability to catch fish and crabs on the trip! My missionary for God's word was less than I had hoped, but that may come later. I pray this book will bring both pleasure and inspiration to my readers. Thanks be to God.

What it all Means

To dream about something that you always wanted to do is common to all of us. Having the privilege to carry it out is perhaps rare. I feel humble for that chance. It is a wonderful thing to be able to plan and carry out a challenge. In the process you learn a lot about yourself. There are those who will scoff at my endeavor and consider it folly and unimportant. And perhaps it is. In my life as Husband, Father, Engineer, I have tried to do well. But I could have always done better. It is better to think you can do better and to keep on trying rather than to think "you have arrived." As you look around the world, you see that others have done more or less than you, by your value scale. But, comparisons are not always helpful. God has a plan for each of us. Each of us is unique. We all will do different things. My hope has always been that one day I will do something greater than ever before. Perhaps my cruises and this book will be a stepping stone to my biggest contribution. Time will tell. In the mean time I satisfied my greatest adventure.

Things to Think About

You should check your insurance policy before you go to Alaska or offshore. Our State Farm boat policy is good to seventy-five miles offshore. I would never do that! You may want towing insurance, too. If you join BoatU.S. you get boat towing insurance while on the water and you can get boat trailer towing insurance while on the road. The BoatU.S. dues will get you many benefits including lobbying to protect us from crazy laws that could keep us off the water.

If you don't have a boat or you want a minimum size one to go to Alaska in, but you don't have a lot of money, buy a used 2159. I see them for sale. I think they are an excellent value. Be sure to get a survey though so you know what you are getting. Keep in mind you may need to replace the engine and outdrive.

A perplexing question is, how often do you replace water-cooled manifolds? You will get answers from three to seven years. A lot depends on how your boat is used and cared for. A better answer is to use the table in the BoatU.S. Catalog which shows probability of failure over time. Pat says he replaces manifolds every 1,600 hours. I had a manifold fail at five years on a used boat, which required an engine over haul. I am planning on eight seasons and seven years on

Day by Day. With an estimated 1,500 engine hours by then, that would be a good time to repower.

Ice is expensive and sometimes hard to find in remote areas. While a refrigerator would be nice, you still need ice if you fish. If you use the refrigerator a lot on 12 volts you can run batteries down. On *Nadja*, we had lots of 12 volt equipment and sometimes we ran both big batteries dead. We were fortunate to have a generator with a separate battery to get things going again. On a small boat there is an advantage of staying simple. That is one reason I stick to an ice box and no autopilot.

A boat trip to Alaska has limitless opportunities for activities depending upon one's appetite. Many publications tout various places. Since you now know me, if you cruised with me day by day in this book, I thought you might like to my opinion on the highlights below.

Best Ports

The best towns or ports along my routes are based upon a lot of factors. They indicate if I would like to live there. They reflect services and access for the small boater. It also considers prices of products and services and how friendly people were when I visited them on my cruises. Beyond that I will not give details on each. You will have to visit, talk to others or read all you can about each port. Significant is that these towns stood out from a list of 20 ports I considered:

1. Sitka, AK
2. Petersburg, AK
3. Ketchikan, AK
4. Nanaimo, BC
5. Juneau, AK

Cozy Ports

Out of the way, small, places are more intimate and are appealing to me in a small boat. They are those fun places to relax when you do not have any other big needs. I found these ports especially attractive:

1. Refuge Cove, BC

2. Echo Bay, BC
3. Duncanby Landing, BC
4. Elfin Cove, AK
5. Walters Cove, BC

Natural Wilderness Areas

My definition of these may not fit any recognized category, but they are in designated protected areas and some or all with cultural significance. They convey a location of beauty, being somewhat unusual, and a place of peace as I experienced them:

1. Glacier Bay, AK
2. Gwaii Haanas, BC
3. Cape Scott, BC
4. Cape Cook Lagoon, BC
5. Checleset Bay, BC

Special Places to Visit

In the following list, I consider all of my experiences in all fifty states, most of Canada and nine other foreign countries. In that context, it reflects what stood out on my trips considering my interests and their unique qualities. Reading the "Sandy Point to Sitka" and "Side Trips" chapters should give you a clue why I may have rated these special places as I did. These stood out in order from a list of thirty sites I considered:

1. Baranof, AK
2. Prideaux Haven, BC
3. Princess Louisa Inlet, BC
4. Blue Heron Bay, BC
5. Tracy Arm, AK

Other Neat Places to Visit

It's difficult to single out every place that I might visit or visit again but these stand as a result of my cruises. Except for Port Alexander, where I have not been, each is remote and has rushing water. Even waters near Port Alexander can be wild, according to *Coast Pilot* and skippers I talk to. Beware in all of these places:

1. Snake River, ID, WA, OR
2. Port Alexander, AK
3. Nakwakto Rapids, BC
4. Fords Terror, AK
5. Nitinat Lake, BC

Favorite Coves and Beaches

If you read *Day by Day to Alaska* you will get a good idea of where these are. I decided against listing my top ones to "give them a break" and the people who live near them. I know how it is to have favorites near our home publicized.

Best Salmon and Halibut Fishing

Many may say, "What does this guy know about fishing?" I have been a good fisherman, but I am certainly not in the top group. Still, I had some experience and perceptions along the way that make me conclude the following have good fishing holes nearby:

1. Langara Island, BC
2. Sitka, AK
3. Barkley Sound, BC

Best Fuel Docks

This may seem like an odd item in this category, but gas docks are critical in this part of the world by boat. One fuel dock operation stood out on my trips for service, price and nozzle operation: Chevron. Price varied widely on my trips. There was less difference in the cost of fuel between 1994 and 1999 than there was in location. Surprisingly, gas was the highest at Gibbons Landing near Vancouver and Roche Harbor in the San Juans. For planning purposes use $2 US per gallon (does not consider the rapid rise in gas price in 2000) times the miles you will travel divided by your boat miles per gallon. On my trips I averaged about $1.55 per gallon. Gas was lowest at Ketchikan, Juneau and Skagway and high outside Vancouver Island, the Central BC Coast and the remote areas of Alaska.

When is the Best Time to Go to Alaska?

May and June are clear choices for me. The long days are a big plus. These months tend to be drier, or should we say less wet! Winds are among the lightest and there are fewer people and less fog. There can be good fishing. Having said all of that you can run into rain, wind, fog and people and the fish may not bite! Remember, you are up North and this an adventure! Summarizing my many years of June boating in three boats, I have these observations in percent of the time: some sun 66; some rain 28; some fog 11; some calm water 64; some rough water 26. Like all weather data, it my not be accurate so beware! You cannot count on it to be always right.

Other Desirables Learned Along the Way:

Large outboard power users and dealers all along the coast seem to favor the 200 hp Yamaha.

For 9.9 hp 4-cycle outboards I have heard a lot of favorable comments about the Honda. Bigger outboards are going 4-cycle to reduce pollution. Buy them!

Differential GPS to allow navigation within fifteen feet would be desirable. BoatU.S. 2000 catalog has a good discussion on this and describes products for this purpose. A backup depth sounder is also highly desirable.

Websites can offer unlimited information. In the Bibliography I have listed a few that may be helpful to trailerable boat skippers and others.

Safety, Tips and Observations (Philosophy)

Safety

Just as in life, many years at sea and in boating circles taught me numerous things. They are valuable and free with the price of this book. Ignore them and they could be costly to you and your world. Nothing on a boat trip can be more important than safety. I devised a series of rules that help me and hopefully will help others:

Rule #1: Safety afloat is always prime consideration.

Rule #2: Use engine blower before starting engine.

Rule #3: Wear a life jacket or vest when you are on deck and not tied to a dock.

Rule #4: When you are the only boat, do not go offshore with an offshore wind.

Rule #5: Use a harness on the windward side when in on deck in open, rough water alone.

Rule #6: In a following sea, put trim tabs up.

Rule #7: In fog, slow down, radar may not see everything—watch ahead.

Rule #9: Men, use a urinal and never drown with an open fly!

Rule #10: If conditions are bad, have dinghy, survival suit and survival kit ready to use.

Rule #11: In a blow at anchor, use more scope, a kellet, and keep a watch.

Rule #12: Make sure passengers and crew are safe, too.

Rule #13: Never do anything foolish, and think about what you are doing before doing it.

Rule #14: Always have a backup plan in case your primary plans fail.

Rule #15: Use chock blocks when launching or retrieving a boat on a ramp.

Rule #17: Before trailering a boat, review the tips in *Chapman*.

Rule #18: Remember Rule #1.

Most of the rules above stand on their own. A few may need expanding.

Rule #5 means the harness you wear will be tied to the boat in such a way that you can still do your deck duty without undue interference. It also means that you must be tied to the boat in such a manner that if you fall overboard you can pull yourself back to the vessel and climb aboard, probably near the stern. Never go on the leeward side or you could be dragged under the boat and drown.

The reason for Rule #6 is to give the boat more stability. In extreme following seas, extended trim tabs could act like fins to help overturn the boat in a broach.

Surprisingly, many men who drown have been found with open flies, suggesting they were urinating over the side when they fell overboard and is the reason for Rule #9.

Rule #10 implies the worst and you may have to abandon ship. Most of us have never been confronted with that so it may be difficult to predict how and when we would act. A number of drownings by crews from capsized fishing vessels have had survival suits on the vessel, but not on the victim. This suggests a rouge wave can make things happen unexpectedly.

My strategy is to get my dinghy into the cockpit, with oars but without outboard, and tie it to the boat with a long line. Into the dinghy I will tie down my survival kit, a jug of water and the water-proof box of flares. If things get worse, I would put on my survival suit while I was still in control of the boat. If I thought I could be in the water for a long time, I would put on my wet suit under the survival suit. I would rather be too warm than die of hypothermia, particularly if the survival suit should get a tear in it.

If the boat is in danger of capsizing and I couldn't control it, I would go into the cockpit and tie the dinghy to my self. I would not want to get knocked unconscious by being slammed around in the cabin. If I ended up in the water, I would head for the dinghy and get away from the boat but still stay tied to it. I would rather not be separated from the boat, because I would more likely be seen by rescuers. On the other hand, I would want to cut myself loose from the boat if it were to sink so that it would not take the dinghy down too. This implies you have a knife handy. But could you open the knife with a survival suit on? Maybe you should have an open knife in a case.

The USCG conducts lots of rescue drills. It would be good training for you to run a drill at a lake and see if you can do all of the above, short of sinking your boat! Don't forget to turn on the EPIRB in an emergency, but not in your drill. Instructions with the EPIRB will tell you how you can test your unit periodically. A first drill probably should be done on a nice day. A second drill might be conducted on a stormy day to add realism. Just don't forget safety during a drill. It would be bad, drowning in a survival exercise!

For Rule #11 it would be good to review *Chapman*.

Rule #14 means that if things go bad, you should think about alternatives: Abort your trip for the day and go back, possibly return-ing home the best way if you have equipment failures; go in a different direction, though it may be longer; finding a safe haven and hole up until conditions are better.

At one point in my book, I suggest a maximum wave (wave height—not swell) a boat may safely encounter might be .4 times the boat length, based upon my observations. This is not scientific, and boat design and wave characteristics all have a bearing on this. In the case of *Day by Day*, a possible maximum wave is eight feet. Knowing that, I will try to avoid waters, where, for instance, the Canadian forecast is for seas to three meters which considers a combination of wave and swell height. With all of the variables, including the inaccuracies of forecasting, I am satisfied with this approach. To me this makes more sense than Small Craft Warnings, which is strictly a function of wind speed and not currents, which make waves bigger or smaller. In the Charlottes, Small Craft Warnings are always in effect because of the location and uncertainty of the weather there.

On most long trips I have three engines—the MerCruiser and two outboards. While the 2½ hp is for the dinghy, it will push *Day by Day* at three knots in the right conditions. I do consider it an emergency power source by lashing the dinghy to the stern with the 2½ pushing. I can steer from the helm. On four occasions with *Day by Day* in seven boating seasons I used the outboard to get me home or to a safe place. Four times on three other boats I needed auxiliary power. Boat enough and it will likely happen. Do not be complacent. Heed Rules #1 and #14.

Traveling by boat requires you to watch more details than going by car. You must make sure the drain plug is in; the fenders are out, then in; the outdrive is up or down; antenna up or down; electronics on or off. You must watch for collisions as every boat travels their own road. You must watch water depth and for floating debris. So if you like it easy, drive a car. If you like fun, skipper a boat! And pay attention!

One advantage of a trailerable boat is, if she does breakdown and you can get her to a port with a road, you can get your trailer and haul her home.

Tips and Tricks

By now, you should have picked up some ideas on how to be a better skipper. Below are some others:

Tip #1: Make sure your drain plug is in before launching your boat! (I never had that problem, but I saw other boats that failed to heed this tip.) Remove the plug when the boat is out of the water to drain the bilge, then put the plug back in immediately. A corollary is to not forget to tilt the outdrive up before hauling out or driving down the road. It is good practice to store the boat with the outdrive down.

Tip #2: If you run your boat weekly, or monthly, you should have fewer problems—that's my experience.

Tip #3: Tow a boat on a trailer monthly and check brakes and lights. (Because you run your car everyday, you have few problems with it. If you ran your boat and trailer daily, you would have fewer problems, than with winterizing, in my opinion.)

Tip #4: Carry a spare boat trailer tire, bearings, grease seal, a bearing buddy and a complete trailer wiring harness with wire connectors and spare bulbs in a water proof locking box on the trailer. (Rich reminds me one day that a long time ago I said, "Sooner or later, you are going to have trailer light problems.")

Tip #5: When not using trailer wiring on your tow vehicle put a wire coupling of the opposite sex on the plug to protect the plug from corrosion. If you have a trailer lighting problem when no lights come on, clean the plug terminals as they tend to get corroded.

Tip #6: Do not bounce a trailer axle off a curb or hit them, as that weakens springs.

Tip #7: Carry a spare trailer spring and a short 4x4 to go between the axle and frame in case you break a spring. (In 1999 I broke two trailer springs. In one case I went 110 miles home with a 2x4 above the axle. A 4x4 works better than a 2x4.) Carry a jack that will lift your trailer. Also carry a large triangle flare kit so that you can warn traffic if you have a breakdown.)

Tip #8: Fasten a strap or line on a chock block that you use to hold your rig on a boat ramp, with the strap long enough to loop over the end of the tow vehicle bumper. When you start up the ramp the chock will be towed along until you get to a level spot.

Tip #9: If you have a roller-bed boat trailer, back the trailer only to the bottom of the rear axle so you keep wheel bearings out of the water. This will help save your trailer from the effects of salt water.

You may need a power winch, and you want to launch the boat slowly in deep enough water. If you have a bolster bed trailer as I do, without rollers, you do not need a power winch. Back in the trailer when hauling out, so that the last six feet of the boat has to be winched up. This way the boat centers properly, which is one advantage of this type trailer. I see many boaters back both kinds of trailers too deep into the water, allowing the boat to drift all around and making it difficult to center the load. Don't forget to tie your boat down, especially if you have a roller trailer. Bolster bed trailers give your boat better support if you tow over long or rough roads. (If you want entertainment, watch boat ramp activity. Some would make great videos!) A brake flushing kit on a trailer is a good item.

Tip #10: Use absorbent pads under the fuel fill when fueling boat in the water or at a gas station—help save the environment and avoid a fine.

Tip #11: Start cruises early in the day to reduce the chances of wind and rough water and to give yourself more time.

Tip #12: Consider following a bigger boat in rough water. This sometimes works if you can take the risk that the vessel may not go where you want. Also the skipper may not want the responsibility of your following if you get into trouble.

Tip #13: When making long passages in open water, never take the boat out of gear or stop the engine. A running outfit is more likely to get going again. (More than once I have had a boat engine not start while on the water, and another time the outdrive stuck in reverse.)

Tip #14: You are on a collision course, if the relative bearing of the other boat remains constant and the distance is lessening, as you steer a steady course. (You want the relative bearing of the other boat to move ahead toward the bow so you go astern of her; or, for the relative bearing to move aft so you will cross the other boat's bow. It is imperative to know the rules of the road in crossing situations— who has the right of way for either a privileged or burdened vessel. *Know your danger zone.* If all of this sounds unfamiliar, see *Chapman*)

Tip #15: Stern first anchorage works well for a lunch hook or when it is rough and you feel safer working in a cockpit. This assumes your anchor is not on deck or you can get your bow-mounted anchor safely into the cockpit. Use a self-tripping anchor when there is possible debris where you could lose an anchor. When dropping a hook, do so slowly to avoid a tangled fluke.

Tip #16: When hauling anchor close to the beach and the wind is blowing you closer to shore, use the auxiliary outboard to idle back into the sea in reverse as you pull anchor. The outboard may need periodic steering adjustments.

Tip #17: You may have to extend the mast light staff if you carry a dinghy top side so that running and anchor lights are seen 360 degrees.

Tip #18: A Micronta auto electrical analyzer from Radio Shack is a handy item for checking battery or alternator condition. It plugs into a cigarette lighter of a boat or tow vehicle.

Tip #19: If you wear glasses when you are on a boat or on a dock, wear a safety strap on them. (Once in the Charlottes as I was helping dock another boat with a very narrow gunnel, I slipped into the drink without a glasses strap or my life jacket! I lost my glasses. Now I follow safety Rule #3 and this tip!)

Tip #20: When your boat is in storage, take cushions home and keep cabinets open. Use a dehumidifier or Damp Chaser. As a minimum, use desiccant in containers and dump water out often.

Tip #21: Mark on US chart catalogs and Canadian catalogues all of the charts you have, for quick reference aboard as what numbered chart to get next.

Tip #22: On our boat I favor rolling charts with the printing out and storing in a Velcro-strap suspended box above the quarter berth. I number charts on both ends for easy identification. When I lay them on the table, the ends curl under the table making it easy to scroll them and to have them stay in place.

Tip #23: Use nonskid place mats on the table to keep charts or other documents from sliding. Use them between charts if you stack charts on the table for the day's use.

Tip #24: Keep on board a generic drawing of your boat's deck plan. On it, number items you carry aboard in the relative position where they are found. Identify what each numbered item represents. (In 1994 going north, I could not find flashlight batteries, although I knew they were on board. So, I bought some at the most expensive place along the way. Of course I found them when I got home! I would not have that problem, if I followed this tip that Rich shared with Sandy Point Yacht Club members when he was Commodore. I now have my drawing in a notebook with other information.)

Tip #25: If you buy a used boat, get a marine survey on it by a surveyor who is a member of the National Association of Marine Surveyors. Doing so may avoid a lot of unhappy surprises.

Tip #26: Running a drain line from the ice box to the bilge in the engine compartment makes for a cleaner smelling boat than draining into the bilge below the cabin.

Tip #27: An outdrive oil reservoir is a must to make sure the outdrive oil is to the proper level and condition. If I had that on *Seaspell*, I may have not have had an outdrive go out in the Juan de Fuca Triangle, causing an expensive repair bill and lost time during my commercial fishing season.

Tip #28: Boats have lots of unused space in out of the way places that manufacturers tend to cover with pretty panels. Rich and I have accessed several of them to great advantage. On *Day by Day*, two deck plates help for small things. One, 9 x 13⅝ inches with a locking cover is below the helm just above the sole. It accesses an amazing amount of storage below the helm, stove and ice box. I could install more.

Tip #29: Rubber-backed outdoor carpet over fiberglass cockpit decks make excellent nonslip coverings that are easily removed and cleaned.

Tip #30: Stacking plastic baskets work great for storing items under a table, above a bilge area and, in my case, after modification on the swim step, for outboard gas tanks as the photograph on the back cover shows.

Tip #31: By making a mounting bracket for the 2½ hp outboard on the swim step, I am able to store it out of the way above the water.

Tip #32: Doel Fins work on some boats to help plane heavy loads at lower speeds. They did on our last two boats (17- and 21-ft). But in each case, they reduced speed at cruising range and for *Day by Day* reduced fuel economy 12 percent. So, they were off after one season. Bayliner does not feel their boats need Doel Fins. They say trim tabs are enough. A better idea that two Bellingham MerCruiser dealers have suggested is putting vertical down fins on each side of the trim tabs, like some bigger Bayliner's have, to reduce the water from escaping out the sides of trim tabs, giving more lift. In 2000 I added these. Preliminary test results are satisfactory. A long cruise is needed for a true test.

Tip #33: One useful item I found for long distance cruising, with our three largest boats, is a speed and fuel consumption curve, which you can make. *Chapman* describes how to make the speed curve using a stop watch and running a measured course such as the one shown on Chart 18424 on Bellingham Bay. Once speed data is plotted on a curve every 500 RPM to engine maximum, I add fuel consumption data to another curve using a different color. You can get the fuel data from the boat or engine manufacturer. When you are done, you have a theoretical gallons per hour plotted by the same RPM increments for speed. From this data you can plot a curve in a third color that represents theoretical miles per gallon. This is useful to determine the most efficient cruising speed, how far you can go on a tank of fuel and what speeds to avoid. Over time, by carefully computing hours and miles run between full tanks, you can verify your data.

Tip #34: When a guest or a crew member aboard a boat, observe how the skipper does things. Be ready to do things the ship's way or ask the skipper if you can assist. Like it or not, the skipper's rule is law on board as long as it is not unsafe, unlawful or immoral. The skipper is also responsible for everything that happens on his or her ship. Feel free to offer suggestions to the skipper if he or she is in the right frame of mind!

Tip #35: It is best not to cruise in the dark. My "rule of moons" is: Cruise in full moon; fish in the dark of the moon.

Tip #36: Keep fish statistics to help you determine what, where and when works for catching fish. For example, a full moon or east winds may not be the best time to fish. Under "Tide and Current Tables" in the Appendix are tide tables that have dots and bar widths that seem to have some validity on best fishing times.

Tip #37: Apply for CANPASS with Canadian Customs and a PIN at US Customs to make it easier to clear customs of both countries.

Tip #38: Keep a professional boat log. It can be interesting recall and a legal document in court if needed.

Tip #39: Whenever you go on a cruise or cross a big body of water, file a float plan with another person or with the Coast Guard. If you don't check in near your ETA, then information is on hand to locate or rescue you.

Tip #40: Filing for state fuel tax refund can save you money. In six years I got $343 refunded.

Observations (and Philosophy)

The longer you live, the more you think you have some ideas that can help society. Here are a few of mine:

Salmon

Important to me are the return to much higher numbers and sizes of wild salmon all along the Pacific Coast. They are a treasure from God we have exploited and destroyed. But there is hope. Near the start of the chapter, "Sandy Point to Sitka and Back," I share an idea how we could get on top of the problem. We should use all of our influence to get the process going that will save fish. In the meantime, where fish are below sustainable growth numbers, there should be a total moratorium on salmon fishing—tribal and non-tribal, sports and commercial. By removing fishing pressure we remove one major factor leading to the decline. It should not be long before we could start fishing again, especially if we identify the critical factors and start correcting them. Fishing methods that allow catching only hatchery marked fish with fins that have been removed might be okay, leaving wild fish to spawn, until the time when all fish are allowed to be caught. The diversity of wild fish is better than hatchery runs. One practice I am strongly against is "catch and release." There is trauma and mortality associated with this technique. We can't afford the losses. Besides how would you like to have a 350 pound NFL lineman drag you all over with a hook in your mouth? So why do I fish and share sport fishing ideas if I want to save the salmon? Fish is a healthy food with a great taste, particularly if it comes from the cold, northern waters. Putting fish on the table is the main reason I fish. Until the rules change, why not fish?

If there is to be a commercial fishery, why not issue only sport-commercial licenses? Gillnets would be banned, but seiners with small nets, reef nets and trollers would be allowed with restricted lures for the later at various times. To fish, a skipper would charge to take tourists with him as his crew, all with licenses. The skipper has money before he leaves the dock. The State has license money from the skipper and all of his crew. Limits would vary depending upon the fishery—maybe one coho, two king, five sockeye, six pinks and ten dogs. After each trip the crew takes the fish they want or they can sell through the skipper to buyers for the market to those who don't fish. Some may go once a year or less. Others may go everyday during a season. There could still be sports seasons.

Closely related to salmon is the herring that they must have. It is a crime we have allowed the herring biomass that once was so plentiful to become almost nonexistent; then we wonder why the salmon have declined. There has been a fivefold drop in herring in the Cherry Point area in Washington. Yet promoters want more growth and development that ultimately can destroy what is left. From California to Alaska there should be a ban on all herring harvesting until herring and salmon return adequately in all waters. No more herring for bait or roe. Let lure manufacturers be challenged for effective replacements.

In the Puget Sound area, salmon have declined as the population has climbed. Whenever I walk across a parking lot and see vehicle oil droppings, ready to be washed into the water making its way to the sea, I wonder how much adverse effect chemical runoff of all kinds have on salmon and herring. Maybe a lot. We need to find out fast and perhaps treat all runoff. I want to save the salmon.

Salmon derbies create an artificial demand for salmon, much of which would not be there if the derbies did not take place. The Port Angeles Salmon Derby, a day on which we were married long ago, is no longer. So is the Sandy Point Derby. All locations should take the heed. Salmon in short supply should not be part of a gamble.

Finally, if you love salmon, get involved. I belong to two groups that are working to save the salmon. There are many groups on the west coast trying to help. Our time, money and influence can make a difference by our being part of the solution to save the Pacific salmon. My observation is that Alaska is doing the best job of salmon management followed by British Columbia. I will be kind and say, Washington State needs the most help to bring back the salmon. In truth, Alaska, British Columbia, Washington, Oregon, California and Idaho need to work quickly and together to increase the quality and quantity of all salmon species. It makes sense to me that fish of origin, at least in numbers, should be caught primarily by that state or province. That means lots of cooperation and enhancing salmon habitat in each coastal area.

The State of Washington should revise their rules for bringing fish back by boat. You can bring fish back from Canada by plane or vehicle anytime, but not by boat, unless a season is open in the water where you land, which sometimes is never. That is discrimination! The law was intended to prevent those along east Juan de Fuca Strait from bringing fish across the strait when Washington waters were closed but they were open in Canada. That does apply to the vast majority who fish up north or fish off the West Coast of Vancouver Island. Speaking of discrimination, why should boaters have to pay customs fees for crossing the border when cars don't? Frankly, I have no objection if all those who cross borders have to pay a user fee if it keeps border operations running smoothly and according to law.

Beaches

Beaches are also a treasure. I see two problems that are destroying them, but I see simple solutions. The first is erosion, much of it natural. I shared with you what happened to our beach at Dockton. At Sandy Point the shoreline is being eaten away. One way to minimize erosion is to collect drift logs along the shore with as many tied to together as possible in a pleasing manner. The effect is the dampening of waves which at times will allow a build up of sand and gravel beneath and behind them. I have observed this happening. It is true that shoreline erosion at Sandy Point accelerated after Cherry Point was developed. We do need to seek out better ideas.

The second beach problem is just the opposite. Some nice gravel beaches at Sucia Island are covered with logs and small debris, which in effect are destroying rare, choice gravel or sandy beaches. In these areas, the drift should be removed where erosion is not a problem and the beaches cleaned. In one Park Reserve in Canada, a manager wants to remove many logs from the beaches. This goes too far, because often they are smooth, picturesque and are nice for sitting. I would rather remove trees that have ugly roots and other detractors that float in.

We should all pick up litter on our beaches and shore side areas. For years we often (and should always) carry a plastic bag and pick up anything that detracts from the natural beauty. Pack it out! In free areas, in particular, it is our small price for using a resource and making it better for others and for our return.

Boats

Boat engines and boats ought to be made for the highest efficiency and fuel economy. Traditionally, boat engines lag automobile technology. It should be speeded up. I am against more government regulations, but we need to be smarter in this area. In the case of *Day by Day*, new boats like her in the future should be twice as fuel-efficient. That seems like a worthy challenge. If nothing else, maybe a lot of boats ought to cruise slower or use hydrofoils to gain the fuel saving and be less polluting. Outboards, by going four-cycle with fuel injection, are making good gains in both areas.

Recalling how sailboats and the Allweather boat get such good mileage, I have an idea. It combines with the concept that most people do not have the time to make long cruises, and neither can they afford very big boats. Why not have a series of places along the Inside Passage where you can charter slower economical boats for cruising for a week? I no longer own snow skis. I find it more economical and less hassle to rent skis since I do not go often. We know people who charter boats to go slowly through the canals of Europe. Cynthia and I rented an electric boat in Austria. Suppose there were ten places along the way from Puget Sound to Skagway and some places outside Vancouver Island to charter energy efficient vessels. The program could work like this: Near an urban area you could become a qualified operator. On your vacation you fly to a remote spot, pick up your boat and enjoy a week of hundred miles of coast. Next year you explore another section. In twenty years you have seen a lot. And maybe it wouldn't cost more than owning a boat. Boats are not cheap! Plus they take time. I figure for every hour you use a boat you spend an hour on maintenance, etc. If you don't, it will be like the guy who replied to me when I was looking for an advertised boat that "Needs some maintenance." He said, "That fits all of the boats in the harbor!"

Someday we may use electric boats. According to BoatU.S. there is a resurgence in this technology, first used in boats in 1880, even before people ran around in cars. Aided with fuel cells in the future, boats may be very quiet, go long distances and be nonpolluting. But they will go slow. *Commercial Fisheries News* in July 1981 pointed out that "It takes about four gallons per hour to plane a ton." And that is fifty times what it takes to go slow. Maybe we should slow down and smell the seaweed!

You may remember I mentioned that others have accumulated data on how boats got their names. I also told you how *Day by Day* and

Fatty Knees were named. Here is a little background how our other boats got their names:

Happy Talk—We built her when we enjoyed *South Pacific* sound track music.

Vikings IV—Our family of four with a Scandinavian name. Rich made us a crest.

Seaspell—That is what the sea does to you. "Do one thing and do it well," that is the motto of the *Seaspell*.

Nadja—Scandinavian sounding name that meant to me, "Never a dull journey afloat."

Tia Too—Named after the best cat we ever had, Tia.

Not forgotten is Shearwater Marine. It is a combination marine repair facility and resort. Impressive! The BC ferry stops here and there is boat taxi service to nearby New Bella Bella. It is comforting to know Shearwater is here, because it is a long ways between Port Hardy and Prince Rupert. You can store a boat here and fish nearby.

Water and Logging

Water use on boats may give us ideas how we can use less at home, since many areas are facing shortages. On board, I use four gallons per day, which includes a portable head and a comfortable two gallon shower every other day, if I am not able to shower on shore. By contrast, at home we use seventy-four gallons per day per person year round. If I only use 5 percent of home use while on the boat, isn't there a lesson here on how we as a nation might figure out how to use less water at home? Or is the lesson, live on a boat?

Logging has long been part of the Northwest. We do need lumber from a renewable resource, which trees provide. And logging can be done responsibly if we keep wide enough stream buffers, build roads properly and use helicopter logging where necessary. Admittedly, there have been many devastating logging mistakes in the past, but, we know how to do it better now and we must. If a site still will harm salmon, we should not log it.

People and Governments

Three individuals along my boating trail from 1950 to 1999, including one each from Oregon, Washington and British Columbia, warned of the dangers of socialism. Lessons I learned from these people are: 1. Wars are started by politicians because it is good for business (somebody profits); 2. Socialism reduces a nation to Third World status; 3. People vote for socialism by their wanting the government to do more for them. In the process, people lose their freedom. Socialism advocates equality, yet freedom and equality are incompatible. One day I was getting my boat trailer brakes worked on in the new Ferndale, Les Schwab Tire Center. While there, I bought the book *Les Schwab: Pride in Performance Keep it Going!*, intended primarily for Les' employees. Les started from a single tire shop and now is the largest independent tire dealer in the US. His effort put him in the Tire Industry Hall of Fame together with those who started Firestone and Goodyear. In his book, which sold twenty thousand copies, Les shows how he grew his business and helped many others. I suggest every young person and everyone in business read this book. It shows what it takes to make it in today's world and how to keep our Nation great. And to that I would add—to keep on boating.

After watching a TV interview with 2000 Pulitzer Prize winner for History, David M. Kennedy, about his book, *Freedom from Fear*, a number of events came clearer to me. It answers, for the first time, why Dad was quickly summoned from his Montana job in August, 1941 just four months before Pearl Harbor. My recall of what the three persons mentioned above had to say is in better perspective. Most of all, and Rich, a retired history teacher will laugh at this one, I want to read Kennedy's 936 page book and learn more about history! The fact that Kennedy was born in Seattle and I heard him describe some of his eleven year effort writing his book makes me appreciate his product all the more. Others may laugh, but you know what? We boaters should know a lot more about life than just about boating and fishing. I want to be more like the live-a-board in Ketchikan. He knew history. As I recall, it was during President John F. Kennedy's memorial service it was spoken to the effect, "What we learn from the past is, we do not learn." So let us and governments apply the lessons of history.

When I think of the Haida I think how friendly they are and how they want to preserve and share their culture. Often these and other Alaskan and British Columbia native citizens have jobs that reinforce their culture while at the same time providing much pleasure for boaters. How sad it is that the US government, through failed policies of massive welfare programs, have hurt many tribal communities. To me, the answer is for all people to get educated and go wherever the best opportunities are for their talents. I am a strong believer that each Native American tribe should have some land (not a reservation) on which they can maintain parks, cultural centers, long houses, museums and perhaps even resorts. Here unique cultures would be preserved and shared. Reservation trust land should become fee land of individual tribal members that can be bought and sold to whomever they want. On some Canadian charts, *IR* appears which stands for *Indian Reserve*. If you go on these lands, treat them with respect and make sure no permits are required to use them.

In the 1970s it appeared to me the divorce rate was higher among boaters. I always thought boating was a great family activity and it can be. My only advice is take it only as far as the family wants it. A strong marriage is more important than a bigger boat or boating excess. Remember, a boat can be "another woman." Why do you think they are referred to in the feminine? It used to be boats had mostly female names. Too much emphasis on boats could be breaking the first commandment of "no other god's before me (God)." Recently, I attended a memorial service for a retired commercial fisherman and neighbor. The Rev. Ottoson had these thoughts to share: Life is short—each day is a gift; people matter more than things; this life is a stepping stone to the life beyond. So, balance boating with life's priorities and life can be a joy and you can have a long, happy marriage. My own thought about a long marriage is that it requires commitment, communication and caring.

Religion

Now that you stayed with me this long, I do not want to end sounding like a preacher, because that I am not. But, I would like to share these thoughts:

Boaters should not forget prayer. If they do not know how, read the Bible. Talk to a minister or a Christian friend. Why pray? There are two paramount reasons for a boater. One is to thank God for creating such a heavenly beauty for us to cruise in along the Inside Passage. No one else could do that. The second reason is to overcome our fears, if the water seems to be overwhelming. In all of my cruising alone and in everyday life, for the most part, I have had a great peace. A peace that comes from being "born again," or having an abiding faith. Some will say being "saved." No matter how you say it, if you experience it, you know there is a power that makes all things better. I have for decades. My real test was when I was diagnosed with prostate cancer. Surprised? Yes! It did not take me long to realize I was going to be okay, no matter how it turned out—live or die. The Bible verse that helped me most was Philippians 4:6, which, thanks to Rev. Charles Stanley of Atlanta on his TV program "In Touch," helped me see, well before my diagnosis, the meaning as "Do not worry—Praise God." That thought has been such a powerful force to me on land and at sea. Both Dr. Stanley, and Dr. Robert Schuller on his "Hour of Power" TV ministry, have shown that from the verses in Philippians 4 we don't need to be anxious. The emphasis is on joy and gratitude, knowing all is well and trusting God rather than asking for something.

Being a cancer survivor is a positive experience. It prepares you for new challenges. In my case, I changed my priorities and my life-style. If you are a man over 40, I would suggest that you see your doctor about getting a PSA and DRE checkup. Early detection of prostate cancer does save lives. Beyond that, I want to be more anchored in the Spirit of Christ. Further in Micah 6:8 we are told what the Lord requires of us: "To be just, kind and walk humbly with our God." If my boat trips and this book seem counter to shared inspiration, may God forgive. I am not there yet.

Our Pastor, Rev. Knight, shared the above thought from Micah one Sunday. Another time she reminded us of these words from Martin Luther, "Anyone who knows the Ten Commandments perfectly knows the entire Scriptures." Further we were told the Ten Commandments are God's policy statements and counter proposals to the world. These statements are wrapped up in Matthew 22: 37-40.

If all of the above seems a little heavy, maybe when you are on the water or anywhere you can remember this from St. Patrick (372-466):

> Christ with me, Christ before me,
> Christ behind me, Christ within me,
> Christ beneath me, Christ above me,
> Christ at my right hand, Christ at my left.

Appendix

Services

Originally, I planned to list services everywhere *Day by Day* cruised. I only mention a few, some of which are not found in other books. This data quickly becomes obsolete and I cannot be as complete as some other publications. Marine atlases and books like Anderson and Carey have helpful services lists. I suggest you look over the Bibliography in this book for services references, as well as other books at marine book stores and departments. Many times you will find free directories of current marine facilities in a given area. The latest *Waggoner Cruising Guide* is excellent for Olympia to Prince Rupert. When you get to Alaska the *Southeastern Alaska Phone Directory* and *The Marine Yellow Pages, Alaska/West Coast* are available free. Boat ramps are found most places and may not be listed in any publication. Sometimes you will need a 4x4 to use them. And don't forget the Internet. You may find the most current information there.

Charts

Few items are more helpful than marine charts. Maps are for cars and hikers. Charts are for boats and unlike maps have water depth and navigational aid information, which is vital, particularly when you are cruising in shallow or rock infested areas. Charts come in various scales from very small to get the big picture with not much detail, to large scale to get a close-up view and more detail, but with not much coverage area. Also, unlike maps, chart distances are measured in nautical miles. Older charts have depths in fathoms. Many newer ones are in meters.

There are a lot of variables that the skipper needs to keep straight. So, how many of what kind of charts do you need? Tough question, because the answer is, it depends. It depends on where you are going and what you will be doing along the way, how big is your boat and how skilled of a skipper are you? If you are going from Seattle to Juneau, you could easily get by with two chart books. If you plan to explore off the beaten path, then some of the largest scale charts would be nice to have.

In a small boat it is impractical to buy every chart available and carry them aboard. Besides the cost is very high. If you can buy electronic charts to use on a laptop that would be good and more economical. You still want to have some paper charts, just in case the electronic data disappear for any number of reasons. In general, here is what I do. First I buy a small scale chart or charts that cover the entire area I want to cruise. Then I buy a chart book, which is more detailed and has charts of some harbors and passages. The chart books will advise you that they are "Not for Navigation." Well, of course they are! Why did you buy it? Why do they have courses plotted on them? The books will say for "Planning only." The truth is they are excellent auxiliaries to charts to help plan and make your voyage. Since they are not official government charts it is safer for the atlas makers to have the disclaimers so they are not responsible if you hit a rock. My experience is chart books are excellent and I use them well beyond their intended use.

As part of my trip planning, after looking at the big picture and seeing the more difficult areas in the chart book, I will look at the free chart catalog at chart dealers. By locating individual charts in the more difficult areas, I then decide which to buy, if any. Over time I find it is less painful to buy a chart now and then, rather than buy a lot at any one visit. New charts come out all the time, replacing older ones. If you want to be on top, buy the latest. I rarely do, unless the new chart has much information that my old one does not. Like I told you in "Side Trip 1", I used a 1939 chart to go to Olympia. Many of my charts are nearly thirty years old. As I cruise, if there are new navigation aids, I will sometimes note them on my chart. It is also possible to buy used charts at consignment stores like Pacific Marine Exchange in Bellingham. Waggoner, Anderson and Rue all have chart listings. Serious skippers should carry the latest editions of *Coast Pilot* and *Sailing Directions* aboard for the areas they are cruising. (I use the original copies I bought.) These are the best sources to read, particularly when you are going into difficult or new areas. These books will reference charts. By reading the area descriptions and looking at a chart, you will be able to tell if you need to buy a particular chart. Be aware, too, there are notices to mariners that frequently update charts and the editions above. Okay, so much for the philosophy. What charts do I need?

To make it easier for you, I give you my minimum charts for each of the cruising areas below where I have been. *Keep in mind going for the maximum, with all of the charts* (paper or electronic) in the area you will cruise is *safest and best.* If you explore or anchor in small bays you will appreciate some additional larger scale charts. Charts in the 3000 series are Canadian.

Cruising area	Chart Code
Sandy Point to Sitka and Back	S
Outside Vancouver Island	V
Side Trip 1 Puget Sound	1
Side Trip 2 Inlets and Passages	2
Side Trip 3 Prince Rupert to Skagway/Glacier Bay	3
Side Trip 4 Prince Rupert to Queen Charlotte Islands	4
Washington Coast	W
Snake & Columbia Rivers	C
Snake River above Lewiston	L

3000; Juan de Fuca to Dixon Ent; S, 2, 4

3001; Vancouver Island; S, V, 2

3002; Queen Charlotte to Dixon Ent; S, 2, 4

3461; Juan de Fuca Strait, East; V, 1

3463; Southern Strait of Georgia; S, 2

3512; Central Strait of Georgia; S, 2

3513; Northern Strait of Georgia; S, 2

3514; Jervis Inlet; 2

3515; Knight-Kingcome Inlets; S, 2

3538; Desolation Sound; S, 2

3539; Discovery Pass-Seymour Pass; S, 2

3541; Toba Inlet-Approaches; S, 2

3543; Cordero Channel; S, 2

3544; Johnstone Strait-Race Passage; S, 2

3545; Port Neville to Robson Bight; S, 2

3546; Broughton Strait; S, 2

3547; Queen Charlotte Strait, East; S, 2

3548; Queen Charlotte Strait, Central; S, 2

3552; Seymour-Belize Inlets; 2

3602; Barkley to Juan de Fuca; V

3603; Ucluelet to Nootka Sound; V

3604; Nootka to Quatsino; V

3605; Quatsino to Queen Char; V

3606; Juan de Fuca Strait; V

3647; Nitinat Lake Entrance; V

3668; Alberni Inlet; V

3670; Broken Group; V

3671; Barkley Sound; V

3673; Clayoquot Sound; V

3683; Checleset Bay; V

3744; Queen Charlotte Sound; S, 2

3784; Hakai Pass; 2

3808; Juan Perez Sound; 4

3853; Cape St James to Cumshewa; 4

3854; Tasu Sound; 4

3868; Port Louis to Langara Island; 4

3891; Skidegate Channel; 4

3895; Langara Island-Masset; 4

3902; Hecate Strait; S

3931; Smith Inlet-Draney Narrows; 2

3932; Rivers Inlet; 2

3934; Smith Sound to Rivers Inlet; S, 2

3956; Malacca Pass to Bell Pass; 4

3958; P.R. Harbour-Butze Rapids; S, 3, 4

16016; Dixon Ent to Cape St Elias; S, 3

17300; Stephens P-Cross S-Lynn Canal; 3

17315; Juneau Area; 3

17316; Lynn Canal; 3

17320; Baranof Island; S, 3

17323; Salisbury to Hoonah sounds; S

17324; Sitka North; S

17360; Etolin to Midway Islands; S, 3

17363; Hobart-Windham bays; 3

17372; Keku Strait; S, 3

17375; Wrangle Narrows; S, 3

17378; Pt. Baker-Protection; S, 3

17387; El Capitan Pass Area; S, 3

17400; Dixon Ent to Chatham Strait; S, 3

17403; Sea Otter Sound; S, 3

17404; San Christoval Channel; S, 3

17405; Craig Area; S, 3

17420; Hecate Str to Etolin Island; S, 3, 4

17428; Ketchikan Area; S, 3

18421; San Juans to Gulf Islands; S, 1, 2

18441; Puget Sound-northern; 1

18448; Puget Sound-southern; 1

18480; Juan de Fuca to Destruction; W

18500; Columbia R. to Destruction; W

18502; Grays Harbor; W

18521 to 18548; 18 Charts Columbia/ Snake R; C

Evergreen Cruising Atlas; S, 1, 2

Marine Atlas, Volume 2; S, V, 2, 3, 4

Snake River Boaters Guide; L

Tide and Current Tables

Next to charts, tide and current tables are very useful for knowing when it is safest to enter some shallow areas or to go though some passages. In Canada the government tables are the way to go. In Washington and Alaska, free and low cost tables at many sporting goods or fuel docks are satisfactory. There are more expensive versions that are valuable. *Tides and Currents* computer program will give you a lifetime of information all along the Inside Passage and then some.

Other suggestions on annual tide and current tables follow:

Tides and Currents for Windows: AK, BC, WA (lifetime)

WXTide32: Worldwide (to 2038); free from www.geocities.com/ SiliconValley/Horizon/1195/

Reed's Nautical Almanac for West Coast: AK, BC, WA

Elliot Sales, *Tide Tables, Dot's Fishing Guide* (dot size): AK, WA

Evergreen Pacific, Tide Guide, including best times to fish (bar width): WA

Canadian Tide and Current Tables, Volume 5: Juan de Fuca Strait and Strait of Georgia

Canadian Tide and Current Tables, Volume 6: Barkley Sound and Discovery Passage to Dixon Entrance

Canadian Tide and Current Tables, Volume 7: Queen Charlotte Sound to Dixon Entrance

Other

Waypoint guides: *Coast Pilot* and *Sailing Directions* give latitude and longitude for many locations from which you can create your own waypoint list. I prefer to determine them from charts so I know exactly where they are so I can arrive at an exact spot. Recording or saving locations with the GPS as you cruise is a good idea so you can put the data in your waypoint list if you may want to return to that location. I find putting waypoints in a spreadsheet works well. I record my GPS name for a waypoint; my own chart name for it; chart number; in four columns show latitude and longitude in degrees and minutes to hundredths of a minute; general area name like San Juans. With this data all in columns, you can do sorts by chart number, general area, etc. to print out your waypoint list for a given cruise. If you take your laptop along you can enter waypoint data when things are slow on your cruise. I rarely find that! The shareware program GPSdb, available from http://gpsdb.com, works with Garmin GPS units to upload/download waypoints and routes. Entering waypoints on the PC is easier and faster then using the GPS keypad.

Glossary

Below are terms used in this book that may have nautical or unique meanings:

0001–2400. Military time in hours and minutes around the clock midnight to midnight.

4x4. Four wheel drive vehicle or 4-inch square timber.

AB AND AL. Name of salmon flasher invented in Port Angeles.

ADVENTURE-GUIDE. The author's adventures while cruising with advice how to minimize risk.

AFT. Rearward in a boat.

AMIDSHIPS. Midway between the sides of a boat.

ASTERN. Behind a boat.

ATLANTIC SALMON. Pond raised salmon introduced from the Atlantic ocean.

ATLAS. See CHART BOOK.

BAYLINER. A builder of popular pleasure vessels.

B&B. Bed and breakfast lodging.

BC. British Columbia, Canada.

BEAM. The width of a boat.

BEAM SEA. Waves parallel to a boat's side.

BIGHT. An indent along a shoreline, or a loop in a line.

BILGE. Lowest place inside a boat's hull.

BOW. Forward end of a boat.

BOW-RIDER. Open bow boat with seats, sometimes with a snap-on cover.

BROACH. To veer or yaw in a following sea so as to lie beam on to the waves with danger of capsizing or swamping.

BUOY. Floating marker on the water.

CALL. Usually a short visit by a ship to a port.

CB. Citizens Band radio.

CG. Coast Guard.

CHINOOK. Large salmon species.

CHUM. Salmon used in pet food.

CHART BOOK. Marine atlas, book of charts or cruising guide.

CLASS III RAPIDS. Water flow with high and irregular waves through narrow passages.

COHO. Bright, lively and desirable salmon species.

CRUISING GUIDE. See CHART BOOK.

DAY BY DAY. Our sixth boat, a 21-ft 1991 Bayliner Trophy with a 4.3 Liter Chevy MerCruiser engine.

DOG. See CHUM.

DRAFT. The depth of water a boat draws.

DRY-DOCK. A dock that can be kept dry for construction and maintenance of vessels.

EGGSHELL. Slang name for fiberglass boats.

EPIRB. Emergency Position Indicating Radio Beacon.

ETA. Expected time of arrival.

FATHOM. Six feet.

FATTY KNEES. The model of our 9-ft sailing dinghy and our name for it.

FORWARD. The front of boat.

FWC. Fresh water cooling.

GEODUCK. A large clam with a long neck.

GILLNETTER. A fishing vessel which uses a gillnet to catch fish by the gills.

GLASSPLY. Boat no longer built.

GM. General Motors.

GPS. Satellite global positioning system device.

GUNKHOLE. Out of the way place along saltwater coasts good for exploring and anchoring.

GUNNEL. Upper edge of a boat's side.

HAIDA. Indian tribe in BC.

HANDI-WIPES. Moist towelettes

HAPPY TALK. Our first boat, a 14-ft 1960 Taft kit-boat runabout with a 35 hp Sea King outboard.

HEAD. A marine toilet.

HELLY HANSEN. A brand of rain gear.

HOOK. An anchor.

HUMPIE. Salmon good for smoking.

INSIDE PASSAGE. Protected waters from Olympia, WA to Skagway, AK.

JUAN DE FUCA TRIANGLE. The area inside Ediz Hook, Race Rocks and Discovery Island.

KELLET. Weight run down rode to make anchor more effective.

KICKER. Small boat with an outboard motor.

KING. See CHINOOK

KNOT (KT). Measure of boat speed in nautical miles per hour.

LINE. A rope.

LIGHTHOUSE. Powerful navigation light usually associated with support buildings and personnel.

LONG-LINER. A fishing vessel that uses long lines with bottom hooks.

MERCRUISER. Leading brand of stern drive with inboard engine.

MIDDEN. Refuse heap often full of sea shells from early encampments.

MOONFOG. Bright fog lighted by the moon.

NADJA. Our fourth boat, a 31-ft 1971 Uniflite sedan with twin Chrysler V-8 v-drives.

NAUTICAL MILE (NAUT MI). One minute of latitude; 6076.11549 feet or 1852 meters or about 15 percent longer than a statute mile.

NE. Wind or compass direction.

NISQUALLY. A Bayliner boat model, no longer in production.

OLD MAN. Skipper of a boat, usually a larger one.

OLYMPIC. A builder of pleasure boats no longer in business.

ONE-LUNGER. One cylinder engine or an engine sounding like it has only one.

OUTDRIVE. Stern drive.

PASS or PASSAGE. A narrow opening along a body of water, or travel by boat.

PC. Personal computer.

PINK. See HUMPIE.

PORT. Left side of a boat when facing forward, or where a boat finds refuge or services.

PSA/DRE. Detection tests for prostate cancer.

PUGET SOUND. Inland salt water body from Olympia to the San Juan Islands.

PURSUIT. Name of a 44-ft limit seiner. (Limited length for certain fisheries.)

REACH. An extended stretch of water.

RED. See SOCKEYE.

RODE. The anchor line.

RV. Recreational vehicle.

SALTCHUCK. Saltwater which I love.

SCAT. Animal droppings.

SE. Southeast Alaska or a wind or compass direction.

SEASPELL. Our third boat, a 22-ft 1972 Bayliner Nisqually with a 302 Ford MerCruiser engine.

SEA SPORT. A builder of quality pleasure boats in Bellingham, WA.

SEINE. A large net weighted at the bottom with floats at the top, used to surround fish.

SEINER. A fishing vessel that uses a seine.

SELF-TRIPPING ANCHOR. Anchor with a sliding ring on the shank.

SENTINEL. See KELLET.

SHE/HER. Respected generic name for a boat.

SILVER. See COHO.

SMG. Speed made good.

SMOLT. Juvenile salmon ready to leave a river for the ocean.

SOCKEYE. Prized canning salmon species.

SOLE. The floor of a cabin on a boat.

SPRING. See CHINOOK.

SS. Steam ship (not many around anymore).

STARBOARD. Right side of a boat when facing forward.

STERN. Rear end of a boat.

SW. Wind or compass direction.

TIA TOO. Our fifth boat, a 17-ft 1987 Stingray bow-rider with a 3.0 Liter Chevy MerCruiser engine.

TLINGIT. Alaska native tribe.

TRAWLER. A fishing vessel that drags large conical nets along the bottom or a pleasure boat with a trawler type hull.

TROLLER. A fishing vessel that drags fishing lures through the water attached to weighted lines.

TROPHY. A Bayliner boat model or a prize fish.

UNIFLITE. Quality boat no longer built in Bellingham.

US. United States.

VHF. Very high frequency marine radiotelephone.

VIKINGS IV. Our second boat, a 16-ft 1967 Larson runabout with a 95 hp Mercury outboard.

WELL-FOUND. Properly equipped.

WHARFINGER. Person in Canada who manages a dock.

WHEEL. Steering wheel, or propeller.

WSW. West SW wind.

YAW. Deviate erratically from a course.

Select Bibliography

Below is a list of helpful publications I have used. Many have later editions. Some are out of print but they may be in used bookstores. Pictures in some of the references show places I visit and describe. Others share experiences on different boats at different times. Selected websites are listed which may offer more current data.

Cruising Information

1978. *Evergreen Cruising Atlas, Olympia to Queen Charlotte Sound.* Seattle: Straub.

1992. *Marine Atlas, Volume 2, Port Hardy to Skagway.* Renton, WA: Bayless.

Allen, Marlene B. May 1997. "Sailing the Charlottes: A Diamond in the Rough Seas", *Nor'westing.* Seattle: Nor'westing Publications.

Anderson, Hugo. 1993. *Secrets of Cruising North to Alaska.* Anacortes, WA: Anderson.

BC Parks. 1994. "Provincial Parks of Vancouver Island" (map 1 : 800,000). Victoria, BC: Queens Printer.

————. 1995. "Coast Marine Parks of British Columbia" (various maps). Victoria, BC: Queens Printer.

Calhoun, Bruce. 1972 *Northwest Passages, Volume II.* San Francisco: Miller Freeman.

————. 1978. *Northwest Passages, Volume I.* Ventura, CA: Western Marine Enterprises.

Canadian Hydrographic Service. 1976. *Sailing Directions, British Columbia, South Portion, Vol. 1.* Ottawa: Government of Canada Fisheries and Oceans.

————. 1991. *Sailing Directions, British Columbia, North Portion, Vol. 2.* Ottawa: Government of Canada Fisheries and Oceans.

Carey, Neil G. 1995. *A Guide to the Queen Charlotte Islands.* Vancouver, BC: Raincoast.

Chapman, Charles F. 1972. *Piloting, Seamanship and Small Boat Handling.* New York: Hearst.

Douglass, Don and Réanne Hemmingway. 1997. *Vancouver Island's West Coast.* Bishop, CA: Fine Edge.

————. 1999. *Exploring the North Coast of British Columbia.* Anacortes, WA: Fine Edge.

Forest Service. 1997. *The Wild and Scenic Snake River Boater's Guide.* Washington, DC: US Department of Agriculture.

Hale, Robert. 1998. *Waggoner Cruising Guide.* Bellevue, WA: Weatherly Press.

Morris, Frank and Willis R. Heath. 1952. *Marine Atlas of the Northwest, Olympia to Skagway.* Seattle: P.B.I.

National Ocean Service 1993. *U. S. Coast Pilot Pacific Coast Alaska: Dixon Entrance to Cape Spencer.* Washington, DC: US Department of Commerce.

National Park Service. 1998. *Glacier Bay Official Map and Guide.* Washington, DC: US Government Printing Office.

Petersen, Dale R. September 1996. "The Mystery of Nitinat Lake", *Nor'westing* . Seattle: Nor'westing Publications.

———. May 1997. "Exploring the Queen Charlotte Islands...Solo", *Nor'westing.* Seattle: Nor'westing Publications.

———. May 1998. "The Circle of Behm Canal", *Nor'westing.* Seattle: Nor'westing Publications.

Rue, Roger L. 1982. *Circumnavigating Vancouver Island.* Seattle: Straub.

Watmough, Don. 1993. *Cruising Guide to the West Coast of Vancouver Island.* Seattle: Evergreen Pacific.

Additional Reading

1950. The Holy Bible (KJV). New York: Harper.

Blanchet, M. Wylie. 1993. *The Curve of Time.* Seattle: Seal Press.

Caldwell, Francis E. 1978. *Pacific Troller.* Anchorage: Alaska Northwest.

Canadian Heritage. N.d. *Gwaii Haanas National Part Reserve and Haida Heritage Site Visitor Handbook.* Canada. Canadian Heritage.

DeForrest, Donald. 1965. *Family Ark.* Dallas, TX: Royal.

Healy, K. 1990. "Queen Charlotte Islands/Haida Gwaii" (map 1 : 250 000). Vancouver, BC: ITMB Publishing.

Forest Service. 1993. *Recreational Facilities, Ketchikan Area, Tongass National Forest.* Juneau, AK: US Department of Agriculture.

Iglauer, Edith. 1988. *Fishing With John.* Madeira Park, BC: Harbour.

Kennedy, David M. 1999. Freedom from Fear: The American People in Depression and War, 1929–1945. New York: Oxford University Press.

Lund, Marten. 1965. *Inside Passage to Alaska.* New York: Lippencott.

Petite, Irving. 1970. *Meander to Alaska.* Garden City, NY: Doubleday.

Schneider, Bill. 1996. *Bear Aware.* Helena: Falcon Press.

Schwab, Les. 1996. *Les Schwab: Pride in Performance Keep it Going.*
Bend, OR: Mavrick Publications.
Spillsbury, Jim. 1995. *Spillsbury's Album.* Maderia Park, BC: Harbour.
Short, Wayne. 1968. *This Raw Land.* New York: Random House.
Upton, Joe. 1977. *Alaska Blues, A Fisherman's Journal.* Anchorage:
Alaska Northwest.
————. 1994. *Through The Inside Passage.* Vancouver, BC: Whitecap.

Websites

www.bcferries.com	British Columbia ferry information
www.boatus.com	Boating catalog and information
www.capjack.com	Computer products for the boater
www.ccg-gcc.gc.ca	Canadian Coast Guard
www.ccra-adrc.gc.ca	Customs Canada
www.customs.ustreas.gov	US Customs
www.fs.fed.us/r10	Alaska Forest Service cabin rental
www.massetbc.com	Masset site with Queen Charlotte links
www.nbctourism.com	British Columbia tourist information
www.nps.gov/glba	Glacier Bay information and reservations
www.state.ak.us	Alaska tourist information
www.uscg.mil	US Coast Guard
www.uscgaux.org	US Coast Guard Auxiliary
www.usps.org	US Power Squadron
www.waggonerguide.com	Cruising guide information
www.westmarine.com	Boating catalog and information

Index

Index

Index

Index

Index

Midden Bay 6
Milbanke Sound 29, 63
Milbrook Cove 136
Miles Inlet 135
military induced error 79
Minstrel Island 15
mission 165, 186, 187
Misty Fiords National Monument 35, 38
Moore Bay 130
Moresby Camp 177, 182
Moresby Island 174
Morse Basin 141, 142
Moses Inlet 137
Mosquito Fleet 102
Mount Fairweather 154
Mount Roberts 149
Mountain Point 35
mountains 15, 54, 119, 123, 126, 127, 135, 141, 145, 147, 149, 152, 153, 154, 158, 160, 170, 176, 184
Murder Cove 44, 162
My Beach 171
mystery 92

N

Nabannah Bay 171
Naden Harbour 180
Nahwitti Bar 68, 69
Nakwakto Rapids 133, 134, 135, 169, 203
Namu 64, 169
Nanaimo 6, 67, 201
National Parks 139
Natural Wilderness Areas 202
Neah Bay 111, 112, 115, 116, 117, 180
Nelson Narrows 137
New Bella Bella 28, 63
New Dungeness Light 115
New Eddystone Rock 38
Newcastle Island 6
Nigei Island 69
Nimmo Bay 133
Ninstints 176
Nisqually 60, 192
Nissen Bight 71
Nitinat Lake 93, 203

Nitinat Narrows 92
Nitinat River 92
Nootka Sound 84
North Iron Rock 25
North Sawyer Glacier 147
Numas Islands 23
Nunez Point 60
Nunez Rocks 60

O

Oakland Bay 99
observations 213, 213–220
Ocean Falls 169, 170
oceans 183
Olga Strait 47
Oliver Cove 28
Oliver Inlet 150
Olympia 97, 98, 122, 151
Olympic Coast Marine Sanctuary 116
Olympic Peninsula 107
only boat 10
Open Bight 136, 137
Opitsat 87
Oregon 119, 173, 214, 217
orientation 153, 154, 176
other neat places to visit 202
Otter Cove 14
Ououkinsh Inlet 77
Owen Bay 128
Ozette 116
Ozette Island 116

P

Pachena Point 91
Pacific Rim National Park 93
Pack Lake 135
Paige Islets 11
park 54, 99, 100, 130
parks 139
passion 184
Pavlof Harbor 158
Pearl Harbor 218
Pearse Canal 143
Peddlar's Cove 78
Pelican 156, 157
Pender Harbour 9, 128
Penn Cove 107
Penrose Island Marine Park 26

Index

T

ISBN 1552123480-0

9 781552 123485